Progress to First Certificate
New Edition

TEACHER'S BOOK

Progress to
First Certificate

New Edition

TEACHER'S BOOK

Leo Jones

CAMBRIDGE
UNIVERSITY PRESS

Published by the Press Syndicate of the University of Cambridge
The Pitt Building, Trumpington Street, Cambridge CB2 1RP
40 West 20th Street, New York, NY 10011-4211, USA
10 Stamford Road, Oakleigh, Victoria 3166, Australia

© Cambridge University Press 1983, 1990

First published 1983
Seventh printing 1988
Second edition 1990
Eleventh printing 1992

Printed in Great Britain by
Bell and Bain Ltd., Glasgow

ISBN 0 521 37957 1 Teacher's Book
ISBN 0 521 37959 8 Student's Book
ISBN 0 521 37958 X Self-study Student's Book
ISBN 0 521 37096 5 Set of 2 cassettes

Contents

Thanks

No book of this kind can be produced by one person alone and in this case countless people have generously contributed their ideas and advice. In particular, I'd just like to say how grateful I am to the following friends, colleagues and teachers:

Jeanne McCarten for guiding the New Edition through from start to finish and for her encouragement, perfectionism and good ideas

Jill Mountain and Kit Woods for their detailed comments on the first edition and for subsequently reading, evaluating and suggesting improvements to the first draft of this New Edition

Alison Silver for her editing expertise and sensible suggestions

Peter Taylor and Studio AVP for their professional skills in producing the recorded material

Peter Ducker for the design of the Teacher's Book

Sue Gosling for her help and advice

And thanks to the following teachers whose detailed comments on the first edition and helpful ideas led to many valuable changes in the New Edition:

Susan Barber, Lake School of English in Oxford

John Bradbury, FIAC Escola d'idiomes moderns in Sabadell, Catalonia, Spain

Susan Garvin, British Institute of Florence, Italy

Roger Johnson and Nick Kenny, British Council in Milan, Italy

Fern Judet, Swan School in Oxford

Lynne White, Godmer House School of English in Oxford

And thanks to the following teachers who kindly wrote about their experiences of using the first edition, some of whom gave us their students' feedback:

H. G. Bernhardt, Tony Buckby and colleagues, J. Carvell, Emily Grammenou, Michael Hadgimichalis, Pearl Herrmann, Jill Jeavons, Katherine Karangianni, Marie Anne Küpper-Compes, Bryan Newman, Cathy Parker and colleagues, Véronique Rouanet, Claire Springett, Andrew Tymn, Robin Visel and J. T. Ward

Finally thanks to the numerous other teachers in many different countries (and their students) who have given us useful informal feedback on the first edition.

Thank you, everyone!

Thanks

From the first edition
I'd like to express my thanks to Sue Gosling and Christine Cairns for all their encouragement and help during the planning, writing and rewriting of this book. Many thanks also to the teachers who used the pilot edition and made so many useful and perceptive comments. Thanks are due in particular to staff at the following schools and institutes: the British Centre in Venice, the British Institute in Paris, the British School in Florence, the Newnham Language Centre in Cambridge, the Studio School of English in Cambridge and the Université II in Lyons.

Acknowledgements

The author and publishers are grateful to the following for permission to use copyright material identified in the text.

Dover Publications, Inc. for the pictograms throughout the book from *Handbook of Pictorial Symbols, 3,250 Examples from International Sources* by Rudolf Modley; J. Sainsbury for the pictogram on p. 64; Venice Simplon – Orient-Express for the map on p. 86; Ordnance Survey and W. Heffer & Sons Ltd for the map on p. 98; Ebury Press for the extract on pp. 128–9 from *Microwave Cookbook* © 1985 National Magazine Company Ltd.

The marking scales on pp. 219 and 226–8 are reproduced with the permission of the University of Cambridge Local Examinations Syndicate from their 'General Handbook of English as a Foreign Language' and from their instructions to oral examiners. No other material in this book has been seen or approved by UCLES prior to publication. The advice given in the Teacher's Book is entirely the responsibility of the author of this book.

Teachers using the Self-study Student's Book of *Progress to First Certificate* may be interested to learn that Cambridge University Press also publishes a Self-study edition of *Cambridge First Certificate Examination Practice 2* adapted by Louise Hashemi. This includes four First Certificate practice tests with answers to the questions, as well as model plans for the Paper 2 and 3 composition questions, tapescripts for all the listening passages, a complete description and explanation of each of the five papers, and suggestions on how to study effectively for the exam.

Introduction

The Teacher's Book of *Progress to First Certificate* **New Edition** contains correct or model answers to all the exercises in the Student's Book, a transcript of all the material recorded on the cassettes, teaching notes on every section of the Student's Book and ideas for extra work and activities. There are also references to supplementary material in other books you may wish to use with the class.

Why a new edition?

Since its first publication, *Progress towards First Certificate* has been an outstandingly popular and effective coursebook and it has been used with great success in First Certificate classes all over the world. But, in the meantime, new ideas have come along, teachers have suggested numerous improvements, amendments have been made to the exam syllabus, and some of the original texts seemed to be getting rather dated (in one text, now replaced, a British Rail fare of £6 was advertised – this had risen to £34 at the time of writing!).

So, what might have simply been an updating of the original edition has become a completely new edition, putting right the shortcomings of the original edition. There are four completely new units as well as many new or revised sections, including new reading and listening texts, communicative activities and exercises – but all the features of the original edition of *Progress towards First Certificate* that teachers and students appreciated and which led to so many successful exam results have been retained.

This completely revised **New Edition** updates the material and enhances its effectiveness. The revisions and improvements are based on comments and reports from teachers who had been using the first edition successfully for many years. The New Edition prepares students for the latest version of the exam, including all the amendments made to the syllabus and the exam papers since 1984. The format of each unit has been changed to provide a more balanced lesson structure and greater flexibility.

The **New Edition** of *Progress to First Certificate* includes:
- Four entirely new units, covering the following topics:
    Nature and the environment
    Science and technology

Books and reading (including work on prescribed books)
News and current affairs
- Revised vocabulary exercises, with more opportunities for students to use the new words they have learnt in discussion tasks
- Many new and up-to-date reading texts, with pre- and post-reading tasks and discussion questions
- Thorough training in composition writing with completely new exercises on the specific skills required for writing good compositions. (The composition sections are near the end of each unit, so that students have more time to consolidate their knowledge of the topic before having to write about it.)
- Systematic treatment of grammar, including thorough coverage of problem areas together with exam-style exercises
- New problem-solving exercises, to help students tackle the directed-writing questions in the Use of English paper as well as problem-solving tasks in the Interview paper
- Many new listening comprehension exercises based on the type of tasks used in the exam, each with pre- and post-listening tasks
- New speaking exercises to prepare students for the Interview paper by means of lively and realistic practice
- Revision exercises to help students keep in mind the language they have learned in preceding units
- Advice, hints and tips on exam techniques
- Entirely new exercises on:
  verbs and idioms (including phrasal verbs)
  prepositions
  word study, word formation and pronunciation

The **New Edition** of *Progress to First Certificate* still retains the most popular and effective features of the first edition:
- Students PROGRESS from exercises which develop the necessary language skills to the kind of exercises and tasks used in the exam
- Most of the vocabulary exercises have been retained, with some additions and amendments, and with new discussion questions to activate newly-learned words
- Ten of the original reading texts have been retained, with new pre- and post-reading tasks and some revised comprehension questions
- Fifteen of the original listening recordings have been retained, with new pre- and post-listening tasks and some revised comprehension questions
- Many of the most popular composition, use of English and interview exercises have also been retained

The **Student's Book** includes all the new material described above. There is also a **Self-study Student's Book (with answers)** – this special edition is

designed for students who are working partly or entirely on their own. It includes the **full text** of the Student's Book as well as:
– Model answers to all the exercises
– Self-study notes giving advice and tips on exam techniques
– Tapescripts of all the listening exercises
The Self-study Student's Book is recommended for adult students and more mature teenage students. If they have this version they will be able to do any of the exercises and check their answers on their own at home, leaving more valuable time in class for the activities that depend on discussion and conversation.

Preparing for the FCE exam

In an examination preparation course there must be a balance between helping students to be successful in the exam AND helping them to improve their ability to communicate with people in English. An examination certificate is of little practical value if the proud holders can't actually use their English in communication! That is why, although the FCE exam itself emphasises writing and reading English in its marking scheme, in *Progress to First Certificate* there are many opportunities for students to speak together, share ideas and communicate with each other in class.

If you have not taught a First Certificate class before, you should familiarise yourself with the format of the exam by looking at the practice tests in *Cambridge First Certificate Examination Practice 3* (CUP, 1989) and its accompanying Teacher's Book. You should also study the latest Regulations, obtainable from your Local Examinations Secretary, which also includes a list of the current books for prescribed reading.

How long does the course take?

The Student's Book contains enough material for about 100 hours' classwork plus homework (about three hours' homework per unit). If you decide to devote a lot of time to the discussion activities you may well need more time. A slow class would need longer than this and every class is likely to have its own strengths and weaknesses which will lead you to spend more or less time on particular sections in a unit. Moreover, some topics may interest your students more than others and consequently there is likely to be more discussion on these than on the ones that are of less interest to them.

If your students are using the Self-study Student's Book, and can spend more than three hours on their homework, you will be able to devote more time to the discussion activities.

The New Edition of *Progress to First Certificate* is a complete course, including sections on grammar, word study, prepositions and verbs and idioms. Each unit contains up to fourteen sections, each of which consists of several parts. The material is designed to be used selectively: some sections can be left out if the class is unlikely to have difficulty with them (or if they are likely to find them too difficult), other sections can be set for homework and checked quickly in class. Ideally, sections which require time for thought and can be done by individual students on their own (preparing reading passages, studying grammar summaries, many of the exercises and the time-consuming writing tasks) should be done for homework, so that more time is available in class for discussion and communication activities.

Working in pairs or groups

Many of the exercises in *Progress to First Certificate* are designed to be done by students working together in pairs or in small groups of three or four. They are not designed to be quickly done 'round the class' with each student answering one question.

There are several advantages to working in pairs or groups:
- Students get an opportunity to communicate their ideas to each other while they are discussing each exercise
- Students are more likely to remember answers they have discovered or worked out by themselves than answers other students give – or answers the teacher announces to the class
- Students working in groups are more active than if they are working as a class: they talk more and do more thinking too. If a class of, say, twenty were doing a ten-question exercise 'round the class' half of them wouldn't answer a single question
- If an exercise is done 'round the class', the lazier students can simply answer 'I don't know' when their turn comes and go to sleep the rest of the time. The weaker students can be lulled into a false sense of security by writing down all the correct answers and kidding themselves that they have 'done' the exercise. The exercises in *Progress to First Certificate* are designed to help students to LEARN, not merely to test their knowledge, and the idea isn't for students to say to themselves 'Another 44 exercises to go and then we've finished!'

The drawback of doing exercises in pairs or groups is that it does take time. However, as many of the exercises can be done as homework, time can be saved by setting some exercises to be done at home. Then, back in class next time, students can begin the session by comparing their answers in pairs or groups, and discussing as a class any problems they encountered.

How does each type of section work?

Vocabulary

Each unit contains a vocabulary section at the beginning of the unit.

A   Before each vocabulary exercise there are some warm-up discussion questions, to allow students to talk about the new topic briefly. These questions are open-ended and, in a talkative class, could lead to a lengthy discussion and you may have to interrupt the discussion to allow enough time for the vocabulary exercise to be done.

B   There is a progression in the vocabulary exercises from:

Questions where the first letter of the missing word is given but the rest is m...............

to:

Questions like this where the whole word is ....

to:

Multiple-choice exam-style questions where there is a choice of four possible ....

replies   sentences   answers   alternatives

The missing words are mostly placed near the end of their sentences to allow students to revise the exercise more easily. This can be done by asking them to cover up the right-hand side of the page with a piece of card or thick paper and to try to remember the words they have hidden.

There are two types of vocabulary items chosen for these exercises:
a) Those which are relevant to the topic and which have been graded as level 4 or 5 in the *Cambridge English Lexicon*, which represents the level of reading comprehension required for the FCE exam.
b) Other words beyond that level which students require to be able to speak and write interestingly and meaningfully about the topic.

Your students are sure to want to find out more words to use in discussion about the topics that interest them most, so time must always be allowed for your students to ask questions on vocabulary. Further vocabulary is introduced in the other sections in each unit and many of the words used in the vocabulary exercise come up again.

C   After the vocabulary exercise there are further discussion questions, to encourage students to use some of the new words they have encountered in the exercises.

Reading

Each unit contains two reading texts with tasks and questions, one near the beginning and one near the middle of the unit.

A   Before the reading comprehension questions there is a pre-reading task, e.g. preliminary discussion questions or some questions about the theme that students may be able to answer from their own previous knowledge. This task helps students to approach the text with more interest and curiosity than if they merely had to 'Read the text and answer the questions'.

B   The reading texts are 'authentic', and not specially written in a simplified style. They are all reproduced in the format in which they first appeared. There is a progression in the exercises from 'true' or 'false' questions like this:

> The texts in this book are printed in the same format
> as they were originally published.   **True**

and open-ended questions like this:

> How are the texts in this book printed?

to exam-style multiple-choice questions like this:

> The texts in this book are
> A   specially written.
> B   selected from magazines, newspapers, etc.   ✓
> C   easy to read.
> D   extremely difficult.

Your students will find that the true or false questions are an entertaining and helpful introduction to the kind of careful reading of texts which is tested in the multiple-choice questions in the exam. The right answers in the multiple-choice questions are the same as 'true' answers, whereas the wrong answers are the same as 'false' answers.

Before they read each text get the class to decide:
- What the text is about *and*
- Who wrote it and for whom *and*
- Where they think it's taken from

  Then they should skim the text (read it through very rapidly to get an idea of what it's about and what the main points are). Then they should read it through more carefully and answer the questions.

It is essential for students to realise that they don't have to be able to understand every single word to answer the questions. They should concentrate on what the writers are trying to say and the information they are communicating. Unfamiliar words in a reading text may be distracting but students should not assume that they are all important and 'worth learning'.

C   After the reading comprehension questions there are further discussion questions, to encourage students to use some of the new words they have encountered in the text and share their reactions to its content with each other.

Grammar

The grammar sections in each unit are designed to revise the main problem areas of English grammar that lose FCE candidates marks in the exam:
   1.3   Present tenses
   2.3   Use of articles: *the*, *a*, *an* and Ø (zero article)
   3.3   The past
   4.3   Modal verbs
   5.3   The future
   6.3   Using the passive
   7.3   Comparing and contrasting
   8.3   Conditionals
   9.3   Relative clauses and joining sentences
  10.3   *-ing* and *to—* (gerunds and infinitives)
  11.3   Reported speech
  12.3   Word order
  13.3   Difficult questions (*You'd better* ..., *I'd rather* ..., *I wish* ..., *If only* ..., *It's time* ..., *I suggest* ..., etc.)
  14.6   Spotting your mistakes

There are also a number of exam-style grammar revision exercises, that review the grammar points covered in previous units and prepare students for the kind of exercises they will have to do in the Use of English paper:
   5.11, 10.10, 12.8, 13.8, 13.12, 14.5 and 14.6.

A   Each grammar section begins with a summary of the basic rules with examples. Some of the examples have gaps for students to complete, so they become more personal and help them to remember the rules more easily – writing things down is a better memory aid than merely reading.

B   The summary or 'presentation' is followed by a series of different exercise types, which give students a chance to practise the structures. These all reflect the kind of tasks that students will have to do in the exam:

- Correcting errors – this is not a Use of English exercise, but one that all students need to perform when checking their own work through:
  There are one mistake in this sentence, for example.
- Exam-style transformation exercises:
  You have to rewrite this sentence.
  This sentence **has to be rewritten**.
- Stories with gaps to fill:
  Students find this kind ....**of**.... exercise difficult, especially ....**in**.... the exam, where there ....**are**.... twenty gaps in a passage.
- One-sided dialogues:
  A: What **is your name** ?
  B: I'm Mr Jones, but you can call me Leo, if you like.
- Letters to be reconstructed from key words:
  It be difficult / decide / what words be missing / this sentence.
  It is difficult to decide what words are missing from this sentence.

Students should realise that the grammar sections consist of REVISION of points that they have covered in previous courses. The summaries given are necessarily brief and simplified and do not cover elementary points or more advanced points. If students require more detailed rules or guidelines they should refer to a reference grammar book, such as *Basic English Usage* by Michael Swan (OUP). Students should be encouraged to ask questions if they are unsure about any points in the grammar sections.

If a class needs to do further work on grammar, the activities and exercises in *Use of English* by Leo Jones (CUP) are designed to be used to supplement the grammar revision sections in *Progress to First Certificate*. The relevant units are suggested in the teacher's notes.

Listing

Each unit contains three recorded listening texts with tasks and questions, one near the beginning, one near the middle and one near the end of the unit.

A   Before the listening comprehension questions there is a pre-listening task, e.g. preliminary discussion questions or some questions about the theme that students may be able to answer from their own previous knowledge. This task helps students to approach the recording with more interest than if they merely had to 'Listen to the cassette and answer the questions'.

Try to 'set the scene' for students before they hear the recording by explaining where the speakers are and what their relationship is (colleagues, good friends, etc.). In class (and in the exam) students will be trying to understand disembodied voices coming out of a loudspeaker and this is much more difficult than being in the same room as a real person who is speaking.

B Many of the listening exercises are based on recordings of 'simulated authentic' speech, broadcasts and announcements. These recordings are 'simulated', rather than taken from genuine conversations and radio programmes, so that they can be short enough to be dealt with adequately in the limited time available in class. You'll find that they retain all the other features of the 'real thing': hesitations, false starts, unclear and fast bits, interruptions and so on. Only a few of the recordings are scripted (for example: a radio news bulletin, a telephone message and a station announcement) – in all the others the speakers are not reading from scripts but talking naturally, and in some of the recordings students will hear people talking spontaneously about their experiences without a script.

There is a progression in the kind of questions asked from:
    True or false questions
to:
    Tasks where the students have to put the information they hear on the tape into visual form, for example marking a route on a map or filling in a chart
to:
    Exam-style multiple-choice and open-completion questions

The progression is also from tasks and questions which are relatively easy towards more difficult tasks and questions. The speed and complexity of the recordings themselves does not change: they are all spoken at a normal speed.

Most classes will need to hear each recording at least twice to extract all the required information. In some cases, where a class is weak at listening, you may need to pause the tape frequently and replay certain sections to help them to understand more easily. However, it is essential for students to realise that they don't have to be able to understand every single word to answer the questions. They should concentrate on what the speakers are trying to say and the information they are communicating, NOT the actual words they are using.

C After the listening comprehension questions there are further discussion questions, to encourage students to share their reactions to the content and discuss the implications of what they have heard. In some cases there is a complete communication activity, related to the theme of the listening text.

Students whose listening skills need to be developed further, or who find listening particularly difficult, may need extra listening practice. The listening exercises in *Ideas* by Leo Jones (CUP) are designed to complement the work in *Progress to First Certificate* and are based on similar topics.

Word study and pronunciation

Each unit contains a section on word formation, an aspect of vocabulary building or pronunciation. Some exercises in these sections are recorded

on the cassettes (shown with [▭] in the Student's Book and the Teacher's Book) and full instructions are given together with a script in the Teacher's Book (and in the Self-study Student's Book).

These sections will help students to cope with Use of English exercises like this:

Although this is certainly difficult it is not ..*impossible*..   POSSIBLE

This type of exercise practises word ..*formation*..   FORM

and helps students to improve their pronunciation (which will be assessed in the Interview) and their spelling (which will be assessed in the Composition and Use of English papers).

The following points are covered in these sections:
1.5 Abbreviations and numbers
2.5 Using prefixes
3.5 Using negative prefixes
4.5 Using suffixes – 1: Adjectives
5.7 Spelling and pronunciation: Vowels
6.5 Helping people to understand: Pronunciation
7.5 Using suffixes – 2: Actions and people
8.9 Spelling and pronunciation: Consonants
9.5 Using suffixes – 3: Abstract nouns
10.8 Compound words
11.7 Word stress + Joining up words: Pronunciation
12.6 Opposites
13.4 Synonyms
14.7 Word-building revision
14.8 Unusual exercises in the Use of English paper

These sections will help students to consolidate what they already know, correct any errors they make and widen their knowledge.

Problem solving

The last question in the Use of English paper is a Directed Writing task – probably the one that causes most candidates the most problems! By encouraging students to associate these tasks with a discussion which involves solving a problem and justifying their solutions, they will become familiar with these tasks and be able to approach them with more confidence. (It is worth remembering that this question only counts for 20 to 25% of the marks in Paper 3, even though it is often more time-consuming than the other exercises candidates have to do.)

In all of these exercises a discussion task comes before the writing task and students are encouraged to make notes before they summarise their discussion in written paragraphs. In later units these written tasks become similar to the exam, where the paragraphs often have to begin with a particular opening phrase.

For more information on writing skills, see the notes on composition below.

Composition

There is a progression in the composition exercises from:
   Tasks where students are free to write as much or as little as they like, using a dictionary and taking as long as they like
towards:
   Tasks where compositions of 120 to 180 words have to be written against the clock without a dictionary, as required in the exam

Each of the Composition sections focusses on one of the types of composition that students are expected to write in Paper 2 AND also on a specific aspect of good composition writing:

Types of composition	*Specific aspects*
1.10 Describing a place – 1	Spelling and punctuation
2.11 Writing a narrative – 1	Including interesting details
3.9 Writing an essay – 1	Making notes
4.10 Writing a letter – 1	Layout of letters
5.10 Describing a place – 2	Starting and ending well
6.11 Explaining a process – 1	Thinking about your reader
7.12 Writing what you would say	Features of spoken English
8.10 Writing a letter – 2	Informal and formal style
9.10 Writing about a prescribed book	Paragraphs
10.11 Explaining a process – 2	Suiting the style to the reader
11.11 Writing a letter – 3	Including only relevant information

In every unit, emphasis is placed on the need for good planning, making notes and checking work through for mistakes before handing it in – aspects of composition writing that are crucial for success in the exam. Students are encouraged to develop their writing skills through short writing tasks, by comparing different versions of compositions and, of course, by writing their own full-length compositions and having them assessed and marked by you.

In marking students' written work (including paragraphs written in the problem-solving sections) it is important to remember how discouraging it is to receive back a paper covered in red marks!

It is better for students to locate and correct their own mistakes, rather than have corrections written out for them. This is particularly important when you believe that a student has made a careless mistake or a slip of the pen.

In many cases, once mistakes are pointed out to students they can often correct them themselves. A 'marking scheme' like the following is recommended, but whatever scheme you use make sure your students are conversant with the system you're using. The symbols shown here would appear on the side of the page in the margin – make sure your students do leave a margin, therefore!

X = 'Somewhere in this line there is a mistake of some kind that you should find and correct.'

XX = 'Somewhere in this line there are two mistakes that you should find and correct.'

An incorrect word or phrase underlined = 'This particular word or phrase is not correct and you should correct it.'

G = 'Somewhere in this line there is a Grammatical mistake that you should find and correct.'

V = 'Somewhere in this line there is a Vocabulary mistake that you should find and correct.'

Sp = 'Somewhere in this line there is a Spelling mistake that you should find and correct.'

P = 'Somewhere in this line there is a Punctuation mistake that you should find and correct.'

WO = 'Some of the words in this sentence are in the Wrong Order, please rearrange them.'

? = 'I don't quite understand what you mean.'

And equally important:
   ✔   = 'Good, you have expressed this idea well!' or 'This is an interesting or amusing point.'
   ✔✔ = 'Very good, you have expressed this idea very well!' or 'Very interesting or amusing point!'

Remember that all learners need encouragement and praise – just as you might sometimes ignore mistakes when students are speaking, perhaps occasionally some mistakes should be overlooked in their written work.

Make sure you allow the students time to read each other's written work: this is particularly important if composition writing is to be considered as more than 'just a routine exercise'. Any piece of writing should be an attempt to communicate ideas to a reader. If students know that their partners, as well as you, are going to read their work, they are more likely to try to make it interesting, informative and entertaining! If you, their teacher, are the *only* reader, the process of writing is much less motivating. Students can learn a lot from reading each other's ideas – and from each other's comments on their own work. In the exam, what is most important is the success of each composition as a piece of COMMUNICATION, not simply its lack of grammatical errors.

It is important to realise that, in the exam itself, candidates are not expected to write 'great prose'. Indeed, no special credit is given for bright ideas, specialist knowledge or entertaining stories – the more imaginative candidates are not rewarded at the expense of the less imaginative ones. Although in the exam each composition is regarded 'as a piece of communication', the best marks do tend to go to candidates whose compositions:
1 are grammatically accurate
2 use vocabulary appropriately
3 are free from spelling mistakes
   Students also need to know that a good composition should not contain irrelevant information and, in the exam, they MUST answer the question asked – not the question they would like to have been asked! Candidates who distort, ignore or misunderstand the question do get penalised for this.
   In preparing students for the exam, they should be encouraged to communicate their ideas to you and each other in writing, just as they do in discussions and other oral activities. Otherwise, the exercise of writing compositions becomes sterile and pointless.

In some cases, model versions of written tasks are given among the communication activities at the back of the Student's Book (see the sections shown with a ● in the list on page 17). In the Teacher's Book (and also in the Self-study Student's Book) there is a model version for every composition task. If you think your students will benefit from seeing any of these, the model versions may be photocopied from the Teacher's Book.

(See page 219 for the official marking scheme used in the FCE exam.)

Prepositions

These sections cover the important uses of prepositions in prepositional phrases and after certain verbs, nouns and adjectives. As these are often just 'things you have to know and remember' rather than aspects of interesting communication, many of these consist of straightforward gap-filling exercises. They can be done at any stage of the unit (i.e. 1.8 doesn't necessarily have to be done between 1.7 and 1.9) or set for homework and checked in class.

The points covered in these sections are:
- 1.8   Using prepositions – Revision (of some basic uses of prepositions)
- 2.8   Position and direction (describing where things are)
- 3.7   Compound prepositions (*owing to*, *because of*, etc.)
- 4.11 Using prepositions – 1: Prepositions after verbs, adjectives and nouns (A–C)
- 5.6   Using prepositions – 2: Prepositions after verbs, adjectives and nouns (D–M)
- 6.7   Using prepositions – 3: Prepositions after verbs, adjectives and nouns (P–W)
- 7.9   Prepositional phrases: AT (*at first*, *at once*, etc.)
- 8.7   Prepositional phrases: BY (*by chance*, *by mistake*, etc.)
- 9.7   Prepositional phrases: IN (*in common*, *in public*, etc.)
- 10.5 Prepositional phrases: ON + OUT OF (*on duty*, *out of date*, etc.)

There are also revision exercises in 7.14 and exam-style grammar/ preposition revision exercises in 11.5, 13.8 and 14.5.

Verbs and idioms

These sections, which come at the very end of units, concern phrasal verbs and the collocations in which certain common verbs are used. Like the preposition exercises, these can be fitted in when there is a little spare time during the unit, or set for homework and checked in class later. As these are basically just 'things you have to know and learn', there is no attempt to make the exercises more communicative.

These sections deal with the following verbs and phrasal verbs:

1.11 Look + See
2.12 Make + Do
3.12 Get
4.6 Come + Go
6.12 Keep + Take
7.13 Put
8.12 Break, Bring, Call + Cut
9.12 Fall + Hold
10.12 Leave, Let, Pull + Run
11.12 Set, Stand + Turn
12.12 Have + Give

Interview exercises and activities

The communication activities and the discussions that follow most of the reading passages and listening exercises are designed to prepare students for what they will have to do in the Interview paper. These speaking tasks follow on naturally from the reading or listening texts. In the problem-solving sections, the discussion activity leads naturally to the directed-writing task. This integration of skills is one of the special features of the New Edition and helps students to see that what they are doing in class is not only going to be relevant to the exam but also useful when they have to use English in real-life situations outside the classroom.

Many of these activities are based on an information gap, where each member of a pair or group looks at different information in the communication activities at the back of the Student's Book (see next page). This information is presented on different pages, so that it's difficult for students to 'cheat' by looking at each other's information. This kind of information-gap exercise develops into a lively, realistic interaction.

Every unit contains a multitude of opportunities for students to use their English in realistic communicative situations, but in several units there is also a section that is specifically directed towards practising the techniques required in the Interview paper:

2.10 Telling a story – Communication activity
3.11 How sweet!? – Picture conversation
6.10 How does it work? – Communication activity
7.10 Staying healthy – Picture conversation
8.4 Getting away from it all? – Picture conversation
11.13 Different kinds of jobs – Interview exercises
12.11 Exam practice – Interview exercises (A complete practice interview)

Students whose speaking skills need to be developed further, or who find speaking particularly difficult, may need extra practice. The communicative activities and discussion exercises in *Ideas* by Leo Jones (CUP) are designed to be used in parallel with *Progress to First Certificate* and are based on similar topics.

Communication activities in the Student's Book

	Description of activity	*Activity numbers*
1.5D	Dictating names and addresses	1 + 10
1.6B	Posters	13 + 20
1.7C	Model notes on gift ideas●	4
1.7D	Model paragraphs on gift ideas●	27
1.9C	Advice on buying something	16 + 23
1.10C	Corrected version of unpunctuated paragraph●	37
2.8D	Following directions	32 + 40
2.10C	Scenes from a film	17 + 24 + 46
2.11A	Rewritten version of breakdown story●	9
2.11B	Rewritten Casablanca story●	3
3.3D	Macabre animal stories	18 + 42
3.6C	Extra information about the weather	15
3.11C	Animal pictures	34 + 44
4.8B	Extra information for problem solving	12
4.12	Transport in the future	2 + 8 + 28
6.5D	Marked-up version of reaction timer passage●	11
6.10	How cassettes and soap work	39 + 47
8.3E	Short break advertisements	19 + 33 + 43
8.9B	Correct spellings of consonant sounds●	25
8.9D	Dictating words	5 + 22
8.10B	Model letters●	41
10.7B	Menu explanations	7 + 35 + 48
10.9C	Refreshing drinks	6 + 29
11.13B	Different jobs	26 + 30 + 45
13.9C	Describing a group of people	38 + 49
13.11B	Dilemmas	31 + 36 + 50
14.13A	Photos from 1933 and 1940	14 + 21

● = These are model versions or correct answers, not information-gap activities.

1 Shopping

The teaching notes for this unit are more comprehensive than later units as they include recommended procedures for the various types of exercise and details of some of the principles underlying them.

1.1 Shopping habits   *Vocabulary*

A   Students work in groups of three or four, or in pairs. With a small class you might ask them the questions yourself and have a short discussion as a class.

The discussion gives everyone a chance to talk about the topic and become interested in it before they do the detailed vocabulary questions in **B**. This is a 'warm-up' activity and should not be allowed to take too long (no more than ten minutes).

If the discussion seems to be getting very animated and everyone is getting interested in the topics you may decide to let them spend longer, but it's probably best to return to the discussion later after doing **B**.

B   In later units, you may prefer to get your students to prepare this type of exercise before the lesson as homework: they would note down the missing words (perhaps in pencil) and look up any unfamiliar words. In this case, as it's the opening unit, they should work in pairs and do the exercise in class, discussing with their partner what words are likely to fit the gaps and then writing them down.

When everyone has finished, make sure they have got the right answers and that there are no spelling problems. Make it clear that in some cases (e.g. in 15 and 25) there may be several possible answers. Discuss what's wrong with any wrong answers they may have given.

Still working in pairs, one student can test the other by reading each sentence aloud and stopping before the missing word: the partner then has to remember the missing word. Alternatively, you could do this while the whole class shouts out the missing words. This kind of 'second go' at the exercise will help them to remember the words better.

Make sure they write down any useful new words that come up, and use the board to encourage this – students are more likely to write words down if you've put them on the board than if they've only been spoken.

▶ Ask the class to suggest more words connected with the topic of shopping. They may also want to ask you questions like this:
  'What do you call it in a shop when you …?'
or 'What do you say in a shop when …?'
or 'What's the name of that thing which …?'
  Suggest that next time everyone goes to town they should look at everything 'through English eyes' and try to put an English name to the things they see. They can report back on this in a later lesson.

Answers

 1 *Example   Make sure everyone knows what to do.*
 2 signature
 3 shopkeeper
 4 shop assistant/sales assistant
 5 counter
 6 help   looking
 7 sale   bargain
 8 total
 9 receipt
10 guarantee
11 shoplifting
12 chemist's/pharmacy
13 trying
14 size
15 fit   long/short/tight/loose/baggy/uncomfortable
16 stock
17 match   suit
18 label
19 market
20 discount
21 greengrocer's
22 hire purchase
23 department store   mail order
24 deliver
25 boring/fun/tedious/enjoyable/exhausting/a waste of time/unpleasant/tiring, etc.

C   Working in pairs or groups of three or four, students treat this section as a kind of problem-solving exercise, in which they discuss the various possible shops. If you anticipate this will be too difficult for them, you could write up a list of the different kinds of shops (but not in the correct order) and add a few irrelevant shops (e.g. shoe shop, fishmonger's, florist's, etc.) as distractors.

Answers (These are all open to discussion – in different countries these goods are sold in different kinds of shops.)

1 *Example   Make sure everyone knows what to do.*
2 stationer's/newsagent's/kiosk   bookshop/bookseller's
3 dairy/grocer's/corner shop   hardware store/ironmonger's/shop that sells crockery
4 greengrocer's   hardware store/ironmonger's/shop that sells cutlery
5 butcher's   hardware store/ironmonger's/shop that sells kitchen equipment
6 off-licence/wine store   hardware store/ironmonger's/wine store
7 electrical dealer's/radio shop   music shop/record shop
8 baker's   grocer's/dairy/corner shop
9 stationer's   stationer's
10 chemist's/pharmacy   chemist's/pharmacy
11 kiosk/newsagent's/sweet shop   post office/newsagent's

D   The final group or pair discussion is based on clothes and the vocabulary required to talk about them. You could start this off by standing up yourself and describing the clothes you're wearing to the class.

Encourage everyone to write down only the words they come across that are both NEW and USEFUL. While the groups are working, you should go round answering questions and making notes of any points you need to explain to the whole class later.

Before finishing this section, ask for questions on any vocabulary that the groups were having difficulty with.

This symbol ▶ in the Teacher's Book indicates an extra activity or supplementary exercises.

▶ There is more work on shopping and describing clothes in *Ideas* by Leo Jones (CUP) Unit 2.

1.2   Enter a different world   *Reading*

A   The aim of the questions in this section is to encourage students to approach the text with a purpose and to use their previous knowledge (and common sense) when they read it.

The questions concern only a few details of the passage but everyone will need to read the whole passage to find the answers. Rather than 'studying' the text they should scan the passage to find the required information – just as if they were looking for information in a reference book.

Perhaps ask them to identify the source of the passage: is it from a novel, or a brochure, or an advertisement, or a magazine article – or what? (It's actually a press handout.)

Answers

1 *Example   Make sure everyone knows what to do.*
2 T   It's a landmark of London (see paragraph 4)
3 T   See paragraph 3
4 F   'anything from a pin to an elephant'
5 T   Look at the royal crest at the top of the page
6 F   It's the second largest

B   These questions check whether everyone has understood some of the details of the text. To answer the questions, they will have to read the text very carefully.

This can be done by students working alone (as homework) or by students in pairs, helping each other to find the answers. If it is done as a solo activity, students should compare answers with a partner afterwards, as suggested in the Student's Book.

Discuss any difficulties with the class and point out that with questions like these the correct answers may depend on the interpretation of the text, not just on the facts. In the exam itself, students may have to answer one or two questions where they have to 'read between the lines' in this way.

Answers (And the words in the text that give the answers)

1 F   'a suitable elephant owner'
2 T   '*no* other store can'
3 F   '500 types of shirts'
4 F   '57 malts'
5 T   'circulating library'
6 T   'funeral service'
7 T   'Los Angeles' – which is in the USA
8 T   '£40 million worth ... annually' – $40 \div 12 = 3\frac{1}{3}$
9 F   '4,000 regular staff rising to 6,000' – they take on 2,000 temporary staff at Christmas
10 T   'will deal with a wider range'
11 F   'from any assistant in the store'
12 F   'the time of delivery will be guaranteed to within one hour'
13 F   'the building ... was started in 1901'

14 F   'reasonable prices'
15 T   'as many cream cakes … as your greed will allow'

C   Students work in groups and discuss the questions. For the benefit of groups who may need some help with this, here are some ideas and prompts:
1 Price: things are not necessarily any cheaper in a department store
   Choice: department stores often stock a wide range of products
   Service: you get personal service in a department store, which you don't get in a supermarket
   Quality: department stores often stock top quality merchandise
   Convenience: you can usually look around without being badgered by assistants
2 Bread, for example, is usually fresher and may be cheaper if you get it from a local baker
3 Can you buy a car or a flat or a book, for example? Or would you have to go to a car showroom/garage, an estate agent or a bookshop for these?

▶ We return to the subject of department stores in 1.10, but you might like to end this section by asking students to say a few words about the poshest department store in their city – how is it similar to and different from Harrods?

1.3   Present tenses *Grammar*

The grammar sections in *Progress to First Certificate* are intended as revision. The examples and exercises in every unit cover the main difficulties that students are likely to have with English grammar. More basic and more advanced points are not covered.

To save time in class, any of the exercises can be done as homework:
– either A to D as homework with E done in class
– or A and B done in class with C to E done as homework

A   The summary of the main uses of present tenses is, like any summary, a simplification. For a more detailed exposition, students should refer to a grammar book, such as *Basic English Usage* by Michael Swan (OUP).
   Students should fill the gaps with their own examples, as this will help them to memorise the rules that are shown. Some suggested examples are given here, but students' own personal examples are likely to be more memorable.

Suggested answers

Permanent or regular actions and situations:
I never **drink coffee before I go to bed.**
Every evening I **watch the news on TV and then I have dinner.**

Temporary, developing or changing actions and situations:
At the moment I **am sitting in class doing this exercise.**
I **am taking** a First Certificate course this year.

Actions or situations begun in the past and still true now or continuing now:
We **have spent two** hours on this unit so far.

B   Students'own more personal examples may be more memorable if they include other members of the class as 'characters' in their sentences! By insisting on negative sentences we are making the task that much trickier.

A few suggested sentences

Thomas doesn't deserve to go out tonight.
These boots don't fit, they're too small.
I don't know what Maria means.   etc.

C   This exercise should be done as homework or discussed by students working together in pairs. This is likely to be the most difficult grammar exercise so far in this unit.

Answers

at the moment – 1	this morning – 1	rarely – 2
from time to time – 3	for a long time – 4	usually – 2
occasionally – 2	hardly ever – 2	frequently – 2
sometimes – 2	once in a while –3	now – 1 (or 2)
every week – 3	today – 1	since Tuesday – 4
generally – 2	for a week – 4	
often – 2	never – 2	

▶   We return to the problems of adverb order in 12.3.

D   The error-correction exercises in the grammar sections will help students to recognise mistakes when they're checking their own written work. This exercise can be done by students together in pairs or set for homework.

B

Answers

1 *Example   Make sure everyone knows what to do.*
2 I am reading
3 I sometimes buy
4 √   *no errors*
5 prefers
6 I have been waiting
7 costs
8 √   *no errors*

E   This can be done by students working in pairs, or set as homework and discussed in class later. The answers given here are suggestions only – many variations are possible. Note that this is a very easy 'complete the dialogue' exercise compared with the ones in later units and in the exam.

Answers

Assistant: *Example   Make sure everyone knows what to do.*
Customer: No, only for a few moments. Could you help me, please?
Assistant: Certainly. What **can I do for you / are you looking for**?
Customer: I'm looking for a pair of jeans in my size.
Assistant: What **size do you take**?
Customer: I take a size 30, normally.
Assistant: Thirty. Well, we have these Levis on special offer.
   Do **you like the look of these / these look all right**?
Customer: Oh, very nice, yes, I like that style very much.
Assistant: You can try them on in the changing room over there.
Customer: Oh, right, thanks. I'll just see if they fit.
(The customer tries them on.)
Assistant: Do **they fit / they seem all right**?
Customer: Yes, they fit perfectly. How much **do thcy cost / are they**?
Assistant: £16.99. Is there anything else you'd like to see?
Customer: Yes, have **you got any jackets/a jacket to match**?
Assistant: I'm afraid we're out of stock of the matching jackets at the moment, but we'll be getting some more in soon.
Customer: When **will they arrive / will you be getting them / will they be delivered**?
Assistant: We're expecting a delivery at the end of the week. If you like, I'll put one aside for you when they come in.
Customer: Oh, thanks very much. And I think I'll keep these jeans on now.
   Do **you take Visa/Access/American Express**?
Assistant: Yes, we take all major credit cards.
Customer: Good, here you are.
Assistant: Thanks. Let me just cut off the label … there we are! And if you could just sign here …

▶ A more advanced point that some students might need to know about:

Notice the special use of the present progressive to refer to unexpectedly or annoyingly frequent happenings:

- He's always/continually/constantly complaining about the weather!
- It's always raining on Saturdays!
- I'm always meeting Chris at the supermarket!

▶ If your students are having difficulties with forming questions accurately, they should do some extra work on this. Units 1 and 2 in *Use of English* by Leo Jones (CUP) provide suitable exercises, and for more general practice of present tenses (including the present perfect and present perfect progressive) Unit 5 contains suitable material.

▶ We return to the use of the present perfect in 3.3.

1.4   I had to go to the shops . . .   *Listening*

A   ☐ This is a suggested procedure for using this recording – a similar procedure should be followed when using the recordings in later listening exercises. (If your class finds listening very easy you will probably decide to omit some of these steps.)

1 To prepare everyone for the conversation they'll hear, ask the class these questions (if they haven't discussed them already):
   - Which do you prefer: large supermarkets or small family grocery stores? Why?
   - Has anyone ever bought goods by mail order?
   - When are the shops in your town or city most crowded or busy?
   Don't spend more than a couple of minutes on this.
2 Set the scene by explaining that Ann and Tim are colleagues who work in the same office. Allow time for everyone to read the questions through before playing the recording. (Don't forget to set the counter to zero, so that you can find the beginning again easily.)
3 Just play the first 20 to 30 seconds of the recording so that everyone can 'tune in' to the theme of the conversation and get used to the unfamiliar voices.
     If you anticipate that the class will find it very difficult to follow the recording – it is a normal-speed conversation and the speakers don't enunciate every word clearly – play the whole conversation through while everyone tries to get the 'gist' of the conversation and gets used to the speakers' voices. To avoid visual distractions, students should

not look at their books during this phase – they'll find it easier to concentrate if they actually close their eyes while they're listening.

4 Tell everyone that they will NOT need to understand every word that's spoken in order to answer the questions.

   Play the recording all the way through. If necessary, PAUSE it once or twice during the conversation to allow students time to gather their thoughts and consider their answers to the questions – they could also discuss their ideas with a partner during these pauses.

5 Before they hear the conversation again, get everyone to compare notes with a partner and find which questions they disagree about or are still unsure about.

6 Play the recording again so that they can check on the answers they missed or were unsure about. Again, PAUSE a couple of times if this will make the task seem less formidable.

7 Again, students should compare notes and check their answers together. Then get everyone to tell you the answers – point out any mistakes they may have made – in this kind of exercise a 'mistake' is a misunderstanding of the speakers, or of the question.

8 To help everyone to realise where they went wrong, replay those parts of the recording that caused misunderstandings. If the speakers spoke very fast or unclearly at those points, read out the words from the transcript opposite – then replay the relevant part of the recording.

9 Play the whole conversation again with no pauses. Get everyone to sit back, close their eyes and listen – this is a valuable stress-free way of getting learners to appreciate and assimilate the rhythms of English conversation, pronunciation and vocabulary.

▶ A follow-up discussion will encourage everyone to use some of the language they have heard in the recording. The discussion could be done as a whole class, or the class could be divided into two or three groups. Start off the discussion by asking these questions:

Which of the speakers do you side with – are you for or against the following aspects of shopping that were mentioned in the recording?
– shopping for food
– buying presents for other people
– buying clothes
– crowded shops and bargain-hunting in the sales
– supermarkets, small shops, mail order, etc.
Do you look forward to being able to shop by computer?

▶ A low-pitched tone is recorded between each section on the cassette. If your cassette player has CUE and REVIEW buttons (i.e. you can hear the recorded voices speeded-up as you rewind), you will be able to hear this tone as a high-pitched *beep* which makes it easy to find where each new section begins on the cassette. So, if you are omitting a section you can find your place more easily. In class, however, using the counter is less disturbing – always set the counter to zero (000) at the beginning of each section.

Answers

1 *Example   Make sure everyone understands what to do.*

2 T	6 T	10 T
3 T	7 F	11 T
4 F	8 T	12 F
5 F	9 F	

Transcript

Narrator: Look at your Student's Book before you listen to the recording. You'll probably need to hear the recording at least twice before you can answer all the questions in the Student's Book.

Ann: Hello, Tim, you look really worn out! What's happened? How come you're so late?

Tim: I'm sorry. I had to go to the shops ... used up my whole lunch hour.

Ann: W ... why didn't you wait till you got home?

Tim: Oh, no, I'm going out this evening. Honestly, I had to queue at that checkout for fifteen minutes, I swear. I only wanted a couple of things.

Ann: Well, how come you didn't go to the fast one if you only had a couple of things?

Tim: Oh no, the queue was even worse there, it always is.

Ann: You know, you sound as if you hate shopping.

Tim: Oh, I don't know ... I don't generally hate shopping as such, I just hate certain kinds of shopping, you know. I don't mind buying clothes and things ... er ... can't stand buying food.

Ann: I like shopping for food. I don't know, I think ... I think, you know, finding a present for somebody else is the hardest thing. You just don't ... you just don't know where to start, you know?

Tim: Oh, I don't mind that. Oh no, I like that, I like buying presents and things, as long as I've got some time, you know. I don't like the sales, mind you, they're the pits.

Ann: Oh yeah! Or the shops, you know, just before Christmas – the crowds!

Tim: Awful! Oh yeah, I hate 'em. What I like ... what I like and what you don't see much of these days is those little shops, you know, little corner shops and things, where you get ... where, you know, where the bloke knows you and you get a ... sort of ... personal service ...

Ann: And they're little and they're crowded and you always have to wait a long time – no, no come on, a big supermarket's the best thing, you've got ... you've got the whole range of everything you might possibly want, the prices are lower, you've got to admit that, come on.

Tim: Yeah, yeah.

Ann: You've got the car park – you can just drive in, load your shopping into the car, drive away again. It's easy, there's no hassle.

Tim: Yes, it's too easy. It's too easy to spend all your money. I mean they … they … sort of … lull you with a … sort of … horrible music and stuff and you end up … I mean there's so much there. You … you buy the stuff you don't really want, you spend all your money!

Ann: Haha. Well, you know, I … I think shopping can be hard work though anyway, I agree with you there. I order a lot of things, you know, from catalogues. You can look through, you know, in your own spare time and phone in and then … and then it arrives at your doorstep. It's all so easy. Now, that's what I like, it's easy!

Tim: That's what I mean! It's too easy. I tell you … it's sending you to sleep, it's brainwashing you. One day we'll have … we'll have computers and we'll be able to order everything we want from our … from our living room and it'll be delivered by robots to our doors. And you'll never leave home, you'll never meet anybody! Not for me, I … I prefer the personal touch.

Ann: Well, I think perhaps we'd better get on with some work.

Tim: Perhaps you're right.

(Time: 2 minutes 25 seconds)

B   This is an extra vocabulary exercise, which can be done by students working together in pairs or groups of three, or set as homework.

Answers

a bottle of mineral water
a box of matches
a can of Coke
a carton (or bottle) of milk
a jar of honey
a bar of chocolate (not really a 'container', but it is how chocolate is sold – note that a 'box of chocolates' is a box containing layers of small chocolates)
a packet of biscuits
a tin (or can) of peas
a tube of toothpaste

Encourage everyone to suggest more of these containers by asking questions like this:
'What kind of container do cigarettes come in?'
'What kind of container does oil come in?'

1.5   Abbreviations and numbers   *Word study*

A   Students should do this exercise in pairs. Suggest that they do the easy ones first and leave the more puzzling ones till later. In this kind of exercise it may be useful for them to do some 'research' by using a dictionary to check the more difficult ones.

The use of full stops in abbreviations in English is often optional – GMT is also sometimes written G.M.T., for example. If the abbreviation consists only of capital letters, the full stops are not necessary and are often omitted in modern English. If the abbreviation is a short form of a longer word, the full stop is necessary.

▶ Point out that the best way to learn abbreviations is by noticing them when you come across them. In most cases, students will have to understand these abbreviations, but not use them – of the ones listed in the exercise only c/o, GMT and RSVP are normally only used in their abbreviated form, the others can be written in their full form if one wishes.

▶ Make sure that one or two (but preferably three or four) English-to-English dictionaries are available to the class during the lesson as a kind of 'reference library'. This will help to foster the habit of using dictionaries and perhaps discourage them from using pocket-size bilingual dictionaries – which sometimes lead to confusion rather than enlightenment.

The following are recommended:
Longman Dictionary of Contemporary English
Oxford Student's Dictionary
Oxford Advanced Learner's Dictionary
Penguin Wordmaster Dictionary
Collins COBUILD English Language Dictionary
Collins COBUILD Essential English Dictionary

Answers

c/o	care of
cont'd	continued
GMT	Greenwich Mean Time
incl.	including/inclusive
info.	information
intro.	introduction
max.	maximum
min.	minimum
misc.	miscellaneous
PTO	please turn over

RSVP	please reply to this invitation (*répondez s'il vous plaît*)
VAT	value-added tax
VIP	very important person (a celebrity)
vocab.	vocabulary
Xmas	Christmas

▶ Ask students to suggest further English abbreviations that they have come across and suggest a few more yourself:

    a.m.   p.m.   i.e.   e.g.   St (Street or Saint)   Rd   Ave   Sq.

B   Students should do this on their own (perhaps as homework) before comparing answers with a partner. Point out that spelling and the use of hyphens are important here.

Answers

333	*Example*	*Make sure everyone understands what to do.*
144		a hundred and forty-four
113		a hundred and thirteen
227		two hundred and twenty-seven
850,000		eight hundred and fifty thousand
5.75		five point seven five
1,992		one thousand nine hundred and ninety-two
$\frac{7}{8}$		seven eighths
$1\frac{1}{4} + 2\frac{2}{3} = 3.9167$		one and a quarter plus two and two-thirds equals three point nine one six seven
$4\frac{3}{4} - 2\frac{1}{2} = 2.25$		four and three-quarters minus two and a half equals two point two five

C   [▭] This exercise practises understanding numbers when they are spoken. Although it is quite difficult, it is an important skill that is often required in real life when exchanging information about phone numbers, addresses, prices and times.

Suggested procedure

1   Perhaps begin by pointing out that, to the ear, there is not much difference between, for example, 14 and 40 or 17 and 70.
2   Play the recording to the class. You will need to PAUSE it frequently: PAUSE for a short time after each number, while everyone is writing; PAUSE for a longer time between each part of the exercise, while everyone compares notes.
3   At the end, play the whole tape again for everyone to double-check what they have written.

Most of the speakers are British, and one of them is American. Examples

1 to 6 are telephone numbers, examples 7 to 12 are normal numbers, 13 to 16 are times and 17 to 20 are prices.

Answers

1 *Example Make sure everyone understands what to do.*		
2 617930	9 40,515	15 7.35
3 01 225 8915	10 14,550	16 7.15 (*or* 7.17?)
4 044 202 892671	11 17,170,660	17 £45.99
5 0473 993313	12 3.142	18 $12.15
6 879615	13 3.45	19 £140 + VAT
7 5,180,477	14 10.50	20 90p
8 617,930		

Transcript

Narrator: Listen to the recording and write down the numbers you hear. The first six are phone numbers.
   1 5180477
   2 617930
   3 01 225 8915
   4 044 202 892671
   5 0473 993313
   6 879615

Narrator: These are just numbers or figures.
   7 5,180,477
   8 617,930
   9 40,515
   10 14,550
   11 17,170,660
   12 3.142

Narrator: These are times of day.
   13 The time's 3.45 p.m.
   14 It's ten to eleven.
   15 It's twenty-five to eight.
   16 It's just after a quarter past seven.

Narrator: And the last four are prices or sums of money.
   17 The total price is 45 pounds 99.
   18 You'll have to pay 12 dollars and 15 cents.
   19 The cost is £140 plus VAT.
   20 You still owe me 90p.

(Time: 2 minutes 30 seconds)

D   ⚙ As this is the first communication activity that the class have encountered, make it clear that the purpose of the activity is to

31

encourage COMMUNICATION – students should NOT look at each other's information during these activities!

To prevent anyone cheating by peeping at the wrong information, divide the class into pairs and get them to decide who will be Student A and who will be student B. Then tell all the student As to look at Activity 1 on page 209 and all the student Bs to look at Activity 10 on page 212.

▶ If you have an odd number of students in the class, one 'pair' should work as a group of three, with two students working together and sharing their information. This can normally be done in all the pairwork activities.

Each student has a list of names, addresses and phone numbers which they must dictate to their partner – the partner has to write down all the information. Some of these names and numbers are easy, others are more difficult.

To start everyone off and show them what they'll have to do, demonstrate by dictating the first address in Activity 1 to the class, in this way:

'Ms Fiona Davison – that's capital M, small 's', FIONA DAVISON: Ms Fiona Davison – 13 Gloucester Road – that's GLOUCESTER: 13 Gloucester Road – Cheltenham – that's CHELTENHAM: Cheltenham GL9 6GT – telephone number: 0242 819232 – all right?'

While the activity is going on, be prepared to answer any questions that the pairs may ask you. Point out that it doesn't matter if you can't pronounce some of the names – as long as you can spell them out to your partner and he or she can understand what you mean, you have succeeded in communicating. And communicating is what this activity is all about.

At the end, each partner looks at the other's information to check that the information has been written down correctly.

▶ To take this exercise further and make it more personal, the pairs can continue the activity by dictating their own names and addresses and the addresses and phone numbers of some of their friends or relations to their partner.

1.6 Advertisements   *Speaking and listening*

▶ For the discussion in D (see below) prepare some large, easily visible advertisements (cut out of magazines or newspapers) for the class to look at and discuss.

▶ Also ask the members of the class to find some advertisements themselves and bring them in to class. They needn't be in English as long as they are discussed in English.

A   The product advertised may not seem terribly useful, but at least it's unusual! Decide together with the class what you would need to tell someone about the advertisement to give them a good impression of it – without reading all the text aloud. This work will prepare them for what they will be doing in **B**.

B   [icon] The purpose of this communication activity is for students to describe what they can see to each other – make sure they don't look at each other's pictures before they start the activity.

Divide the class into pairs (or pairs and one group of three): one student looks at Activity 13, the other at 20.

The picture in 13 shows a young couple photographed against a fast-moving background. They are clearly having fun and we are meant to feel how wonderful it would be to experience the same feelings – 'You Can't Beat The Feeling!' is the slogan of this Coca-Cola poster.

The picture in 20 shows eight sweet little children, standing in a row and looking straight at us. They're all wearing funny, fashionable clothes. Two of them have woolly hats on with Mickey Mouse ears. The product advertised is printed on one of their schoolbags – Benetton.

C   [icon] Play each commercial separately – if everyone can answer the questions easily, go on to the next. Point out that it is not necessary to understand every word. (After all, who listens to every word in a radio commercial?) They only need to note down the answers to the questions. Point out that the commercials are all authentic and may contain unfamiliar vocabulary.

PAUSE between each commercial for everyone to compare notes and to check the answers. Make sure everyone looks at the next set of words and gaps before they listen to the recording.

At the end, find out from the class which of the products advertised they would or would not buy.

Answers

1 10 a.m. to 5 p.m.
2 olive oil   olive oils   natural
3 cool   hot   portable   conditioners   sweat
4 spring   orange   seriously
5 fries   hamburgers   pineapple   anything   ketchup   more   more
   waste   thick   smooth   dinner

Transcript

1
Harrods would like to suggest five places to spend this Bank Holiday Monday,
August 29th: our ground floor, our first floor, our second floor, our third floor
and our fourth floor. Harrods: open 10 a.m. to 5 p.m. for people who would
like to spend this Bank Holiday spending.

2
Have you discovered that wonderful Italian, Filippo Berio? I mean Filippo Berio
Olive Oil, of course. Pure olive oil is perfect for frying and extra virgin olive oil
is divine in salad dressings. Filippo Berio is just so incredibly versatile that
naturally you wouldn't choose to cook without it. Filippo Berio Olive Oils: the
natural choice.

3
Man:	The heatwave was all over the front pages, I was my usual cool self.
Woman:	Darling, the heat in the office is unbearable. I need someone to cool me down quickly
Man:	The lady was hot. It was another job for the Heatbusters. In less time than it takes an ice cube to melt, a portable air conditioning unit was installed and working. The lady simmered down.
Woman:	You Heatbusters are so wonderful! Why don't we s ... ?
Man:	It was time to leave. Portable air conditioning on hire. For written details call Freefone Heatbusters – no sweat.

4
noises
1st man:	No, no they're not right. Sorry.
2nd man:	How about – *noise*?
1st man:	Oh, no, no, no, no.
2nd man:	What exactly are you trying to achieve?
1st man:	Well, the sound of an orange dropping, preferably a big juicy Citrus Spring orange.
2nd man:	How about – *noise*?
1st man:	Mm, what was that?
2nd man:	Well, it's actually a grapefruit but ... um ... I reckon if I work on it ...
1st man:	Hmm, people'll spot it. How about the second half of the melon with the first one we had? *noise* Not really.
2nd man:	I could do you a raspberry.
1st man:	No thanks, Mike.
2nd man:	Look, why don't you just say it tastes great? You know the sort of thing: 'A sparkling blend of spring water and natural orange juice'. Um, I mean, this is a seriously fruity drink.
1st man:	If it was that easy, we'd have done it, Mike.
2nd man:	More?
1st man:	Yeah, keep going. *noises* No. No. Interesting. No ...
3rd man:	Citrus Spring – *noises* – the seriously fruity drink.
1st man:	That's it! Perfect!
2nd man:	Love it.

5

Men: Doowahbeketchup, bedoowah, bedoobedoobe ...
Girls: Gee, Lucy, was that Dirk Studebaker outside your house last night?
Lucy: Uhuh.
Girls: What on earth did you do to get him out of his car?
Lucy: Can't you guess?
Girls: Oh, Lucy, you didn't!
Lucy: Yes, I did!
         I cooked him dinner: frankfurters and fries,
         with two hamburgers and for a surprise,
         we had some gammon with a pineapple ring,
         that's what I cooked him.
Girls: Did you miss anything?
Lucy: Don't think so.
Girls: Was the ketchup on the side of his plate?
Lucy: It was Heinz, it was Heinz on his plate.
Girls: Well, ah well, oh well, oh
         give me more, give me more
         of that Heinz Ketchup taste.
         Eat it all, eat it all,
         'cause it's too good to waste.
Men: I do like a dollop of ketchup, of Heinz ...
Girl: Are you seeing Dirk again tonight, Lucy?
Lucy: You betcha!!
All: Heinz is the ketchup, so thick and so smooth,
         Heinz is the ketchup for dinner for two ...

(Time: 3 minutes 50 seconds)

D   Use the advertisements you have cut out of magazines to show the class, together with the ones they have brought. Perhaps ask each member of the class to say a few words about his or her ads before dividing the class into groups of four or five.

Get each group to decide on their No. 1 and least favourite ad. When they're ready, ask them to report to the class on their decisions. Be ready to help with vocabulary to talk about particular ads.

E   This part, though potentially enjoyable, can be omitted if time is short. Start the ball rolling by describing your own favourite/least favourite commercial.

1.7   **Which gift?**   *Problem solving*

The problem-solving sections in *Progress to First Certificate* are
equivalent to the Directed Writing questions in the Use of English paper.

In this part of the exam, candidates have to extract information from
a text, advertisement, picture or diagram and then rewrite some of the
information in their own words, usually following an awkward opening
phrase, like: 'If I were Chris I'd ... '

A   This preliminary discussion in groups of three or four will help
students to warm up for the work they will have to do.

B   After reading about the products and noting down the main
attraction of each, they should tell their partners which one they would
prefer to receive as a gift.

C   The profiles of the two friends, Chris and Jo, will influence the
decisions they'll be making.

Emphasise that MAKING NOTES is an essential part of any writing task
– it gives students a chance to arrange their ideas in a sensible order and
to decide on the order in which they will present them.

Make sure everyone has completed their notes before they look at the
model notes in Activity 4.

The model notes are intended as a 'basis for discussion and
comparison' – they are not 'perfect notes'. Different people have
different ways of making notes.

▶   We return to techniques of making notes in 3.9, but it is emphasised
over and over again in the problem-solving and composition exercises.

D   Normally, writing paragraphs is best done as homework but here,
so as to make sure everyone knows what is expected of them, both
paragraphs should be written in class.

Perhaps point out the potential problems that students may have with
using *would* in their paragraphs.

Encourage everyone to read a partner's work (see page 4 in the
Introduction).

Then they should look at Activity 27, which contains two model
paragraphs. Everyone should compare their work with the models and
discuss the differences. It is important to realise that the models are not
'perfect answers' and that many variations are possible – indeed brighter
students may well find aspects of them that they want to criticise.

▶   To make the task more personal and realistic, perhaps ask the students to write another paragraph about their own preference OR to choose which gift they would give to a REAL friend of theirs.

1.8   Using prepositions – Revision

This exercise covers some common uses of prepositions and adverbs that everyone should already know. Doing the exercise may reassure them that prepositions, though clearly a problem area, are not totally obscure. Subsequent exercises will include a mixture of known, half-known and unknown uses of prepositions.

This can be done in class, with everyone comparing answers at the end, or as homework.

Answers (Note that more than one answer is possible in some cases.)

1	*Example*	*Make sure everyone knows what to do.*	
2	of	18	by/on
3	of	19	off
4	for	20	for
5	for	21	with
6	about/on	22	at
7	on	23	about
8	off	24	by to
9	by	25	in
10	of	26	of
11	at/over	27	off
12	for	28	of
13	by	29	at
14	out of	30	over
15	off	31	on
16	on	32	under/over
17	off	33	with

Make sure any problems or questions are cleared up before finishing this section.

1.9   Buying a camera

A   Before everyone listens to the recording, they should use their own knowledge of photography (and common sense) and note down in pencil any information that they expect to be given. Using a pencil (and having a rubber handy) means that they can correct any mistaken preconceptions when doing **B**.

B   Follow a similar procedure to the one outlined for 1.4 on page 25. Set the scene by explaining that they're going to hear a conversation in a camera shop.

Play the recording twice but allow time for everyone to compare answers between playings.

Answers

```
┌──────────────────────────────────────────────────────────────────┐
│  ACME INSTAMATIC CAMERA £29̶9̶5̶                                   │
│  INSTRUCTIONS                                                       │
│  1  Load film cassette.                                            │
│  2  Set film speed to  100      or  400          SPECIAL          │
│  3  Press WIND lever till   1     appears in    OFFER £19.95      │
│     the small  window                                             │
│  4  Set focus to symbol of  people     for close-ups             │
│     or  mountains   for landscapes.                              │
│  5  Press shutter very  slightly                                 │
│     If  green       light appears, shoot picture.                │
│     If  red         light appears, switch to  flash              │
│  6  Wind film on for next shot.                                   │
└──────────────────────────────────────────────────────────────────┘
```

Transcript

Salesman: ... camera? Yes, certainly, madam, this one actually is on special offer this week. It's a good deal at 19.95, so ... er ... you know, you've struck it lucky. Er ... I suppose you'd like to know a bit about ... er ...

Customer: Oh please, yes. How ... how do you load it?

Salesman: How it loads? OK, well look, you ... first of all, it's dead simple, anyone can sort of operate these, you know, they're really ... even I can, you know ... ha ha ... I hope! Anyway, you open it up at the back here, OK? That's where you put in the film cassette. No problem, you just press that and it closes up. And then you set the film speed, you see, if you've got a fast film or a slow film you want to use it either to 100 or 400 and you use this switch here, you see, where it says 100, where it says 400.

Customer: When do you want to use 100 and when do you want to use 400?

Salesman: Well, it depends. I mean, if it's very dark, for example, you'd use 400 or if it's, you know, it's ordin ... most often you'd use 100, you know. But if you've got any problems, just ask whoever you're going to buy the film off, OK?

Customer: Uhhuh.

Salesman: So then the next thing you want to press the Wind lever until the number 1 appears. You see, in the little window there.

Customer: That's for the first picture?

Salesman: That's right, you've got it, you've got it. You see, it's dead simple. And then you set the focus to the picture, you know, depending on who you're going to take photos of, right?

Customer: Uh ... no.

Salesman: Well, I mean, say ... say you want to take a picture of me ...

Customer: Yes.

Salesman: That's just a portrait picture, you see. You turn it to People ...

Customer: Oh right.

Salesman: There, right? If you want to take a big landscape, then ... then you put it on Mountains ... dead easy.

Customer: I see, I see. Close-ups or landscapes?

Salesman: That's right, yeah. Then you ... then you press the shutter very slightly ... yeah ... as you look at the subject. Now if the green light appears – do you want to hold it? Here ...

Customer: Yes. Right, thanks ... I've got it.

Salesman: Right ... OK, now if you look through there, if a green light appears in the frame ...

Customer: Oh yes, it's appeared!

Salesman: That's right. Well, you go ahead and shoot, you see. But you won't have any luck at the moment because there's no film in there, you see.

Customer: Ha ha.

Salesman: Anyway, if the red appears in the frame, then you have to switch to Flash before shooting.

Customer: Flash?

Salesman: Yeah, well, you just press that little button there and a little, you know, flash thing comes out but you have to buy ...

Customer: Oh I see ...

Salesman: ... have to buy ... you know ... it's quite straightforward.

Customer: Have to buy a bulb?

Salesman: Yeah, you have to buy a bulb, yeah. And then finally when you've finished, you just wind the film on before the next shot.

Customer: Oh, that's marvellous. Very simple. Oh, I think I'll have it. Thanks very much.

Salesman: Jolly good, OK, madam. How are you going to pay? By cheque or cash?

Customer: Oh ... um ... could I pay by Access, please?

Salesman: Certainly.

(Time: 2 minutes)

C ▐▜▌ Divide the class into an EVEN number of pairs (and no more than three groups of three). Later they will have to recombine as groups of four to six, so an even number is essential.

Half the pairs look at Activity 16, the others at 23.
- Those looking at 16 will be discussing what advice they'd give to

someone who is going to buy A NEW CAMERA or A PERSONAL STEREO and who has never owned one before.
- Those looking at 23 will be discussing what advice they'd give to someone who is going to buy A NEW BICYCLE or A NEW WATCH and who has never owned one before.
Everyone should make notes.

When everyone is ready, rearrange the class into groups of four (each pair with another pair who have been doing a DIFFERENT section). They then role-play the roles of 'first-time buyers' and ask the 'experts' for advice.

▶ Instead of deciding on advice to give to first-time purchasers of a camera/walkman or bike/watch, students could decide on another product they really do have some knowledge of.

1.10   Starting out . . . *Composition*

Parts **A** to **C** in this section can be done as homework or by students working in pairs in class. These parts deal with some important micro-skills that students require when writing a composition.

A   The 'typical spelling mistakes' are underlined below:

My brother is <u>ninteen</u> years old.
One day he's <u>hopping</u> to go to <u>Amerika.</u>
It was a realy <u>wonderfull</u> meal!
I <u>recieved</u> your letter this morning.
He <u>want</u> to improve his <u>knoledge</u> of <u>english.</u>
Concorde <u>flys</u> <u>accross</u> the Atlantic in 4 <u>ours.</u>
Some people find <u>speling</u> <u>especialy</u> <u>dificult.</u>

★   These notes in the Student's Book are 'useful tips' and 'points to remember' or, later in the book 'advice on exam techniques'.
   The importance of checking written work through carefully is a point that will be emphasised over and over again.

B   Point out that capital letters are used incorrectly as well as apostrophes, commas, etc. The punctuation mistakes are corrected in this version of the text:

Harrods is London's most famous department store. You can buy almost anything there and it's one of the landmarks of London. People come to eat at its restaurants and look round its 214 departments, but not everyone comes to buy. Many of the people who go there are just

having a look at the enormous range of goods on display and at the other customers.

▶ This might be a good time to make sure that everyone knows the names of the most common punctuation marks in English:
   colon, exclamation mark, inverted commas, hyphens, etc.
Perhaps write them all up boldly on the board and ask everyone to tell you what they are:

! ? . , ; : ' ' " " — — ( )

C   There is a punctuated version of the unpunctuated paragraph in Activity 37. Point out that some variations are possible.

▶ If your students need to do more work on punctuation, see Unit 7 in *Use of English*.

D   Now we come to the main writing task. This preliminary discussion explores some of the points that might be made in the composition exercise in **E** below.

E   Follow the instructions given in the Student's Book for this part. The actual writing could, if convenient, be done as homework, but in this case the advantages of doing it in class are that you can offer help where needed and the feedback from a partner can lead to useful changes before the work is handed in.
   Collect the written work and, when marking, add some notes of advice on what aspects of each student's work should be improved.

▶ Before marking your students' written work, look again at the Introduction, pages 11 to 14.

▶ It might be a good idea to keep copies of this written work for future reference. It can be very encouraging for students to see how much their work has improved about half-way through the course, when motivation is dropping off.

1.11   *Look* and *see*   *Verbs and idioms*

A   This section, which can be done by students working in pairs or as homework, deals with some common synonyms of LOOK and SEE. Point out that, as we are dealing with synonyms, several variations are possible. If it is done as homework, make sure plenty of time is allowed in class to discuss the problems or queries that arise.

Answers

1 *Example   Make sure everyone knows what to do.*
2 watched   7 watch
3 gazed/looked   8 seen
4 see/recognise/notice   9 see
5 recognise   10 looks
6 noticed/seen/recognised

B   With this kind of exercise, students should be encouraged to do the phrasal verbs they know first before trying the ones that are more puzzling. The use of English-to-English dictionaries is recommended here.

Point out that many phrasal verbs can be replaced with equivalent 'normal verbs' – as this exercise shows. Quite often the phrasal verb is more informal than its 'normal' equivalent.

Answers

1 *Examples*
2 *Make sure everyone knows what to do.*
3 looking for
4 Look out
5 look up to
6 see to
7 looking into
8 saw through
9 look up
10 look in
11 look through it/look it through
12 looking forward to

The difference between particles (e.g. look **out**) and prepositions (e.g. look **for** something) should only be discussed with students who have very analytical minds! Some of the verbs we have described as 'phrasal verbs' are, strictly speaking, prepositional verbs or phrasal-prepositional verbs!

The ★ note in the Student's Book may lead to some questions – ask everyone to find more examples of each type of phrasal verb in exercise **B**, which they have just done.

More examples of the four types of phrasal verb:
1 The same as a verb + preposition:
   look for   look into   and also   *answer for   watch for*
2 Intransitive phrasal verbs (with no object) –
   none in this exercise, but: *go away   come back   the plane took off*
3 'Separable' phrasal verbs:
   see off   see through   look through   and also   *pick up*
   take off a coat
4 'Inseparable' phrasal verbs (these include the ones with a preposition
   and a particle):
   look forward to   see to   and also   *do with   do without*

Notice that, structurally, type 1 and type 4 are the same.

▶ For more practice in using phrasal verbs, see Units 38 and 39 in *Use of English* by Leo Jones (CUP).

Finally . . .

▶ Ask everyone to tell you what parts of this unit they found:
● Most difficult and least difficult
● Most useful and least useful
● Most interesting and least interesting
This will help you to plan how to organise the time you will spend on subsequent units.

▶ For more listening and speaking activities on the topic of shopping, see Unit 2 in *Ideas* by Leo Jones (CUP).

2 Leisure activities

2.1 Entertainment and sport
Vocabulary

A Don't spend too long on this warm-up discussion, but do spend a little time writing up the hobbies, games and sports that the members of the class are interested in or take part in.
Perhaps make four lists:

Hobbies	*Indoor games*	*Sports*	*Entertainments*
stamp collecting	bridge	basketball	watching TV
painting	chess	athletics	cinema
etc.	etc.	etc.	etc.

(Depending on your students' real interests)

▶ Keep the list on the board in case you want to do the extra activity suggested at the end.

B This exercise can be prepared before the lesson as homework and then discussed in class – or everyone can do it together in pairs in class. Perhaps point out that questions 4 to 17 concern entertainment and 18 to 24 concern sports.

Answers

  1 *Example Make sure everyone understands what to do.*
  2 recreation/relaxation
  3 collecting   taking
  4 comedy
  5 thriller
  6 plot
  7 director
  8 screen   stage
  9 reviews
10 audience
11 musical
12 interval   performance
13 video
14 villain
15 channel

16 hi-fi/stereo/record player/compact disc player/personal stereo/
   Walkman, etc.
17 pop/rock 'n' roll/opera/folk music/jazz/classical music/
   orchestral music, etc.
18 match
19 referee   whistle   applause   crowd/fans/supporters (NOT audience)
20 team   supports
21 cup   prize
22 draw   score
23 court   course
24 baseball/basketball/hang gliding/windsurfing/volleyball/badminton/
   athletics/soccer, etc.

C   Perhaps arrange the class into similar interest groups (tennis players
together, footballers together, etc.). If the members of the class are quite
young, the boys and girls could be in separate groups, perhaps.

   If this part is set for homework, each student should find out about all
the sports he or she is interested in, using a dictionary.

▶ Students might be asked to grade all the sports, entertainments and
games that you have written on the board. They could put them in order
according to how much they like each one or give a number out of five
according to whether, in their opinion, it is extremely interesting/
exciting (5) or extremely dull/boring (1).

Ask them this question:
● What do you particularly enjoy or hate about each sport that has
  been mentioned?

2.2   Fitness or fun?   *Reading*

A   Trying to guess the answers will help everyone to apply their
previous knowledge to the theme of the text. Finding the answers in the
text gives a purpose to reading the text – normally people only read a
particular magazine article from choice, not because someone has told
them to.

   Parts **A** and **B** could be set as homework, to save time in class.

Answers

1 walking
2 beer
3 health and fitness clubs
4 sports and leisure centres

B   After discussing the answers to the task, get the class to discuss the final 'big question' in the article:
● Should sport be something you take seriously or should it just be fun?
And also, perhaps:
● How much training should amateur sports people do?
● Should children at school be compelled to take part in sports?

Answers

Annual expenditure per head of population:	
Motor vehicles	£180
Beer	£150
Spirits & wine	£140
Smoking	£110
Electricity	£90
Gas	£75
Bread	£75
Sports	£60
DIY goods	£50
Newspapers & magazines	£40
Pets	£25
Gambling	£20
Bingo	£5
Cinema	£2.50

Number of people who regularly take part in leisure activities: (total population of UK 55 million)	
Walking	9.5 million
Snooker & pool	4.7 million
Indoor swimming	4 million
Outdoor swimming	4 million
Darts	3.8 million
Fishing	1.7 million
Going to football matches	1.3 million
Keep fit, aerobics & yoga	1.2 million
Football	1.2 million
Squash	1.2 million
Golf	1.2 million

C   This follow-up discussion gives everyone a chance to compare their own country with Britain, as described in the article. Perhaps also get everyone to share information about the involvement of their own family in leisure and sports activities – and of their circle of friends – as well as people in their country.

2.3 Articles   *Grammar*

A   Hopefully, this quick reminder will be enough to deal with this problem area. If necessary, refer to *Basic English Usage* or *Practical English Usage* for more information.

Answers

These are countable nouns: suitcase   lesson
These are uncountable nouns: bread   butter   food*   blood   milk*
    salt   money   luggage   accommodation (countable in US English)
    mathematics   education   health

These could be either:

glass (windows are made of glass / a glass of milk)
fire (fire is a great danger / what a nice fire!)
room (there's no room / this is a nice room)

* Note that in some special cases these words can be countable:
  Hamburgers and frankfurters are fast foods. (i.e. kinds of fast food)
  Three coffees and two chocolate milks please. (i.e. ordering in a café)

B To begin with, if your students will find this part difficult, put a list of possible examples (from the answer key below) on the board as clues. To save time in class, everyone could prepare this as homework.

Note that this is a summary of quite a complex area and that there are exceptions to some of the rules of thumb that are given.
These are some common exceptions:

the High Street, the Strand, the Matterhorn, the Jungfrau

Suggested answers

THE

Ipswich Town is the best football team in the world. (many variations possible!)
What time does **the sun/moon** rise?

How many students are there in **the class/school/college?**
We are taking **the (First Certificate)** exam in **June/December.**

The director of the film *Psycho* was Alfred Hitchcock.
- **the** Pacific, **the** Rhine, **the** Nile, **the** Mediterranean, etc.
- **the** Alps, **the** Rockies, **the** Cyclades, **the** Philippines, **the** West Indies, etc.
- **the** National Theatre, **the** Royal Opera House, **the** Hilton, **the** British Museum, **the** Odeon, etc.

A
- A leisure pool usually has **a wave machine/a water slide.**
- She's **a relation/cousin/colleague** of Peter's.
- She's such **a delightful/charming/rude/fussy** person.
- My father's **an accountant/a baker/a seaman.**
  My mother's **a teacher/managing director/housewife.**
- **A manager/teacher/politician/An army officer** has to be a good leader.

Ø – zero article
- **Dictionaries/Computers/Reference books** are useful.
  Discos/Lorries/Aircraft/Children are noisy.
- Mars, Venus, Asia, West Germany, China, Texas, Bavaria, etc.

- Greek, Chinese, Welsh, Arabic, Guaraní, etc.
- Everest, Mont Blanc, Lake Constance, Lake Superior, etc.
- Richmond Park Avenue, Shaftesbury Road, Regent Street, etc.
- Queen's Park, Liverpool Street Station, Heathrow, etc.

▶ Ask everyone to write eight sentences, each using one place name from the examples in **B**.

C   Remind everyone that this error-correction exercise is similar to what they should do when checking through their own written work.

Answers

1 *Example   Make sure everyone understands what to do.*
2 I'm looking for some accommodation with an English family.
3 More women are involved in politics in Britain than in other countries. (not true, by the way)
4 Most people agree that women can do the same work as men.
5 To get to the library, go along Elizabeth Road and take the first right.
6 Violence is a very great problem in the world today.

D   If you anticipate that your class will find this exercise very difficult, the task can be made easier by reading the whole story out to the class before they do it themselves. While they're listening they should look at the exercise in their books but NOT take notes or write anything down. As this is the first one of these fill the gaps exercises, though, it might be best to let them try doing it in pairs and see how they get on. It could also be set for homework.

Complete story

Last week I went to **an** exhibition of Ø paintings at **the** Tate Gallery in London. I'm not really **a** great art lover but I'd read **some/a lot of/lots of** good reviews of **the** exhibition and I was keen to see it. When I arrived, there were already **some/lots of/a lot of** people waiting outside for **the** doors to open. I joined **the** queue and in **the** end **the** doors opened and we went inside to see **the** show.
   Now, I must be honest and admit that many of **the** paintings disappointed me. Although I spent **a lot/lots of/some** time looking carefully at Ø each one, I had **some** difficulty in understanding what **the** artist was getting at. Finally, as I was looking rather stupidly at one of **the** paintings and trying to decide if it was **the** right way up or not, **an** old gentleman came up behind me and started to explain **the** whole thing to me. He kindly answered all of Ø my questions and we talked for over **an** hour. Then he said he had **an** appointment and had to go, so we

shook hands and said goodbye. I went round **the** gallery once more and now I found that all **the** paintings seemed really beautiful.

It was only as I was leaving **the** gallery that I found out who **the** old man was – his self-portrait was on **the** posters advertising **the** exhibition!

E Perhaps point out that headlines and notes don't obey quite the same rules as normal prose in English.

Answers

1 *Example   Make sure everyone understands what to do.*
2 Please don't send the results of the exam to my/an address in the UK.
3 Bring an example of a good and a bad advertisement to (the) class tomorrow.
4 The President of France and the Queen will open / have opened / opened the Channel Tunnel.
5 A group of taxi-drivers have won a million pounds in a/the lottery.
6 A man has found a valuable painting in a garden shed.

▶ If your class finds the use of articles particularly difficult to master, they could do the exercises in *Use of English* Unit 23. For further reference, *Basic English Usage* (sections 38 to 45) is recommended.

2.4   What sort of films do you enjoy?   *Listening*

A If you anticipate that your class will find the conversation very difficult to understand, let them hear the first couple of minutes without worrying about the questions. Even if they're likely to find it reasonably easy, let them hear the first 20 seconds or so to let them get used to the voices, then rewind the tape to zero and play the whole thing.

Be prepared to PAUSE the tape if everyone is getting panicky! Remind them that they don't have to catch all the words to be able to answer the questions.

As Bob's voice is much harder to understand than Susan's, you can make the task much easier by getting everyone to note down only Susan's likes and dislikes during the first playing, then to listen for Bob's during the second playing.

See the suggested procedure for 1.4 for more ideas on how to handle the recording.

Answers

	BOB	SUSAN		BOB	SUSAN
Thrillers	√	✕	Harrison Ford	√	√
Action films	√	✕			
Horror films	✕	✕	Clint Eastwood	√	✕
Love stories	√	✕			
Films with			Sylvester Stallone	√	✕
subtitles	√				
Comedies	√	√	Robert Redford	✕?	√
Cartoons	√	✕			
Black and			Eddie Murphy	√	√
white films	✕	√			

(Although Bob doesn't actually say what he thinks about Robert Redford, his tone of voice *might* be interpreted as being disparaging, perhaps.)

Transcript

Bob: ... all right ... er ... so what do you feel like doing this evening? We could ... er ... have a meal – are you hungry?

Susan: Nnn ...

Bob: I know, do you feel like ... um ... how about going to the cinema?

Susan: Ah, that's a good idea, yes. I ... I'd love to see a film, I haven't been to the cinema for ages.

Bob: No, no, I haven't either. OK, what ... what sort of films do you like? Erm ... how about thrillers? I enjoy a really good thriller. What was that one with ... um ... that one with Harrison Ford, you know about ... you know, that strange sect? *Witness*. Harrison Ford – he's always good, isn't he?

Susan: Yes, *Witness*, yes. Now I like Harrison Ford and ... er ... I don't know about *Witness*, no. Mmm ... I'm ... it was a good film, but I'm not really very keen on that ... that ... sort of ... kind of film.

Bob: Mm, so th ... then ... then you won't ... what if I suggested action films, you wouldn't like that either?

Susan: Action? Wh ... what do you mean by action films?

Bob: You know ... um ... w ... er ... Clint Eastwood, that sort of thing.

Susan: Oh, no, no, I can't stand films like that.

Bob: Oh, I like those, you see ... um ... violent – *Rambo* 1, 2, 3.

Susan: Oh no, definitely, no, no, definitely not, no. I can't stand old ... um ... whatsisname ... um ... Sylvester Stallone. I can't stand it when you see people getting killed and all the violence and everything, no. I think it's pointless and horrible.

Bob: Well, n ... I ... I quite ... I quite like him. I don't mind you see, I don't mind some violence on the screen though, it's not real life after all. But if it's well, if it's too bloody I have to shut my eyes. Bit squeamish.

Susan: Oh, absolutely, but you know the worst films of all th ... are horror films. Ugh! I went to see a horror film – now what was it called? – um ... *Nightmare on Elm Street* Ohh! Did ... I went to see it last year ... er ... I had to keep my eyes shut almost the whole way through the film.

Bob: Yeah, I know, that sort of film gives me nightmares, I just ... So what ... what ... what *do* you like, what shall we go and see? I mean, love stories? I quite like a good love story.

Susan: No, no! Can't stand romantic films. *Unless*, unless Robert Redford's in them.

Bob: Oh, come on! Susan, you don't like him, do you? I'm really surprised!

Susan: Robert Redford, he's my absolute favourite! I absolutely adore him.

Bob: Haha.

Susan: Actually, I don't really like American films at all really, no. I quite like foreign films, but not when they've got subtitles.

Bob: Oh, I disagree with you there, I mean, I don't mind subtitles at all. In fact I prefer it, I like to hear foreign languages being spoken. I quite like French or Spanish films, for example. Now, what does that leave us? Comedies? You must like comedies, surely.

Susan: Well, yes. I love comedies. Now, one of my favourites is Eddie Murphy.

Bob: Ah, now then, now then, he's brilliant. Did you see *Coming to America*?

Susan: Oh, yes! Wasn't it brilliant! And what about *Crocodile Dundee*, did you ... did you see *Crocodile Dundee*?

Bob: Oh, I did. I didn't ... I didn't really enjoy that quite as much.

Susan: You didn't enjoy *Crocodile Dundee*?

Bob: Oh, it was ... well ... stupid, wasn't it? Unbelievable, I thought.

Susan: Oh, come on, that was the whole point!! It *was* a comedy you know!

Bob: Oh, yeah, I take your point but I didn't enjoy it, OK? Well ... er ... that doesn't leave us much, does it?

Susan: Not really.

Bob: Cartoons – you know, Walt Disney? Kind of thing. I love cartoons. But you don't see many new ones these days, only the old Walt Disney ones.

Susan: Oh, did you see that Roger Rabbit film?

Bob: *Who Framed Roger Rabbit?* Oh, that was fantastic, wasn't it? The way the real people and the ... the cartoon characters acted together, it was fabulous.

Susan: Oh, actually you know, I didn't really enjoy it. Do you know, I don't really understand what the attraction is of cartoons, I ... I really don't. You know ... what I really like, no, what I really like are the old black and white films. You know, the classics, the Humphrey Bogart, the Hollywood classics.

Bob: Mm, well, I've got to confess I prefer modern films really – I don't like black and white – well – it's old-fashioned.

Susan: Well, I don't really know what we're going to do, do you?

Bob: No.

Susan: Do you know what? I ... I don't think we should go to the cinema at all. I think we should go out for a meal instead.

Bob: I'd quite like to go to the cinema. Have you got a local paper, so we can see what's on?

Susan: Oh! Well, I don't know, I haven't got a ... a paper. I know, why don't we just ring up the cinema and find out what's on?

Bob: You've always got the best ideas. Then we can decide properly and sort out exactly …

(Time: 4 minutes 10 seconds)

B ⊂▭⊃ The times come thick and fast, but we're only interested in the evening performances – as in reality, one would only need to find out some of the information given in a recorded message like this.

After hearing the recording, ask the class which of the films Bob and Susan did decide to go to, based on the preferences expressed in their conversation earlier.

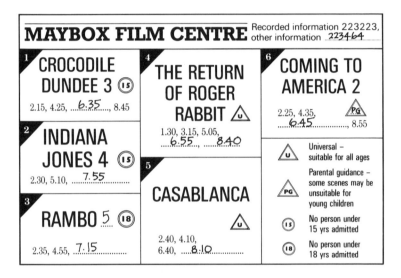

MAYBOX FILM CENTRE Recorded information 223223, other information ..2234-64.....

1 CROCODILE DUNDEE 3 Ⓘ⑤
2.15, 4.25, ..*6.35*..., 8.45

2 INDIANA JONES 4 Ⓘ⑤
2.30, 5.10, ...*7.55*.........

3 RAMBO 5 Ⓘ⑧
2.35, 4.55, ..*7.15*.........

4 THE RETURN OF ROGER RABBIT △ⓤ
1.30, 3.15, 5.05, ..*6.55*.., ..*8.40*..

5 CASABLANCA △ⓤ
2.40, 4.10, 6.40, ...*8.10*.........

6 COMING TO AMERICA 2 △ᴾᴳ
2.25, 4.35, ..*6.45*.........., 8.55

△ⓤ	Universal – suitable for all ages
△ᴾᴳ	Parental guidance – some scenes may be unsuitable for young children
Ⓘ⑤	No person under 15 yrs admitted
Ⓘ⑧	No person under 18 yrs admitted

Transcript

Narrator: You'll hear a recorded message.
Recorded voice: … now be repeated. Thank you for calling. This is the Maybox Film Centre with recorded information on films showing from today until Thursday next.

Screen One is showing *Crocodile Dundee 3* starring Paul Hogan, Certificate 15: showing at 2.15, 4.25, 6.35 and 8.45.

Screen Two is showing *Indiana Jones 4*, starring Harrison Ford, Certificate 15: performances begin at 2.30, 5.10 and 7.55.

Screen Three is showing *Rambo 5*, starring Sylvester Stallone, Certificate 18: performances at 2.35, 4.55 and 7.15.

Screen Four is showing *The Return of Roger Rabbit*, Certificate U: performances at 1.30, 3.15, 5.05, 6.55 and 8.40.

Screen Five is showing *Casablanca*, starring Humphrey Bogart and Ingrid Bergman, Certificate U: performances at 2.40, 4.10, 6.40 and 8.10.

Screen Six is showing *Coming to America 2*, starring Eddie Murphy, Certificate PG: performances at 2.25, 4.35, 6.45 and 8.55.

If you require further information, please call this number: 223464. This programme information will now be repeated. Thank you for calling. This is the Maybox Film Centre with recorded information on films showing from today …

(Time: 1 minute 45 seconds)

▶ Ask students to find out what's really on locally and decide what to see. If feasible, recommend where English language films/TV programmes/videos can be seen locally.

▶ Ask everyone to discuss in groups the kinds of films and film actors they like and dislike. Write up on the board some of these useful expressions that can be used when talking about likes and dislikes:

I'm very keen on …   I love …
My favourite sort of film …   I prefer … to …
The best kind of film is …
I think … is great/wonderful/fantastic.

I'm not very keen on …   I can't stand …
I don't know what people see in …   I really hate …
I think … is awful/terrible/dreadful.

2.5   Using prefixes   *Word study*

This word-formation exercise can be prepared as homework or done by students working together in pairs. You may need to explain some of the meanings, but not unless people are confused – they should be encouraged to work things out for themselves and use dictionaries:

co = with
mid = in the middle
over = too much
under = not enough
re = again
self is connected with *oneself* or *itself*, but can't be explained easily – ask
    the class to look at the examples and see what they have in common
sub = below
un = doing the opposite action – not quite the same as *un* in *unkind*
    (= not kind) or *unfamiliar* (= not familiar)

A   Note that the use of hyphens is slightly problematic and in some cases the words can be written as one word or with a hyphen.

⟫→

53

Answers

co	co-driver
mid	mid-afternoon, mid-morning, mid-winter, midway
over	overcharge, overexcited
under	underdone
re	rearrange, remarry
self	self-control, self-service
sub	sub-standard
un	unbutton, unfold, unscrew, unwrap

▶ Ask everyone to write sentences using the 'new' words in the list in **A**. (The 'new' words are ones that students haven't come across before which they think will be useful and are worth learning.)

B

Answers

1 *Example   Make sure everyone understands what to do.*
2 co-author
3 overconfident
4 mid-sentence
5 rebuilt
6 underpaid
7 overworking
8 unlock
9 sub-zero   mid-winter
10 overeat   overweight

2.6 Safety at sea   *Listening*

A   Students should use their previous knowledge and common sense to predict the answers to the questions and then listen to the recording to confirm what they already suspect, rather than receive a huge amount of new information.

B   🔲 Students listen to the recording and answer the questions.

▶ Find out how many people in the class have experience of a water sport: water skiing, diving, windsurfing or sailing. What do they enjoy about it? How safe is it?

Answers

1 Match the signals to the pictures:
   a) 'I am OK.' – picture C
   b) 'I need assistance.' – picture A
   c) 'I have a diver down. Keep clear and proceed at slow speed.' – picture B
   d) 'Faster!' – picture F
   e) 'Slower!' – picture E
   f) 'Speed OK.' – picture G
   g) 'Back to jetty.' – picture D

2 nod your head
3 shake your head

4 Advice to the water skier:
   a) watch the skier   drive the boat
   b) above water
   c) start
   d) let go of the rope and sit down
   e) curl yourself into a ball
   f) they can help to keep you afloat

Transcript

Jenny: After a series of accidents involving water skiers, it's clear that there need to be stricter rules and controls. Chuck Brown is a lifeguard. Chuck, what advice would you give to people who are taking part in water sports?

Chuck: Well, Jenny, er ... first of all you have to know the signals that ... er ... you should use if ... if you get in trouble. Now, it ... it's difficult to hear shouts alone above the noise of waves, er ... boat engines, breathing apparatus if you're wearing that, and so on.

Jenny: I see, could you give us some examples?

Chuck: Well, if you're diving ... er ... you need to use these signals. Now, 'I'm OK,' is the hand up with thumb and forefinger making an O, like that. Um ... the 'I need assistance' ... er ... signal is ... er ... you put the fist up and you move it from left to right above the water. Now, er ... if ... you're on a boat you should be flying the right international signal which is a flag. Um ... Flag A: that's white on the side nearest the mast and it's blue on the other side.

Jenny: And what does that mean?

Chuck: That indicates 'I have a diver down ... er ... keep clear and proceed at a slow speed' for other boats around.

Jenny: Yes, and what about skiers?

Chuck: Well ... um ... anybody who's going to be water skiing should be taught several signals. First of all, the signal to go faster: you hold your palm up and motion upwards *or* just nod your head.

C

Jenny: Yes.

Chuck: The signal for slower is the palm down, you motion downwards *or* you shake your head. Now, if you want to indicate that the speed's OK, you give the OK signal with your thumb and forefinger making the O, as ... er ... I just told you about. If you want to go back to the jetty, just point with your arm downwards. Like that, down towards your side like that.

Jenny: I see, uhuh. Well, so much for signals. But water skiing can be quite dangerous, can't it?

Chuck: Well, not if you follow the basic safety procedures and you know what you're doing. Um ... well, there are three points really. There should always be two people in the boat. Now, that's one person to watch the skier and the other to drive the boat ... er ... they call him the helmsman. Um ... before you start, your ski-tips must be above the water, so you don't get dragged down immediately. If you're the skier you have to give a clear signal to the helmsman (that's the driver, the person who's driving the boat) when you're ready to start.

Jenny: And I suppose even the best water skiers fall into the water quite often, what should you do if you fall?

Chuck: When you fall! Well, if you start to fall forwards you should let go of the rope and sit down. Um ... if you're falling sideways, you should just curl yourself up into a ball. And very important: recover the skis immediately. Get a hold of those skis because they can help to keep you afloat.

Jenny: I see, right. Well, thank you very much, Chuck.

Chuck: Not at all.

(Time: 3 minutes 15 seconds)

2.7 The Month in View   *Reading/Problem solving*

The text here is a magazine article. It contains a number of difficult words and references to names with which students will be unfamiliar – but they will be able to do the tasks WITHOUT this knowledge. This section will help students to cope with a difficult text in spite of the difficulties.

A   This part gets students to scan the text for particular information. Encourage them to do this quickly, without worrying about unfamiliar words. It can be done by students working together in pairs.

▶ This kind of reading skill may need further practice. A good way to do this is to get students to search for specific information in a newspaper, by asking them questions like: 'Which airport did the plane take off from?' and 'What was the temperature in London yesterday?'

Answers (And relevant words or information that provide the clues.)

1 Nov 16 – burglary   Agatha Christie
2 Nov 10 – French
3 Nov 4 – invented   ballpoint pen   safety pin   etc.
4 Nov 23 – Bomb   nuclear war
5 Nov 4 – Painters   paintings
6 Nov 26 – Sixties   since the war
7 Nov 18 – women   women

B   In this part students have to find the relevant programme and then check whether the information given accords with the statement in the Student's Book. Discourage students from asking questions about the vocabulary and about the names of the performers and actors.

Answers

1 *Example   Make sure everyone understands what to do.*
2 F – he copies other painters' styles
3 F – the character wants to escape from home
4 T
5 T
6 F – the writer finds humour in the situation
7 T
8 F – it's on twice a week
9 T
10 T

C   This part gives everyone a chance to give their own views, and leads on to **D** which is a Directed Writing task.

D   Before they write the two paragraphs, get everyone to make some notes on the points they will make, based on what they have been discussing in C. The writing is probably best done as homework.

Make sure everyone looks at another student's work and makes COMMENTS. You'll probably need to explain the kind of comments that would be helpful and which your students are capable of making:

1 Reactions to the text – 'That's interesting, I didn't know you liked so-and-so.'
2 Questions about the content – 'You say that it would be boring, why do you think that?'
3 Questions about things you don't understand – 'I can't read this word – what does it say?' or 'What do you mean here – I don't quite understand.'

4 And POSSIBLY (but not necessarily) also comments on mistakes – 'I don't think you've spelt this word right.'

Model paragraphs

These are not definitive, just suggested versions of what students might write. If your students might find it helpful, these paragraphs could be photocopied and shown to the class.

```
The programme I'd most like to see is 'Year of the
French'. This interests me because I like to find out
about the way people in other countries live and their
attitudes. I've never heard of Marie-Paule Belle, but I'd
like to find out more about French pop music. Friday's
programme about a skiing policeman sounds fascinating,
too.

The programme I'd least like to see is 'Stuntman
Challenge'. Although stunts in films are always exciting,
it's their place in the story that makes them worth
watching. The idea of people challenging each other to do
dangerous things seems pointless and stupid to me, not
thrilling.
```

© Cambridge University Press 1990

2.8 Position and direction   *Prepositions*

A To make sure everyone knows what they're supposed to do, demonstrate the position of the pen or pencil you're holding in different positions. (If you don't mind putting on a little performance, you could get everyone to imagine that you're pointing at a fly or mosquito as it buzzes round the room, alighting in various positions – but you'd have to do the sound effects yourself.)

Then get members of the class to use their pens in the same way, while everyone listens and you correct any errors and answer questions.

▶ Further practice can be given by taking into class a handful of paperclips and 'hiding' them in different parts of the room. Members of the class then have to SAY WHERE each one is, but they are NOT allowed to point at it or pick it up.

B and **C** You could get everyone to add a few more letters to the rectangle by telling them where you want them to put W, X, Y and Z. Your students may need a bit of help with phrases like:
    just a little

slightly
about a third of the way from
almost touching   etc.
Go round the class while they're doing C and offer help when requested.
At the end ask for questions.

Answers

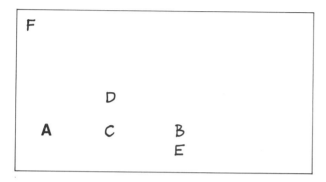

D   Student A looks at Activity 32 and B (and C in a group of
three) looks at 40. One partner has a drawing of a fox, the other a
drawing of a rabbit superimposed on the grid. The idea is to explain the
ROUTE that a pencil should take on the grid to draw the same picture.

Make sure that no one peeps at the other's picture and that they
explain the route WITHOUT identifying what the drawing is supposed to
represent. Your students may need some help with the vocabulary
required to describe different kinds of lines:

horizontal, vertical, diagonal, curved, parallel, straight

▶ Divide the class into groups. Make sure that at least one member of
each group knows something about chess – if not, rearrange the groups.
This information can be drawn on the board:

The groups have to decide together:
1 Where the chess pieces should be placed on the board before a game of chess can start.
2 What moves each piece is allowed to make during a game of chess.
3 How each piece can take another piece.
If they're in difficulty, they should ask a member of another group to help them.

NOTE: No one needs to be an 'expert' to do this activity. A group of non-experts or people who only know a little about chess may have a much more lively discussion and use a greater variety of prepositional phrases than a group who are all chess buffs!

▶ There are more exercises on position and direction in Units 8 and 9 in *Use of English* by Leo Jones (CUP).

2.9 The jogger's wallet *Listening*

This is a very straightforward listening exercise. Its main purpose is to introduce the theme of telling a story, which students themselves will have to do in the communication activity in 2.10 and, in writing, in the composition exercise in 2.11.

First everyone hears the story and agrees on the correct sequence of pictures (not too difficult!).

Then play the tape again so that students can concentrate on some of the techniques that are used by the speaker. It can be treated as a 'model' for what they will be doing in the next section. They should also notice how the speaker involves his listener in the story.

▶ For homework ask everyone to think of a story that has happened to a friend of a friend of theirs. They will be able to tell this story to their partners in 2.10 **B** – see below.

Answers

The correct sequence of pictures is: E F C D A B

Transcript

OK, OK. Now listen to this then. Now, this ... this is a story about a friend of mine, a New Yorker who ... he lives near Central Park, so every morning he goes out jogging. Right? He goes out jogging. Now he was jogging this morning, this one morning very early at his usual ... the way he usually ran, you know, jogging along there, and he was surrounded by, you know, lots of others, there are always lots of people jogging in Central Park. And suddenly, out of nowhere, this jogger ... kind of bumped into him and ... and shot past him. Well, he didn't think much except that ... er ... suddenly ... he thought he felt something ... he felt something missing, so he discovered ... he tapped his pocket and he discovered that his wallet was missing. Huh? So he said to himself, 'Now, this has never happened to me, this ... I've got to ... I ... I can't let this happen.' So he saw the guy that had hit him and said, 'That ... he must have been the one,' and he ran up to him and he ... and he grabbed him and he ... and he shook him and he said 'Give me that wallet!' like that. Well, the guy was terrified, it was really threatening, and the other guy obviously wasn't stronger than him and ... and thank God he didn't pull a knife or anything like that. And s ... immediately, immediately the guy reached in his pocket and he produced this wallet which my friend took and felt very happy about it, pocketed the wallet and ran home.

Well, hc ... he went home, and he took his shower as he usually did to get ready to go to work and then he got his ... putting his clothes on and he patted his jacket pocket a ... and ... it w ... in his pocket was his own wallet. The wallet he had taken in the guy ... from the guy, the wallet was in his back pocket belonged to somebody else – he'd taken the other guy's wallet! He felt dreadful!

(Time: 1 minute 45 seconds)

2.10   Telling a story   *Communication activity*

A   After the discussion, ask each group to report to the class on what they talked about. In a small class this could be a whole-class discussion.

B   This activity is best done as a class, so that everyone can pool ideas. It may be more interesting to change the setting of the story to somewhere closer to home – in a local street, on a train or bus or in a lift, for example.

Draw everyone's attention to the kind of questions that a listener or reader might ask – telling a story usually happens as part of a conversation, not a monologue.

C   ⚏ Student A looks at Activity 17, B at 24 and C at 46. Each person has three scenes from a film – one of which is the same as another person's.
1   To begin with, each person should sit quietly and form an idea of how the scenes might fit together into a story. Then they should tell their version to the others, beginning: 'This is what happened ...'
2   When all three have done this, they should look at the other people's scenes and decide on a story that will fit all six pictures.
3   Get each group to tell their version of the story to the rest of the class.

2.11   **Writing a narrative**   *Composition*

We considered the role of the listener in 2.10, now we consider the reader of a narrative. Keeping the reader interested is essential if you're writing a narrative.

A   To begin with everyone reads the car breakdown story and decides together how it could be improved. There are no grammatical errors or spelling mistakes – what is wrong is that it lacks detail and is very boring to read. Moreover the precise times and distances are irrelevant and distracting.

Activity 9 contains an improved version of the car breakdown story. After reading it, students are asked to underline the main changes that have been made. There are no 'correct answers' to this as it is a straightforward task, designed to draw students' attention to the language used.

Ask if anyone can suggest any further changes which might make the improved version even better.

B   Now the same task is done with the Casablanca story. Again there is an improved version to look at later, in Activity 3.

The first version uses the past tense (which makes it seem a true story, rather than the plot of a film) and is pretty dreary to read. The improved version contains extra information, which has to be underlined – this is to draw attention to the details and there are no 'correct answers'.

Ask if anyone can suggest any further changes which might make the improved version even better.

Perhaps point out that the plot of a film or book is generally told in the simple present tense.

C   Students should write their own composition as homework, but it may be best to discuss the kind of things they could write about in a class discussion beforehand.

D   Before collecting the stories for marking, get everyone to read one or two other people's stories and comment on them.

▶   We return to writing narratives in 12.4, but it would be a good idea to get students to write a composition on a different topic in **C** as an extra composition assignment later on in the course.

2.12 *Make* and *do* *Verbs and idioms*

A This section revises some collocations with MAKE and DO. It can be set as homework or done in pairs in class.

Answers

Bill made ...
    Shirley laugh   a cake   a noise   a mistake   an arrangement
    a comment   a decision   a good impression   me an offer
    a promise   a statement
Shirley did ...
    Bill a favour   the washing-up   her duty   the shopping
    an exercise   her homework   a good job   badly in the test
    her best   very well   nothing at all

B It may be helpful for students to know the definitions given in the Answers below. Note that these are rough-and-ready definitions – consult a dictionary for more detail and further examples. This exercise presents just a selection of the myriad idiomatic phrasal verbs with DO and MAKE, but any more would be confusing and discouraging at this level.

Answers

1   do with = need or want
2   doing up = redecorate (we can also do up a shoelace or coat)
3   done   out of = cause to lose by cheating or trickery
4   do without = manage without having something

5   make out = see with difficulty
6   make up for = repay or compensate for
7   making for = going in the direction of / heading for
8   making   up = invent a story
9   made off with = steal

▶ For more listening and speaking activities on the topics of entertainment, hobbies and sport, see Units 8, 10 and 20 in *Ideas* by Leo Jones (CUP).

3 Nature and the environment

3.1 Plants and animals

Vocabulary

▶ To start everyone off, do a quick brainstorm and ask the class to suggest some local mammals, birds and insects they might see in the wild locally (e.g. sparrows, dogs) – and some animals they'd normally only see in a zoo or on TV (e.g. lions, crocodiles).

A This part can be set for preparation as homework, using a dictionary. When everyone has compared ideas with a partner, pool ideas as a class – write up only the words that you consider to be worth learning.

Some suggested answers

1 *Example   Make sure everyone understands what to do.*
2 Fruit: apple, plum, pineapple, apricot, melon, raspberry, strawberry, blackcurrant, cherry, etc.
3 Vegetables: cabbage, potato, cauliflower, aubergine, onion, etc.
4 Trees: fir, beech, palm, cypress, eucalyptus, etc.
5 Flowers: buttercup, daffodil, crocus, dandelion, orchid, etc.
6 Wild animals (mammals): lion, wolf, fox, elephant, deer, monkey, dolphin, etc.
7 Domestic animals: cow, sheep, chicken, horse, donkey, etc.
8 Pets: cat, dog, canary, hamster, gerbil, etc.
9 Birds: blackbird, robin, stork, crow, swallow, kingfisher, etc.
10 Young animals: cub, kitten, lamb, foal, etc. (not many of these)
11 Reptiles: snake (adder, python, cobra, etc.), crocodile, tortoise, turtle, etc.
12 Insects: bee, mosquito, cockroach, beetle, locust, moth, flea, etc.
13 Fish: trout, sole, sardine, cod, anchovy, red mullet, etc.
14 Other sea creatures: lobster, mussel, squid, prawn, shrimp, jellyfish, etc.

B This could be prepared at home and checked through in class. Allow time for any queries about related vocabulary to be raised.

Answers

1 *Example   Make sure everyone understands what to do.*
  (The percentage of people employed in agriculture is much higher in
  some countries: Greece 30%, Italy 9%, India 60%, Spain 14%.)
2 harvest   crops   picked
3 mountains
4 hunting
5 pollution   poisons
6 forecast   intervals
7 fog
8 misty
9 temperatures   frost
10 gale/storm/hurricane/night/evening
11 breeze   shade
12 thunder   lightning
13 shower
14 scenery   valleys   climate
15 coast   cliffs

▶ Finally, to activate some of the vocabulary ask the members of the
class these questions:
● What kind of agriculture is common in your country?
● What are people's attitudes to animals and nature in your country?
● What is your own attitude to hunting and shooting animals and to
  fishing?
(There will be further opportunities for discussion later in this unit.)

3.2   The balance of nature   *Reading*

The tasks in this section focus on coping with unfamiliar vocabulary in a
passage and on distinguishing between key words and less important
words. The use of dictionaries should not be permitted during these
activities.

A   This is a warm-up discussion. Students from Mediterranean or
hotter countries may find the fauna and flora of a Northern European
woodland somewhat exotic.

B   Everyone reads the passage quickly through to get the gist. No
dictionaries allowed.

C   This focusses on the key words in the passage – the ones that contain important information and which are repeated. If students don't understand them, they won't be able to fully appreciate the passage.

Answers

natural community (i)	species (h)	link (f)
woodland (a)	tissues (e)	organisms (c)
dominated (b)	flesh (d)	decomposers (g)

D   These are less important words – students can probably appreciate the passage fully without knowing exactly what they are. This is an easy exercise, designed to show students that they CAN work things out by looking at the context; the passage actually *says* that a caterpillar is an insect, for example.

Answers

oak (a kind of tree)	aphid (a kind of insect)
bramble (a kind of large plant)	caterpillar (a kind of insect)
moss (a kind of simple plant)	lacewing (a kind of insect)
lichen (a kind of simple plant)	shrew (a kind of small animal)
algae (a kind of simple plant)	vole (a kind of small animal)
trunk (part of a tree)	fungi (a kind of simple plant)
snail (a kind of small animal)	

E   After spending so long on the previous parts, the true or false questions should present few problems.

Answers

TRUE statements: 1   3   4   5   8
FALSE statements: 2   6   7

F   The closing group discussion touches on issues like pollution, cutting down trees, reclaiming 'waste' land for agriculture or building, etc.

___

3.3   The past   *Grammar*

A   To save time in class, the examples could be studied and the gaps filled as homework.
      Answer any queries and clear up any doubts before going on to **B**.

Suggested answers

SIMPLE PAST:
> I **saw** a film about animals on TV last Wednesday evening.
> In 1988 I **spent** my summer holidays in **Italy**.

PAST PROGRESSIVE:
> We **were playing** cards when the lights went out.
> As the sun **was shining** we decided to go for a drive.
> While you **were waiting for** the bus, we walked all the way here.

USED TO:
> Before the war, more people **used to work** on the land.
> When I was a child, we **used to have** a dog.

PAST PERFECT:
> It rained all day but I **had forgotten** to pack an umbrella.
> After I **had read** the book, I made some notes on it.
> They were still friends even though they **had been** apart for ten years.

PRESENT PERFECT:
> We **have** already **studied the first** two units in this book.
> She **has made** five phone calls since lunchtime.
> **Have** you (**ever**) **visited** Britain?

B   This could be done by students working together in pairs, or they could do it alone and then compare answers with a partner later.

Answers

1 *Example   Make sure everyone understands what to do.*
2 I **went** to the zoo last weekend.
3 When **did you leave** school?
4 Where **did you go** on holiday last year?
5 She **was** born in 1975.
6 Our family **used** to live in a smaller flat when I **was** younger.
7 Our broken window **hasn't been** mended yet.
8 The rain started **while they were playing** tennis.

C   This can be set as homework, or done in pairs or alone.

Suggested answers (Some variations are possible.)

1 *Example   Make sure everyone understands what to do.*
2 When the farmer had started his tractor, he began to plough the field.
3 While I was walking in the country it began to rain / the rain began to fall.

4 After we had had lunch, we went for a walk by the river.
5 They used to have a dog (but they haven't got one now).
6 Before I went to the zoo (last year), I had never seen a real tiger. /
  Before I saw a tiger in the zoo last year, I had never seen one.

D ⬚ Student A looks at Activity 18, student B at 42. Each has a
gruesome story about an animal to read and then tell, using past tenses.
   To prevent people simply reading their story out loud to their partner,
everyone should tell the story in their own words from notes, with books
closed.
   One story concerns a pet cat, the other a pet canary, both of which met
unfortunate ends. Both of them allegedly happened to 'friends of a friend'.
   Alternatively, this can be done as 'pairs of pairs' – i.e. an even number
of pairs. Each pair would prepare the story together and then split up to
tell the prepared story to another student.

▶ There is more work on past tenses in *Use of English* Units 3 and 4.

3.4   The Earth at risk   *Listening*

First of all, ask the class what they already know about the risks facing
nature and the environment – a subject that is always in the news but
which may have passed some students by, perhaps.

▶ A map of the world might be helpful during this section, particularly
if you suspect that your students may not know the whereabouts of
some of the countries mentioned.

A As well as preparing them for the theme of the recording, this will
mean less distraction during the listening.

B ⬚ It will take more than one listening to fill all the gaps.
Although this is quite a difficult broadcast to understand, the task
should help students who might otherwise find it intimidating.
   The recording is probably too long to be played non-stop. Two
suggested places to take breaks are shown in the Transcript below – this
would split the task into three parts: questions 1 to 4, questions 5 to 10
and question 11 onwards. Alternatively, pause the tape before each of
the interviewer's questions.
   Note that, in spite of the disclaimer about the paper used in books,
recycled paper is more environment-friendly as its manufacture requires
less energy and causes less pollution than the smooth white paper used
in a textbook.

▶ Follow up the listening exercise with a discussion about the content of the interview. Perhaps ask these questions:
- Which of the points made were you already aware of?
- Which of the points do you agree with? Or disagree with?
- What other 'solutions' can you suggest to the problems described?

Answers

1 firewood   domestic
2 rain
3 soil
4 wheat   maize
5 tropical forests
6 food   Europe   America
7 poor   exhausted
8 the USA   furniture
9 rare plants   medicines
10 world
11 Nepal   India   rainfall
12 1 ten   twenty   international
   2 controlled
   3 softwoods   hardwoods

Transcript

Interviewer: Brian Cowles is the producer of a new series of documentaries called 'The Earth at Risk' which can be seen on Channel 4 later this month. Each programme deals with a different continent, doesn't it, Brian?

Brian Cowles: That's right, yes, we went to … er … we went to America, both North and South and then we went over to Africa and South-East Asia.

Interviewer: And what did you find in each of these continents?

Brian Cowles: Well … er … starting with … er … Africa, our film shows the impact of the population on the environment. Generally speaking, this has caused the Sahara Desert to expand. It's a bit of a vicious circle … er … we find, people cut down trees for firewood and their domestic animals eat all the available plants – and so consequently they have to move south as the Sahara Desert expands further south. I mean, soon the whole of Mali will become a desert. And … er … in East Africa: here the grasslands are supporting too many animals and the result is, of course, there's no grass – nothing for the animals to eat.

Interviewer: Mm, yes, I see. Um … and the … the next film deals with North America?

Brian Cowles: That's right. In the … er … USA, as you know, intensive agriculture requires a plentiful supply of rain for these crops to

69

grow, I mean if there isn't enough rain the crops don't grow. And growing crops stabilise soil, without them the top soil just … it just blows away. I mean, this is also true for any region that is intensely farmed – most of Europe, for example. But the USA is the world's breadbasket – American farmers grow huge quantities of extra wheat, maize and soya beans to feed the world – consequently, if there isn't enough rain there, other countries can't buy enough food for their people to eat.

(Questions 5 to 10 ↓)

Interviewer: And what did you find in South America?

Brian Cowles: In South America (a … as in Central Africa and Southern Asia) tropical forests are being cut down at an alarming rate. Th … this is done so that people can support themselves by growing food or to create ranches where cattle can be raised to exp … to be exported to Europe or America as tinned meat. The problem is that the s … the soil is so poor that … um … that only a couple of harvests are possible before this very thin soil becomes exhausted. And it can't be fed with fertilizers like agricultural land in Europe.

Um … for example, in Brazil in 1982 an area of jungle the size of Britain and France combined was destroyed to make way for an iron ore mine. I mean, huge numbers of trees are being cut down for export as hardwood to Japan, Europe, USA … I mean … to make things like luxury furniture. These forests can't … er … they can't be replaced – the forest soil is thin and unproductive and in just a few years, a … a jungle has become a waste land. Tropical forests contain rare plants (which … er … we can use for medicines, for example) and animals – one animal or plant species becomes extinct every half hour. These … er … forest trees … I mean … also have worldwide effects. You know, they convert carbon dioxide into oxygen. The consequence of destroying forests is not only that the climate of that region changes (because there is less rainfall) but this change affects the whole world. I mean, over half the world's rain forest has been cut down this century.

(Questions 11 and 12 ↓)

Interviewer: So, Brian, would you agree that what we generally think of as … er … as er … natural disasters are in fact man-made?

Brian Cowles: Yes, by and large … er … I mean, obviously not hurricanes or earthquakes, but take flooding, for example. I mean, practically every year, the whole of Bangladesh is flooded and this is getting worse. You know, the cause is that forests have been cut down up in Nepal and India … I mean … higher up-river in the Himalayas. Trees … er … would hold rainfall in their roots, but if they've been cut down all the rain that falls in the monsoon season flows straight into the River Ganges and floods the whole country. The reason for flooding in Sudan is the same – the forests higher up the Blue Nile in Ethiopia have been destroyed too.

Interviewer: Well, this all sounds terribly depressing. Um ... what is to be done? I mean, *can* anything be done, in fact?

Brian Cowles: Yes, of course it can ... er ... first, the national governments have to be forward-looking and consider the results of their policies in ten or twenty years, not just think as far ahead as the next election. Somehow, all the countries in the world have to work together on an international basis. Secondly, the population has to be controlled in some way: there are too many people trying to live off too little land. Thirdly, we don't need tropical hardwood to make our furniture – it's a luxury people in the West must do without. Softwoods are just as good, less expensive and can be produced on environment-friendly 'tree farms', where trees are replaced at the same rate that they are cut down.

Interviewer: And, presumably, education is important as well. People must be educated to realise the consequences ... um ... of their actions?

Brian Cowles: Yes, yes of course. But educating people who are struggling to survive is difficult. I mean, you can't say 'Don't cut down these trees because you'll only get one harvest' – one harvest will keep them alive for another year.

Interviewer: Yes, I see, well, thank you, Brian.

(Time: 5 minutes 35 seconds)

3.5   Using negative prefixes   *Word study*

This section deals with negative prefixes. Perhaps remind students that they have already come across **un–** in 2.5 in verbs like *undress* and *undo*.

A   If necessary, explain that **mis–** means 'incorrectly' or 'wrongly'. Note that all the **il–** and **ir–** forms that students need to know at this level and for the exam are listed in the Student's Book and these are the only examples that they need to learn.

Answers

un–	uncomfortable, unexpected, unfamiliar, unknown, unlucky, unpopular
in–	inaccurate, inconvenient, intolerant, invisible
im–	impatient, impersonal, improbable
dis–	disapprove, dislike, disobey
mis–	mispronounce, misspell

▶ Ask everyone to write five sentences using the new and useful words they have come across in this section.

B   Make sure everyone realises that they will have to alter the grammatical form of some words to fit the contexts given.

Answers

1 *Example   Make sure everyone knows what they have to do.*
2 impatient
3 inconvenient
4 unreasonable
5 inefficient
6 misunderstood
7 misspelt
8 disliked

▶ We return to this aspect of word formation in 12.7. For more work on negative prefixes and opposites, see *Use of English* Unit 33.

3.6   What's the weather going to be like?   *Problem solving*

Make it clear to everyone that they should imagine that Alan, Betty and Colin are 'globe-trotting friends' of theirs.

A   🔲 The purpose of this part is to give further practice in understanding phone numbers when they're spoken (as already practised in 1.5), as well as providing information that will be required for **B** and **C** below. The actual phone numbers are not relevant to the later parts of this section.

Begin by asking everyone how they feel if they have to leave a recorded message on an answering machine.

Each message can be played and replayed individually, rather than all three together.

Answers

Alan
Monday	London: 01 444 3456
Tuesday	Paris: *no number*
Wednesday	New York: 0101 212 909 3900

Betty
Monday	Oslo 101 47 2 776 2121
Tuesday	Rome: 010 39 6 685 3890
Wednesday	Brussels: 010 32 2 861 1970

Colin

Monday	Los Angeles: 0101 213 345 8729
Tuesday	Geneva: *no number*
Wednesday	Vienna: *no number*

Transcript

Narrator: You'll hear three recorded messages from your friends.

Alan: Hello, this is Alan. Listen, I'll be in London on Monday, Paris on Tuesday and New York on Wednesday and Thursday. You can get in touch with me in New York on Wednesday at this number: 0101 212 909 39 double 0. I'll go over that again: 0101 212 909 39 double 0. In London, that's Monday, the number is 01 treble 4 3456, well you know that one. In Paris I won't be … er … contactable on the phone.

Betty: Hi, this is Betty. I'm just leaving now … er … and I'm going to be in Oslo on Monday, er … in Rome on Tuesday and in Brussels on … er … Wednesday and Thursday. Now … um … if you need to get in touch, my phone number in Oslo is 010 47 2 776 2121. Er … now … in Rome it's 010 39 6 685 3890. Oh … er … and in Brussels it's 010 32 2 861 1970.

Colin: Er … hello, this is Colin. Um … look, I'm going to be in Los Angeles on Monday, er … then in Geneva on Tuesday and in Vienna from Wednesday for the rest of the week. If you need to get in touch, my number in Los Angeles is: zero 1 zero 1 31 … no, oh, let's start that again: that's zero 1 zero 1 213 345 8729. Um … but you won't be able to get me on the phone in Geneva or Vienna, I'm afraid.

(Time: 2 minutes 20 seconds)

B   Now everyone has to note down the details of the weather that Alan, Betty and Colin can expect, according to the forecast. This task and the one in **C** practise extracting relevant information from written data.

Everyone will probably have different ideas about the kind of clothes each person should pack!

C   The weather summary in Activity 15 shows the temperatures and weather that different parts of the world experienced on the Wednesday of the week in question. When the pairs or groups have decided which place (of the ones visited by the friends) had the worst weather and which friend was most lucky with the weather, find out if everyone in the class agrees.

⋙→

Answers

This chart summarises the relevant information that has to be gathered in **B** and **C**.

FORECAST	Monday	Tuesday onwards	Actual weather on Wednesday
Alan			
London	cloudy 18	thundery showers	sunny 22
Paris	sunny 24	mostly sunny	fair 21
New York	rain 28	rain at times	fair 36
Betty			
Oslo	cloudy 22	rain at times	sleet 4
Rome	sunny 26	warm and sunny	sunny 25
Brussels	cloudy 18	warmer, sunny	hail 15
Colin			
Los Angeles	cloudy 21	dry and sunny	fair 17
Geneva	cloudy 22	mostly sunny	fog 14
Vienna	sunny 20	showers then fair	fair 17

D   After reading the postcard from Alan, everyone has to write two postcards in a similar style, describing the weather in each place. Point out that writing an informative postcard is a similar task to writing a paragraph.

If time is very short, different groups could write different postcards and then 'send' them to another group.

The model postcards may be photocopied for your students, if this will be helpful. If they have managed to do the task adequately, this would not be necessary.

Model postcards

> Brussels, Wednesday evening, 22 June
>
> Dear Eddie,
>
> Arrived here this morning from Rome. Here at lunchtime there was a hailstorm and it was quite a contrast from the lovely sunny weather in Rome yesterday and of course, as I expected, it's much cooler.

But Rome was an even greater contrast from Oslo. As you know, I was there on Monday and the forecast had said it might rain but that it would be reasonably warm — but in fact it was freezing and there was sleet!! As I only had a light raincoat I was glad I was only staying there for one day.
I'll see you in a couple of days.
        Best wishes,
                Betty

Vienna, Wednesday 22 June

Dear Eddie,

Well, here I am in Vienna after stopping over in Geneva on my way from Los Angeles. They say the sun always shines in Southern California, but while I was there it wasn't very nice at all — everyone said it was more like winter there. Yesterday in Geneva it wasn't too bad — mostly sunny in fact and quite warm but it was foggy when I left this morning. Here in Vienna it's not very warm but at least it's dry.

I'll call you on Saturday when I get back.
    Best,
        Colin

© Cambridge University Press 1990

▶ You could also ask everyone to role-play a phone call between one of the travellers and a person staying at home, finding out what the traveller is doing and what the weather has been like.

3.7   Compound prepositions   *Use of English*

This should be 'revision' for most students, but be prepared to step in with explanations where necessary. The exercise could be done as homework and checked later in class, to save time.

Answers

1 *Example   Make sure everyone knows what they have to do.*
2 apart from/except for
3 by means of
4 except for/apart from
5 due to
6 According to
7 ahead of
8 on behalf of
9 instead of
10 in addition to/as well as
11 As for
12 As regards

▶ Get everyone to write five sentences, using the most useful 'new' compound prepositions.
Can they think of any others? Here are a few fairly common ones:
   away from   because of   in front of   out of   in spite of   despite

3.8   The Greenhouse Effect   *Reading*

Begin by finding out how much everyone already knows about the Greenhouse Effect. To save time, they could read the text and perhaps do **A** or **B** as homework.

A   This is a scanning exercise: the gaps in the captions are to be filled by finding the relevant information in the passage.

Answers

1 fossil fuels   trees   atmosphere
2 heat   space   trapped
3 vapour   absorbs
4 surface   reflect   snow
5 store   warming   expand

B   Perhaps point out that the questions refer to information that is given in the text – this may contradict students' own knowledge of the subject. Indeed, according to some experts, the effects of the changes to the Earth's atmosphere may be even more catastrophic than this magazine article suggests.

Answers

TRUE statements: 1   2   5   6   7   8
FALSE statements: 3   4   9   10

▶ Follow up the comprehension exercises with a discussion about the effects of man's interference with the environment. Within your students' lifetimes, what changes in global and local climate are likely to take place? Will these be for the better – or for the worse?

3.9   Making notes   *Composition*

▶ This section could equally well be done AFTER the listening and discussion activities in 3.10.

▶ Give anyone a chance to explain why they're *against* making notes before writing a composition and get the others to convince them they are mistaken. We will continue to emphasise the value of making notes throughout this book – time spent doing so is never time wasted. Point out that in one's own language this may be less necessary than it is in a foreign language.

A   Ask everyone to suggest further points that they might make on the topic of recycling:
e.g. BOTTLES – recycling glass bottles uses almost as much energy as manufacturing new ones. Plastic bottles should also be recycled.
   No particular style of notes is recommended here – students should be encouraged to experiment with various styles to find out which suits them best. The second type, sometimes called a 'mind map', is particularly suitable for making notes on a lecture or on a text you have read.

B   When the pairs have made their notes, get them to compare them with another pair's. Perhaps collate everyone's suggestions on the board in one of the preferred styles.

▶ Instead of writing notes on one of the three topics suggested in the

Student's Book (whales, experiments and zoos) you may prefer to follow up some of the topics from other sections:
1 Rain forests (3.4)
2 Greenhouse effect (3.8)
3 One of the topics discussed in 3.10

C   The model notes and two model 100-word paragraphs opposite are on the topic of zoos. They may be photocopied, perhaps to give students some ideas of how to approach one of the other topics.
  Before they hand in their work, give everyone a chance to read someone else's composition.

▶ Discuss what difference it would make to the communicative effect of the composition if the second paragraph came first. Does the reader conclude that, on balance, the writer is 'for' or 'against' zoos in the model composition, for example?

Ask the class to look at each other's compositions and comment on how the communicative effect would change if the paragraphs were reversed.

Model notes

<u>"CLOSE ALL ZOOS"</u>

I AGREE BECAUSE...
- unpleasant, depressing - especially old-fashioned zoos
- cruel to keep animals in small cages - lions: Africa, open spaces
- climate - winter: tropical animals
- entertainment (like circus) - people laugh at animals performing (bananas, swinging, etc.) & people make animals nervous - don't respect them

I DISAGREE BECAUSE...
- modern zoo parks - large enclosures
- scientific research
- preserving + breeding rare species - stop some becoming extinct
- education about animals - better than films or books

Model composition

Some zoos are rather unpleasant, depressing places. This seems to be particularly true of the more old-fashioned ones where large animals are kept in tiny cages for the amusement of the public. This kind of zoo is cruel - a lion is an animal that lives in the open spaces of Africa and cannot enjoy being a prisoner. In the winter, zoos in colder countries do not provide a warm enough environment for animals from hot countries. Worst of all, it seems to me, is the way some zoos are regarded as places of entertainment, like circuses, where people are encouraged to laugh at animals as they 'perform' their funny tricks (eating bananas, swinging from rubber tyres, and so on), make them frightened or angry by teasing them and don't respect them as our fellow creatures.

On the other hand, it seems to me that people who say that <u>all</u> zoos should be closed are overstating the case. Many modern zoo parks do keep animals in large enclosures and try to make them feel at home. Some zoos are valuable centres of scientific research, where rare species can be preserved and encouraged to breed. In many cases, this policy has led to the reintroduction of animals into areas where they had almost become extinct. Zoos are also a unique form of education, where children (and adults) can learn about the behaviour of animals in a more effective and enjoyable way than seeing films or reading about them.

3.10   For or against?   *Listening*

▶ This section could be done before 3.9, if more convenient.

A   💾 The brief discussions students hear in this part will lead to
longer, more personal, discussion in **B**. The three parts can be played
and replayed separately.

Set the scene by explaining that the people are being interviewed in a
street – a kind of opinion poll is being taken.

Answers

1 'Keeping pets in cities'
   Points FOR: Dogs can protect you from thieves and intruders
                      Dogs can be good company
                      Take their owners for walks
   Points AGAINST: Cruel to keep bird in cage
                      Cruel to keep dog shut indoors all day
                      Dogs pollute pavements + parks – unhealthy for
                        children and sports
2 'Everyone should stop eating meat'
   Points FOR: Cruel to kill animals, e.g. young lambs
                      Unnecessary to have meat – protein from nuts,
                        beans, etc.
                      Land used to raise animals could be used for
                        growing corn or wheat – just as good for you
   Points AGAINST: Meat very important biologically + is tasty
                      You can't tell people not to eat meat if they want to
                      Most vegetarians eat fish – also cruel?
3 'There should be stricter worldwide control of pollution'
   Points FOR: Pollution is a world problem – rivers, air, oceans
                      Pollution crosses frontiers
                      Ozone layer being destroyed by gases in aerosols –
                      forbidden in some countries, permitted in others
   Points AGAINST: Not such a big problem – only a tiny amount of
                      pollution on a worldwide scale.
                      Oceans and space immense – can absorb all this
                      stuff
                      Pollution concentrated in certain areas
                      Local people should protest and clean it up

Transcript

Narrator: You'll hear three conversations. Here's the first.

Interviewer: Excuse me, could I just stop you for one moment and ask you both please your opinion on ... um ... pets? What is your opinion of keeping pets in the city?

Man: What? Dogs and cats? Well, I've got a dog and ... er ... I'm all for it. A dog can protect you from thieves and intruders and ... um ... he's very good company, he's a very lively little dog and ... er ... of course, he takes me for walks! Haha. Gives me all the exercise I need ...

Woman: Yes, yes, but ... I mean ... it is ... it is ... cruel to keep a bird in a cage, I mean, or even a dog ... a dog that's shut inside all day. I mean, particularly in London, dogs pollute pavements and ... and in the parks ... I mean ... they're really unhealthy for children, people running, for sports ... I mean ...

Man: But don't you think this is something to do with the owner, how he actually ...

Narrator: Two.

Interviewer: Excuse me, do you agree that everyone should stop eating meat?

Man: Yeah, I do, I think it's really cruel to kill animals because, I mean, we see these nice woolly lambs, right? And they're less than a year old when they're actually taken off to a slaughterhouse and killed. I mean it's unnecessary to have meat for protein. I mean, we can get protein from nuts, beans, that sort of thing. Look at it from the agricultural point of view: to raise one cow you need all that land and all that land could be used for growing corn or wheat – just as good for you.

Interviewer: Thank you.

Woman: Well, I ... no I'm sorry, I don't agree at all. I mean, I ... I think ... well, yes all right it may be cruel to ... to slaughter very young animals but I think meat's very important biologically, I think we need it. And it's tasty ... I mean ... there's no way you can replace that with anything else, is there? I mean, that soya protein stuff it is just horrible. The other thing is, I don't think that you can actually tell people what to do. You see, you can't tell everybody not to eat meat if they want to, there's nothing you can do ...

Man: Well, I'm not telling them.

Woman: Well, yeah, well, that's what this lady's suggesting, isn't it? And ... and what about fish? Now, have you noticed, most vegetarians will eat fish, now why isn't that considered cruel? I mean, think about it ...

Narrator: Three.

Interviewer: Er ... excuse me, I wonder if you could spare a moment, please? Do you think there should be stricter worldwide control of pollution?

Woman: Oh yes, I certainly do. Um ... many countries have strict control but others haven't as yet and I think it's high time they had because it is a world problem. Um ... pollution goes into our rivers, the air, the oceans, it crosses frontiers. The ozone layer is being destroyed by gases in aerosols that are actually forbidden in some countries and ... and permitted in others. It's permitted in our country and I think it's disgraceful, something should be done about it before it's too late.

Interviewer: Right, thank you. What about you, sir?

Man: Ha, well I don't think it's such a problem as these prophets of doom would say – sorry about that, honey! Look there's only a tiny amount of pollution happening on a worldwide scale. Th ... the oceans are immense, space is immense, it can absorb all this stuff. Pollution is concentrated, I'll give you that, in certain areas, now it's up to the local people in those tiny areas to protest against it and to clean it up!

Interviewer: Thank you very much ...

(Time: 3 minutes 30 seconds)

B   Perhaps remind everyone of some useful expressions that they can use in their discussion and write them on the board:

It seems to me that ...	I don't agree that ...
I'd say that ...	It's not true to say that ...
I agree that ...	It's ridiculous to say that ...
Don't you think that ...	

3.11   How sweet!?   *Picture conversation*

In the exam, part of the Interview will involve talking about a photograph. This section gives everyone a chance to get used to doing this and to finding things to say – monosyllabic answers are not recommended in the exam!

Typically in the exam candidates are asked to:

- Describe or compare the people, the setting and/or the activity
- Discuss two or three points relevant to the picture(s)

Students should realise that, in the exam, such questions are not just ABOUT the content of the picture but are designed to encourage them to give opinions.

A   The class should be divided into an even number of pairs. Perhaps show how Yes/No questions are a lot of work for very little reward:

Interviewer: Do you think that the people in the picture are happy?

Candidate: Er ... no.

Interviewer: Would you agree that animals are treated as part of the family in some countries?

Candidate: Well, yes.

And of course this is equally true of normal conversations.

B   Students now work as pairs of pairs (each pair with another pair) as they try out their questions. Point out that prompting often encourages people to say more.

C   [image] Now students are back in pairs, applying the principles they have discussed to a one-to-one conversation. Student A looks at Activity 34, student B at 44.
Activity 34 shows a kitten with its paws on the keys of a typewriter.
Activity 44 shows a smiling man with an enormous spider on his arm.

3.12 *Get*   *Verbs and idioms*

A   This can be done in pairs in class, or set as homework. Make sure everyone realises that they may have to change the grammatical form of GET to fit the context. Perhaps point out that in British English the forms are: *get, got, got,* and in American English: *get, got, gotten.*

Answers

1 get rid of	6 get the joke
2 get better	7 get ready
3 got a headache	8 got home late
4 got the sack	9 get to sleep
5 getting dark	10 get someone else to do it

B   Suggest that everyone identifies the ones they know first before tackling the unfamiliar ones. If you think it will be helpful, point out the synonymous expressions given among the Answers below.

Answers

1 *Example   Make sure everyone understands what to do.*
2 get on with = live happily together
3 get round to = find time
4 get out of = avoid
5 get   across = communicate   getting at = suggest
6 getting   down = make someone feel depressed
7 get around/round = find a way of solving
8 get by = survive
9 get off = alight
10 getting on = manage/make progress
11 get through = make connection on phone
12 get together = meet/assemble

4 Transport and travel

4.1 On the move   *Vocabulary*

▶ To introduce the topic, perhaps get everyone to list as many different modes of transport as they can and then grade them in order of preference. Ask why/when they prefer cycling to going by bus, for example.

A   To save time in class, sections **A** and **B** could be prepared at home and then checked through by students working in pairs during the lesson. Imaginative students may be able to come up with amusing variations.

Notice the US English terms, which may be of interest to your class – though not necessary for the exam.

Answers

1	fares	11 engine bonnet (US hood)
2	trams (US streetcars)	12 way roundabout
3	tunnel	13 lights lane
4	return (US round trip)	14 caravan (US trailer/mobile home)
5	pavement (US sidewalk)	15 straight
6	footpath	16 space
7	petrol (US gas) motorists	17 car sick
8	seatbelt/safety belt	18 sign
9	boot (US trunk)	19 pedestrian crossing
10	mirror off	20 trip journey journey

B   This part is similar in style to the FCE exam, except that in Paper 1 there are only four alternatives to deal with.

▶ Make sure everyone looks at the WRONG alternatives in this part – and in such exercises in later units. There are many useful words among them. Ask the class to explain WHY the wrong answers are wrong in each context.

For example, in **B1**:

● Why is *by-pass* wrong in this context?
   Because a by-pass goes round a city or town – like a ring road, in fact.

- And why is *highway* wrong in this context?
  It's not completely wrong, it's just not a British English term – but it could be used in American English.
- And why is *main road* wrong in this context?
  Because a main road is a general word for an important road – not as wide as a motorway.
- And why is *main street* wrong in this context?
  Because a main street is an important road in a town or city, not one that goes a long distance.

Answers

1 motorway (US highway/freeway/interstate)
2 tube (US subway), also *underground*
3 coach (US bus)
4 turning
5 brake

C The purpose of the exercise is to help students who are confused by the plethora of nouns that are used to describe different forms of travel. Only approximate definitions are given in this exercise; for more exact definitions and examples consult a dictionary. Note that the definitions aren't watertight: in certain circumstances, for example, we can refer to a fairly long journey as a *trip*.

Answers

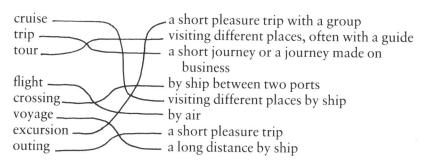

cruise — a short pleasure trip with a group
trip — visiting different places, often with a guide
tour — a short journey or a journey made on business
flight — by ship between two ports
crossing — visiting different places by ship
voyage — by air
excursion — a short pleasure trip
outing — a long distance by ship

D This discussion in groups of three or four will help to activate some of the vocabulary that students have come across in this section.
While the groups are discussing the questions, go round the class listening out for mistakes they are making that are relevant to the topic. For example:
'I enjoy going by foot.' ×
'I had an interesting travel to London.' ×
'The street from Milan to Rome is very busy.' ×

Make a note of any such errors you overhear and point them out to the class after they have finished the discussion.

▶ Finally, ask everyone if they have any further questions on vocabulary to do with transport and travel.

4.2   The Orient-Express   *Reading*

This passage contains quite a lot of difficult vocabulary. The questions in **A** and **B** will help students to understand the main points in spite of this.

A   To do this task, students only need to find the relevant information in the text. First though, they should read it through to get a general idea of what it's all about. To save time, this could be prepared at home beforehand.

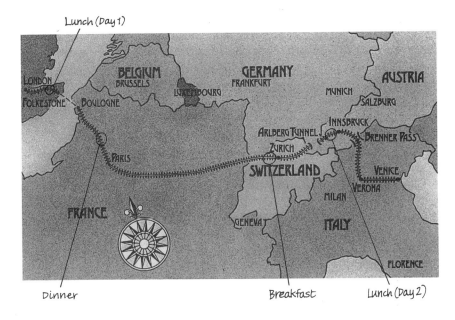

B   To encourage everyone to 'justify' their decisions, ask them to underline in pencil the relevant lines that give the answers.

Answers

TRUE statements: 2   5   6   9   10
FALSE statements: 1   3   4   7   8

C   This part draws attention to the style of the passage, which contributes to its communicative effect. Perhaps give further examples of phrases from the passage before students work on this in pairs.

Some selected phrases

- magnificent English 'Pullman' cars waiting grandly
- lunch in all its splendour with the Alpine panoramas in all theirs
- Exquisite food flawlessly served in surroundings of magnificent opulence
- Courteous and professional to a fault
- Course after tantalising course cooked to perfection by superb French chefs
- with your cabin miraculously transformed
- reading lamp left thoughtfully aglow
- your steward will tiptoe past your cabin
- dizzying Arlberg Pass and its 6½ miles of amazing tunnel
- Towering forests, and peaks you have to crane to see, alternate with pretty waterfalls and rushing streams to take your breath away

D   To start everyone off, perhaps describe a journey you have made, making it sound as attractive, exciting and interesting as possible! This could be your journey to work/school or something more exotic.

4.3   Revision of modal verbs   *Grammar*

A   This part should be prepared at home before the lesson, if possible. The rules summarised in this part are quite complex, both linguistically and conceptually.

Suggested answers (With remarks on possible difficulties.)

Ability/inability:
I can't find my pen anywhere – **Can/Could** you help me to **look for** it?
I **was** unable **to** finish all my work yesterday, but I hope **to finish/to be able to do it** tomorrow.

▶ Some students may have difficulty with the use of *was able* rather than *could* in positive sentences. For example:
He thought he could climb the mountain easily. = He thought it would be possible (but perhaps he didn't succeed)
He was able to climb the mountain easily. = Past ability + success

87

D

Possibility/certainty/impossibility:

Your bus **can't have** been two hours late, surely?

Might it be difficult to get a seat at such short notice?

Jane is always so careful, she **can't have/couldn't have** forgotten to check the timetable – the train **must have** been delayed.

▶ Note that the ideas of 'certainty' and 'impossibility' can also be referred to as 'deduction' (e.g. *You must be joking./You can't be serious.*). Strictly speaking, if you are perfectly certain about something you wouldn't use a modal verb at all:

It will rain today. = I am certain it will rain.

She was joking. = I know she was joking.

His plane didn't land on time.

▶ Some students may have difficulty distinguishing between the idea of possibility that something is **not** true:

That may not/mightn't be correct. = It's possible that it's not correct.

He may not/mightn't have done it. = It's possible that he didn't do it.

and **impossibility**:

He can't have done it. = It's impossible that he did it.

That can't be correct. = I'm sure it's not correct.

Permission/refusing permission:

You **mustn't smoke** when you're in a non-smoking seat.

You **weren't allowed to/couldn't use** a calculator in the maths test because it was against the rules.

Obligation or responsibility:

You **don't have to/needn't stand up** on the bus unless all the seats are occupied.

In the exam **do we have to/have we got to/must we write** in pen or are we allowed to use pencils?

You **ought not to/shouldn't spend** so much time listening to music when you **ought to be/should be** working.

▶ Some students may have difficulty with expressing different degrees of obligation. These are very fine distinctions and may not be worth worrying about, particularly as in many cases *must, have to, have got to, should* and *ought to* are interchangeable.

For the benefit of students who require a straightforward (though simplified) explanation, the differences can be explained as follows:

MUST expresses strong obligation:

You must go home now. = I am ordering you to go.

I really must leave. = I am ordering myself to go.

HAVE TO expresses obligation from 'outside':

I have to finish this today. = According to the rules or someone's orders.

Don't you have to leave before 6? = (perhaps) You've got a train to catch or an appointment somewhere else.

HAVE GOT TO is equivalent to HAVE TO.

SHOULD expresses a duty or what is the right thing to do:

You should be careful on the way home. = I advise you to be careful.

I should work harder. = It would be the right thing for me to do.

OUGHT TO is equivalent to SHOULD.

▶ Some students may have difficulty understanding the distinction between lack of obligation:

You needn't do it if you don't want to. = There's no obligation to do it.

and an obligation not to do something:

You mustn't do it. = There is an obligation not to do it / You are forbidden to do it.

B   If necessary, do the first two or three together as a class before the rest are done by students working together in pairs.

Sentences with errors corrected (Some variations are possible.)

1 You don't need to / needn't worry about meeting me at the station, I'll get a taxi.
2 Ought I to / Should I phone the airport to find out if there might be / are any delays?
3 Were you able to find the papers you lost?
4 I don't/won't have to show my passport to get a rail ticket.
5 I was able to / managed to buy my ticket after queueing for five minutes.
6 You needn't / don't have to write anything down unless you want to. (If the original sentence ended … *unless you really want to*, it wouldn't really be wrong.)
7 I checked the timetable so I can't be wrong about the departure time!
8 You don't spend as much time as you should on your homework.
9 Could/Can you tell me where I can catch a bus to the railway station?

C   Perhaps point out that this is the kind of exercise they may have to do in the exam. It can be done in pairs or as homework.

Answers

1 You shouldn't eat food as you walk down the street in Japan.
2 I shouldn't have spent so much money on records.

3 Do I have to pay for my ticket now?
4 Can you tell me how much luggage I am allowed to / I can take on the plane?
5 Her car can't have broken down again.
6 You needn't stand / won't have to stand on the train if you have a reserved seat.
7 You must have made a mistake when you added up the total.
8 Will you be able to get to the airport at 6.30 a.m.?
9 You needn't have / shouldn't have travelled first class.
10 We couldn't go / weren't allowed to go onto the platform.

D With exercises of this kind, if your students find them particularly difficult, you can make the task less formidable by reading out the complete story to the class while they listen with pencils down. Then they can approach the task with more confidence, knowing the story.

Complete story

1 **Have** you ever driven a van? I *2* **did** once. It *3* **was** just after I left college and I *4* **had** got myself a temporary job as a delivery man. When I accepted the job I thought I *5* **would** have to sit beside a driver, chat to him and help him to carry things from the van to the houses, but no, I *6* **was** on my own and I *7* **had** to drive the van and carry everything by myself. It *8* **might** have been very strenuous but after no more than a week I *9* **had** got used to it and I *10* **was** able to relax and enjoy the driving. But I *11* **must** say that I *12* **was** very glad when I *13* **had** finished after six weeks. It *14* **would** have been rather boring in the long run. I *15* **can** imagine that someone who *16* **has** to do that kind of job permanently *17* **doesn't** mind getting held up in traffic hold-ups as much as I *18* **do**, but something really *19* **ought** to be done to improve road conditions: it *20* **must** be so frustrating having to spend half your working life sitting in traffic jams. If you *21* **could** read a book or something it *22* **wouldn't** be too bad, but of course that *23* **is** impossible. All you *24* **can** do is listen to the radio and smoke too much!

▶ For more work on modal verbs, Units 10, 11 and 12 in *Use of English* contain a number of suitable activities.

4.4 Getting the message

Listening

A 🔲 Perhaps set the scene by asking about everyone's experiences of hearing loudspeaker announcements in public places. Tell everyone not to worry about the unfamiliar place names – in real life such announcements are full of place names.

The recording will probably have to be played at least twice for students to get all the information required.

Answers

1 a) Lyndhurst Road: Remain on platform 4
  b) Portsmouth: Go to platform 2
  c) Romsey: Go to platform 3

2 a) Poole: Yes
  b) Dorchester South: Yes
  c) Christchurch: Yes – and you must change at Brockenhurst

3 a) Parkstone: Change at Bournemouth
  b) New Milton: Change at Brockenhurst
  c) Millbrook: Remain on platform 4 for the next stopping train

Transcript

Narrator: Imagine that you're waiting on platform 4 at Southampton station and listen to this announcement.

Announcer: This is Southampton. Southampton. The train at this platform, platform 4 is the 17.38 Network Express to Weymouth, calling at Brockenhurst, Bournemouth, Poole, Hamworthy, Holton Heath, Wool, Moreton, Dorchester South, Upwey, and Weymouth. Change at Brockenhurst for Sway, New Milton, Hinton Admiral, Christchurch, and Pokesdown. Change at Bournemouth for Branksome and Parkstone. Remain on this platform for the next stopping train calling at Millbrook, Redbridge, Totton, Lyndhurst Road, and Beaulieu Road. Cross the footbridge to platform 2 for Netley, Fareham and the Portsmouth line. Cross the footbridge to platform 3 for Romsey and Salisbury.

(Time: 1 minute 20 seconds)

B 🔲 Perhaps start off by asking what kind of recorded information students can get in their own country over the phone: weather, entertainments, tourist information, etc.

Make sure everyone compares their answers with a partner and, if necessary, play the recording again to clear up any disagreements.

Answers

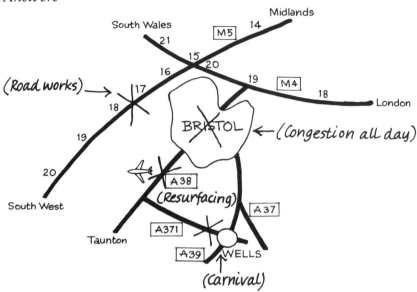

Transcript

Recorded voice: ... now be repeated. This is the road report for the Bristol area for Saturday 24th November, compiled by the Automobile Association. There are emergency road works on the southbound carriageway of the M5 motorway between junctions 17 and 18. These are likely to last throughout the weekend. Southbound traffic will be diverted to the northbound carriageway and there are likely to be long delays in both directions, particularly on Saturday.

Delays can also be expected on the main A38 Bristol to Taunton road near Bristol Airport due to resurfacing work on Saturday afternoon and Sunday.

The Carnival at Wells on Saturday afternoon is likely to cause delays to traffic on the A371 to the west of the city, but traffic on the A39 and A37 is unlikely to be affected.

Motorists are also advised to avoid the centre of Bristol all day Saturday, where traffic connected with the International Power Boat Races is likely to cause severe hold-ups.

There was a serious accident on Friday evening on the M4 between junctions 18 and 19 causing long delays to traffic. Both carriageways have now been reopened and no delays are expected on this motorway.

That is the end of this recorded road report, which will now be repeated. This is the road report for the Bristol area ...

(Time: 1 minute 25 seconds)

4.5   Using suffixes – 1: Adjectives   *Word study*

A   Point out that the word stress changes in the **-ical** words, but not in any of the others:
biólogy→ biológical   grámmar→ grammátical   álphabet→ alphabétical
geógraphy→ geográphical   etc.

Also point out that words ending in **-ible** (see the ★ note in the Student's Book) aren't the same as the ones ending in **-able** because -ible isn't a suffix.

Answers

-al	musical professional traditional
-ical	alphabetical grammatical mathematical
-able	breakable comfortable enjoyable obtainable washable
-ful	colourful hopeful painful restful successful thoughtful
-less	careless fearless restless useless
-ish	foolish greyish oldish smallish tallish youngish
-y	bumpy draughty noisy rainy sleepy smelly sunny

B

Answers

1 *Example   Make sure everyone understands what to do.*
2 thoughtful
3 musical
4 childish
5 sunny
6 readable
7 geographical
8 reddish
9 unreliable
10 unforgettable

▶ For more work on forming adjectives by using suffixes, see *Use of English* Unit 30.

4.6   *Come* and *go*   *Verbs and idioms*

A   Point out that *come/bring* and *go/take* are used in similar circumstances. If your students are confused, draw a diagram on the board:

fetch ⤺ take → bring ←
         go →   come ←

Answers

| 1 come | 2 go | 3 take | 4 Come   bring |
| 5 carry | 6 delivered | 7 fetch | |

B

Answers

1 came across	7 gone off
2 came up against	8 has gone off
3 came about	9 went off
4 go with	10 went in for
5 comes in goes out	11 Come on
6 has been going out with	12 go on go over

4.7   Avoid the queues   *Reading and discussion*

A   The communicative effect of the advertisement depends on word-play – very common in British advertising. Reading the text is a lead-in to a discussion about travelling.

Answers

1 Eleven Qs are missing.
2 British Airways flights to Paris, Amsterdam and intercontinental destinations (i.e. flights beyond Europe).
3 It's very large and so it's less busy and there are fewer queues.
4 You can wheel your trolley directly to the car park (no lifts, stairs or escalators), which holds 3,200 cars and is easily accessible.
5 Terminal 1.
6 There is a frequent bus service.

B   In this discussion activity, the questions everyone will be considering are just the type of questions they might be asked in the

Interview about their experiences and opinions. Students with no
experience of flying or long-distance travel should be encouraged to say
what they *imagine* it would be like to go by plane, ferry, etc.

4.8   InterCity services   *Problem solving*

A   This activity needs quite a lot of time and may provoke a fair
amount of discussion. It requires students to extract and collate
information from various sources – in real life this would be even more
complex, probably. In the exam such a task might well come up in the
Directed Writing section. It might be a good idea to pair students who
claim to be 'hopeless with maps and timetables' with students who are
more confident about it.

   With this kind of task, there may be several possible routes and times
which are equally suitable.

   To save time in class, students could be asked to study the timetables
and work out their routes, etc. before the lesson. In class, different pairs
could be told to start with a different friend's travel arrangements and
then, when ready, move on to consider the others'. Note that Conny's
arrangements are relatively straightforward.

   Make sure everyone realises they should allow at least 40 minutes to
travel between London stations by Underground.

Model notes on each person's route (These could be much briefer.)

ALAIN

Trains

The 07.55 is the ideal train, but he'd probably miss it –
if he did catch it he could catch the 10.30 from Euston,
arriving at Glasgow at 15.44. 08.55 probably OK unless
ferry late – arrives London 10.19. Allowing 40 minutes to
cross London, he might just make the 11.00 from King's
Cross, if not he'd get the 11.35. That means he'd arrive
in Glasgow at 17.18 or 18.21, changing trains in
Edinburgh. A more relaxing way might be to go to Euston
and catch the 13.00 direct train, arriving in Glasgow at
18.30, but if he's really in a hurry that's not the best
one.

Planes

Catching the 08.55 from Portsmouth and taking the
Underground to Heathrow Airport would get him there in
time to catch the 12.15 plane, arriving at Glasgow
Airport at 13.25 and then by coach to central Glasgow
arriving about 2 p.m. If he caught the 07.55 from
Portsmouth he could even be there by 1 p.m.

BOBBY

```
The best route is the direct one (especially if he's got
a lot of luggage) and he may just catch the 10.17 and be
in Manchester at 14.05. But by the time he gets through
customs it may be 10.30 or later, so he can get the
Gatwick Express at 10.35 or 10.50, arriving Victoria at
11.05 or 11.20. The train to Manchester from Euston at
12.50 will get him there at 15.25. He might just make the
11.50, which arrives in Manchester at 14.36.
```

CONNY

```
The best direct train is the 06.17 from Bristol, arriving
in York at 10.46. No point in going via London.
```

© Cambridge University Press 1990

B   The extra information in Activity 12 suggests that there is a possibility that each friend will be delayed. Each pair now has to modify the travel arrangements they have made.

Model notes on each person's route (These could be briefer.)

ALAIN

```
If the ferry is two hours late, he might just make the
09.55, but even if he missed it and caught the 10.55 that
should get him in London in time to catch the 13.00 from
Euston. Alternatively, the 13.15 plane from Heathrow
would get him to the centre of Glasgow by 3 p.m.
```

BOBBY

```
If he's three hours late, he can get the 13.47 direct
train, arriving in Manchester at 18.05. If he misses that
he could get the 14.20 Gatwick Express and then get the
16.00 from Euston, arriving in Manchester at 18.33.
```

CONNY

```
If she misses the 06.17, she'll have to go via London.
The 07.40 arrives at Paddington at 09.06 and then she can
catch the 10.00 from King's Cross, arriving in York at
12.11. However, to be on the safe side, the earlier 07.00
from Bristol would be better, enabling her to catch the
09.35 from King's Cross, arriving in York at 11.54.
```

© Cambridge University Press 1990

C   If time is very short, students could be asked to write just two of the postcards or letters (Alain's is the most difficult and Conny's the easiest). To help everyone get started, the first part of the letter to Alain could be done as a class, writing up everyone's suggestions on the board.

Model letters/postcards

Dear Alain,
    When you get to Portsmouth, you should get the bus
from the Ferry Port to the railway station. You might
just make the 7.55 to London, but if not there's another
train at 8.55. When you arrive at Waterloo, get the
Underground to Heathrow Airport and you'll be in time to
catch the 12.15 plane, arriving at Glasgow Airport at
13.25. There's a coach from there to the centre of
Glasgow and you'll get there at about 2 p.m. If you
caught the 7.55 from Portsmouth you could even be there
by 1 p.m.
    If you don't want to go by air, and you do catch the
7.55, you could catch the 10.30 from Euston direct to
Glasgow, arriving at 15.44.
    If your ferry is late, there are trains at 5 minutes
to every hour from Portsmouth to London Waterloo,
arriving about 1½ hours later. From there you can take
the Underground to Heathrow (planes leave there every
hour) or go to Euston and catch the 13.00 which arrives
in Glasgow at 18.30.
        Have a good journey!
            All the best,

Dear Bobby,
    If your plane lands at Gatwick on time, you should
hurry through customs and try to catch the 10.17 direct
train, which will get you to Manchester at 14.05. If
you're a bit late, you should take the Gatwick Express
(every 20 minutes) to London Victoria. Then take the
Underground to Euston, where you can take the 11.50 or
the 12.50. If all goes well, you'll arrive in Manchester
at 14.36 or 15.25.
    If your plane is delayed, there's another direct
train from Gatwick Airport station at 13.47 which would
get you to Manchester at 18.05.
        Have a good journey!

Dear Conny,
    If you have to get to York in good time for your
interview at 12.30, you should take the direct train via
Birmingham, leaving Bristol at 6.17 a.m. and arriving in
York at 10.46. There's no point in going via London.
    If you missed that, you'd have to go via London. The
best train to take is the 7.00 to London and then take
the Underground to King's Cross to catch the 9.35 from
King's Cross, arriving in York at 11.54.
        Good luck with your interview!
            Best wishes,

4.9   How do I get there?

A Before playing the recording, perhaps find out everyone's experiences of one-way systems in the town or city they're studying in, as motorists, cyclists or pedestrians.

Answers

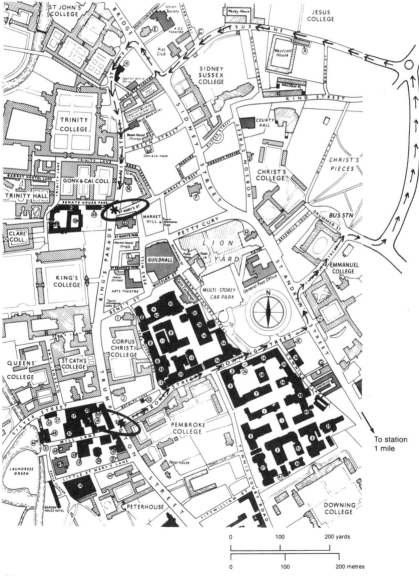

Transcript

Woman: Hallo, Acme Agency. Can I help you?

Driver: Yeah, I hope so ... um ... look, I'm bringing round some deliveries this morning. I think you're expecting them and ... er ... I've got a bit of a problem. Um ... I'm in Trumpington Street in a van at the moment but I can see up the road ... er ... to King's Parade that it's a one-way street and I ... I ... I don't have a clue as to how to get to you. Is there anyone in your office who can ... um ... you know ... ?

Woman: Yes, yes, I can probably help you. Whereabouts exactly are you in Trumpington Street?

Driver: Er ... by ... er ... Pembroke Street. Um ... yeah, that's right. Because I've got this map here but it's a very stupid map because it has ... it doesn't tell you where the one-way streets are, you know.

Woman: Yes and ... and some of the ... streets have become pedestrian precincts. It's changed a lot recently.

Driver: Yeah.

Woman: Look ... um ... go up Pembroke Street ... Yes ... Do you see that?

Driver: Yeah ... yeah, sure.

Woman: And that becomes Downing Street ... Yes ... Now follow along Downing Street until you hit a T junction ...

Driver: Yes.

Woman: St Andrew's Street?

Driver: St Andrew's Street.

Woman: That's right. Now turn left into St Andrew's Street and then immediately right down ...

Driver: Immediately right? That's Emmanuel Street.

Woman: That's it. Past Emmanuel College. Then keep going and if you go straight to the end of Emmanuel Street, you'll see on your left the Bus Station.

Driver: Right. Got you.

Woman: Now don't ... don't turn into the Bus Station. Turn right away from the Bus Station and then left ... er ... first left.

Driver: Well, that's a bit dodgy 'cause I haven't got that on my map, but carry on, carry on.

Woman: Ah, well, maybe you should draw it in.

Driver: Yeah, all right.

Woman: Right ... go back to the bottom of Emmanuel Street.

Driver: Right.

Woman: Now turn right round the corner of Emmanuel College and draw in a road directly opposite going first left. That road will curve round with Christ's Pieces, which I think is marked on your map, on your left. Christ's Pieces on your left.

Driver: Quite right.

Woman: Right, in fact Christ's Pieces is set into a park and there's a car park on your right. Now keep going straight ahead until you hit a roundabout.

Driver: Yeah.

Woman: And then take the second exit.

Driver: The second exit. OK.

Woman:	That will bring you into Jesus Lane. Can you see that?
Driver:	Ah, I can see Jesus Lane, that's at the top of my map, yeah, right.
Woman:	Fine. Follow Jesus Lane right round, Sidney Sussex College will be on your left ...
Driver:	Yeah, with you.
Woman:	And you hit a T junction. Right, Sidney Street's on your left.
Driver:	Yeah, that's Bridge Street and Sidney Street?
Woman:	Bridge Street and Sidney Street, right. Turn right into Bridge Street and then take the first left down St John's Street.
Driver:	Yes!
Woman:	Go down St John's Street, along Trinity Street, where St John's Street becomes Trinity Street, right? Right to the end there and we're on the corner of Trinity Street and St Mary's Street. Can you see it?
Driver:	Yes, yes, no problems now. Well, thanks very much. I'll be there in a few minutes I hope.
Woman:	OK.
Driver:	If I don't get lost again, eh?
Woman:	Yes, good luck!
Driver:	Bye.
Woman:	Bye.

(Time: 2 minutes 40 seconds)

B   To start everyone off, demonstrate how you would explain the best pedestrian route between two places on opposite sides of the map. Students should mark the route with little arrows → → as you're speaking.

▶   Instead of, or as well as, using the street plan of Cambridge, use a map of the city or town your students are studying in. Get them to explain the best routes to the various points of interest.

4.10   Layout of letters, directions   *Composition*

A   When everyone has studied the two versions of Jan's letter to Alex, get everyone to share their ideas with the rest of the class:
● Which letter do they prefer?
● Why?
● Which parts of each are more helpful and which parts are less helpful? (They could perhaps underline the helpful parts in ink and the unhelpful parts in pencil.)

Suggested answers

This is clearly a matter of opinion, but some of the more helpful bits of the *first letter* are perhaps:

'Ask the driver to tell you'
'I enclose a map' + the map itself is very useful

And some of the less helpful bits are:
'expensive' – how expensive?
'cheap, but slow' – how slow?
'you'd have to change twice' – where?
Jan doesn't recommend a best option

Some of the more helpful bits of the *second letter* are:
'there's no easy way'
'I'd suggest taking the underground'
'When you come out of the station …' etc. – the clear directions
'there's a stop opposite Greenwood Station'
'If you get lost … phone me at work' + the number

Some of the less helpful bits are:
'You'll have to change twice' – where?
No map

B   Now students have to write an informal letter to a friend from abroad. Point out how such a letter should be laid out in English.

There is no model composition, as the two letters in the Student's Book serve as models in this case, and show how personal letters are laid out.

4.11   Using prepositions – 1   *Use of English*

This can be done in pairs, or prepared as homework and checked in class. If students use a pencil to fill in the gaps, they can later rub out what they have written and do the exercise again at a later date as revision.

Answers

1 for	6 in	11 of
2 with about	7 from	12 on
3 for	8 for	13 of
4 of	9 about	14 of
5 with about	10 from	15 for

▶   There are further exercises on prepositions used after certain verbs, adjectives and nouns in 5.6 and 6.7. *Use of English* Units 27 and 28 contain more work on this area.

4.12   **Transport in the future**   *Communication activity*

▐▓▌ After everyone has had time to make notes, divide the class into groups of three (or four). Each has different ideas about transport in the future to study:
Student A has information about bicycles in Activity 2.
Student B has information about electric vehicles in Activity 8.
Student C (and D) has information on public transport in Activity 28.

Draw attention to the useful expressions in the Student's Book before they exchange ideas.

▶ The topic of this discussion could also be an extra composition task.

▶ For more listening and speaking activities connected with travel and transport, Unit 7 in *Ideas* is recommended.

5 Somewhere to live

5.1 Make yourself at home!   *Vocabulary*

A Warm-up discussion.

B Many of the gaps can be filled with a variety of words; a few of these are suggested in the answers below.

Answers

1 swimming pool/games room/study/large garden, etc.
2 neighbours
3 detached/semi-detached/terrace/two-storey/family
4 storeys   floor
5 accommodation
6 outskirts   suburbs
7 move   cottage/farmhouse, etc.
8 mortgage (US home loan)
9 rent   landlord/landlady
10 cupboards (US closets)/storage space
11 bookcase   shelves
12 central heating   living room/lounge
13 wardrobe/chest of drawers
14 cosy/spacious/homely (GB)/welcoming/tidy, etc.

C Make sure the meanings and uses of the 'wrong' answers are covered while doing this part. For example, with question 1 you could ask for suggestions like this:
- What's the difference between *a cellar* and *a cave*?
    A cave is in a cliff or mountain, *a cellar* is under a house.
- Why are *attic* and *loft* wrong in this context?
    Because they're at the top of a house, not in the basement.

Answers

1 cellar	3 drive	5 lawn
2 blinds	4 shed	

D The last questions lead into the next section: Different places.

5.2   **Different places**   *Listening and speaking*

A [cassette]

Answers

1 In a small flat in the city centre.
2 In a small semi-detached house in the suburbs, 10 km from town.
3 The garden, the lack of noise and the shops nearby.
4 Walking to work, the entertainments and the facilities.
5 The noise and the traffic.
6 Travelling to work and being dependent on public transport or a car.
7 In a larger flat in the city centre.
8 In a little cottage in the country.

Transcript

Charles: I'm going to have to do something about my flat, you know.
Ruth: Why?
Charles: It's just much too small ... I live in the middle of the city centre, you see.
Ruth: Oh I see, well I live in a small ... semi-detached house in the suburbs. It's about ten kilometres out of town.
Charles: Oh, do you like it?
Ruth: Oh, I love it. I like having a garden, being able to sit in it and relax. You know, away from the noise of the city. And good shops, there are good shops nearby, I like that.
Charles: Course I like being able to ... to walk to work ... I've got all the entertainments and the facilities of the ... you know, living in a city, they're all nearby like the cinemas and banks, shops, those sorts of things, you know.
Ruth: Oh yes ... But ... er ... isn't it noisy?
Charles: Oh yes, it's terrible. Oh, well, that's what I dislike about it: the noise and the traffic.
Ruth: Mm, but still if you live out like I do, I ... there's still disadvantages. I dislike having to travel into the city to work and, you know, I'm always dependent on public transport or I have to go by car.
Charles: Yeah, I think the ... thing that I really ... er ... feel most about my flat is that it's just not big enough and I ... You see, you talk about sitting in the garden, well I've ... I haven't even got a balcony ... Well, really I just wish I ... you know, what I'd like to do most of all is get a bigger flat but still be in the middle of t ... of the city.
Ruth: I ... I'd like not to have to go into the city at all. I wish I could afford to give up work and go and live somewhere in the country. You know, that's my dream: a little cottage in the heart of the country.

(Time: 1 minute 20 seconds)

B   This is a straightforward picture conversation. Students should work in groups of three or four. Perhaps begin by getting everyone to guess where each place actually is.

5.3   The future   *Grammar*

A

Suggested answers

PREDICTIONS + GENERAL FUTURE:

I'm sure the weather **will improve** towards the end of the week.
She is very clever, so I expect that she **will do well in** her exams next summer.
If you don't hurry up, the bus **will have left/gone** before we get to the bus stop!

Following a time conjunction:

If you **write them down,** you'll find it easier to remember the new words.
When my friend **arrives / gets here,** I'll tell her all about my plans.
By the time our guests **arrive/turn up,** all the food will have been eaten.

▶   Perhaps point out that, in CONVERSATION, the short form '*ll* is often used after names and question words:

Thomas'll be there.   Alison'll know the answer   Who'll tell us?

but usually only WRITTEN after pronouns:

Thomas will be there.   Alison will know the answer.   Who will tell us?
He'll be there.   She'll know the answer.

FUTURE EVENTS THAT WE CAN 'SEE COMING':

Look out! That dog **is going to** bite you!
Look at those black clouds – it **is going to rain** soon.

INTENTIONS AND PLANS:

I **am going to do** the work later, when I've got more time.
Your room is in a terrible mess – when **are you going to tidy it?**

ARRANGEMENTS:

I can't meet you this evening because **I'm going to a concert.**
Mr and Mrs Jones **are coming** to dinner tomorrow.

⟫→

FIXED EVENTS ON A TIMETABLE OR CALENDAR:
   The plane from London **lands/gets here** at 9.30.
   Tomorrow, according to my diary, the sun **rises/sets** at 5.09.

PROMISES, SUGGESTIONS AND OFFERS:
   Give me your suitcase and I **'ll put it** in the boot of the car for you.
   I'll **pay you back/repay** the money you lent me next Friday.

▶ An extra point on *will* v. *shall*:
Point out that, in these examples, either can be used, but *won't* and *will*
are more common:
   I won't/shan't tell anyone our secret.
   We will/shall never know the answer.
   We won't/shan't forget your birthday next year.

B

Corrected sentences

1 If the telephone rings, I'll answer it.
2 After the floor has been cleaned, I'll polish the furniture.
3 This evening I'm going to/I'll tidy up my room.
4 By the time you get home we will have finished dinner.
5 We'll be waiting for you when your plane lands at the airport.
6 Elizabeth is going to have a baby next month.
7 The new by-pass will be finished in the spring.
8 You won't be able to unlock the door if you don't remember your
   key.

C   This kind of exercise is similar to the 'letter from notes' type of
question in the Use of English paper. Make sure everyone understands
what they have to do by looking at the examples together.

Suggested answers (Some variations are possible. In the places
marked with a * *going to* can be used.)

1 *Example   Make sure everyone understands what to do.*
2 Our latest news is that next week we are moving* house!
3 Our new flat is on the outskirts of the city.
4 The flat (itself) is not any larger but we'll be able to grow vegetables
   in the garden.
5 We hope there won't* be any problems with noisy and nosy
   neighbours, as there are now.
6 We'll* be glad to escape from the noise and traffic in the city centre.
7 My journey to work will* take longer, but I'll* enjoy the fresh air
   and privacy.

8 We'll* (be able to) take the dog for a walk across the fields every evening.
9 On Sunday 14th we're having* a flat-warming party.
10 Will you be able to come?
11 We're looking forward to seeing you any time after 7 p.m.
12 P.S. You won't (be able to) find our new flat without some directions.
13 If you phone me I'll tell you how to get there.

▶ For more practice on future forms, Unit 16 in *Use of English* is recommended.

5.4   A nice place to live   *Reading*

A   To save time in class, students should be encouraged to read the passage at home before the lesson and perhaps do this comprehension exercise too.

Answers

TRUE statements: 2   3   4   5   7   8
FALSE statements: 1   6   9   10

B   Make sure everyone understands the expressions in the questions before they hunt for synonyms in the passage itself.

Answers

1 *Example   Make sure everyone understands what to do.*
2 courteous   6 manners
3 squeezing   7 needless to say
4 agents   8 citizens
5 award   9 consolation

C   This discussion gives an opportunity to explore what kinds of behaviour are considered polite in different countries – the concept of what is polite is by no means universal. In some cultures, for example, sniffing or sneezing loudly are considered rude, in others they are acceptable behaviour.

5.5   **High-rise buildings**   *Listening*

A   Before playing the recording, find out how many members of the
class actually live (or work) in high-rise buildings. How many storeys
does a building have to have to be considered a high-rise building?

🗔 In this exercise, as there is a lot of writing to do, it may be
helpful to PAUSE the tape occasionally before the interviewer's questions.
Otherwise students may miss the next answer if they're still busily
writing.

Between playings give everyone a chance to compare notes.

Answers

NOTES

Where and when was the first skyscraper built?
Chicago in 1883
Why was it built?   1   High price of land
                    2   Cheap steel
                    3   Invention of the lift (elevator)
Where is the world's tallest apartment block?
Lake Point Towers, Chicago
Where is the tallest in the UK?
Shakespeare Tower, Barbican, London
How do people who live in tower blocks feel?
Isolated and lonely
What kind of flats are vandalised?
Council flats
How can vandalism be prevented?
   1   Encourage tenants to be proud of their homes
   2   Not housing families in high-rise blocks
   3   Building more low-rise flats
   4   Blowing up vandalised flats

Transcript

Interviewer: … over the past few years there seems to have been a swing
               against the popularity of high-rise buildings. Professor Hill, why
               do you think this is?
Professor: Well, first of all, I think we must make a clear distinction between
               residential and commercial buildings, OK?
Interviewer: Yes.
Professor: The first skyscraper was itself an office block built in Chicago in
               1883 and there were really three reasons for this being built.
               Firstly, the enormously high price of land; secondly, there was a

	fair amount of cheap steel about. And the third reason was that they'd invented the passenger elevator, the lift, in 1857.
Interviewer:	So they could get to the top?
Professor:	Exactly, yes. And where land is in fact still very expensive – especially in the centre of cities – high office buildings are still being built. And some companies get prestige from operating from a large modern beautiful building.
Interviewer:	Yes, well, what about … um … dwellings?
Professor:	Well, some luxury flats are still being built and the highest in the world is at Lake Point Towers in Chicago … um … the highest in the United Kingdom is the Shakespeare Tower, Barbican, in the City of London. But in the public sector housing – that's council flats – they're no longer being built at the rate they were in the 60s and early 70s. And the reasons for this are quite numerous: people feel very isolated in them and lonely and they have this terrible feeling of being cut off from the real world.
Interviewer:	Understandable.
Professor:	Yes, and so many of these flats were getting vandalised and smashed up – the windows were being broken, lifts damaged and so on. And oddly enough perhaps this doesn't seem to happen in privately-owned blocks, they … they tend to be much more secure. But perhaps that's because they've got porters or even guards to protect them.
Interviewer:	Yes, what do you think can be done to prevent vandalism?
Professor:	Well, vandalism can only be prevented by encouraging the tenants to take a pride in where they live, to feel that they own their environment. Not housing families in these large high-rise blocks – perhaps only single people or at least only childless couples. And … um … building more low-rise accommodation and, I have to say, that … er … in the last resort if all else fails, by blowing up the blocks which attract the vandals.
Interviewer:	That seems a wee bit drastic.
Professor:	Well, in many cases, it's the only thing that can be done.
Interviewer:	Well, Professor Hill, thank you very much.
Professor:	Thank you.

(Time: 2 minutes 35 seconds)

B   The discussion in groups of four or five gives everyone a chance to discuss to what extent similar problems arise in their own country – what kind of security systems are used, for example?

5.6 Using prepositions – 2 *Use of English*

If students fill the gaps first in pencil, they can later erase them and do
the exercise again as revision at a later time.

Answers

1 deal with	8 introduce you to
2 depends on	9 involved in/with
3 engaged to married to	10 hope for
4 forgive Bill for	11 interested in
5 exchanged it for	12 confidence in
6 insisted on	13 lack of
7 interfere with	14 longing for

5.7 Spelling and pronunciation: *Word study*
Vowels

This section concerns homophones and other spelling difficulties. Note
that the examples are all R.P. (Southern British English 'Received
Pronunciation') and that in other accents some of the words may be
pronounced differently.

A   This is a gentle lead-in to the subject. It can be done as a class or by
students working in pairs.

Answers

guest   break   hole   steal   through

B   First of all, go through the list of phonemes and the way they're
spelt, saying groups of words aloud and getting the class to repeat them
after you.
   This exercise is nothing like as difficult as it looks: the words that have
to be added are grouped together and separated by a blob: •. What
everyone does have to do is decide on the correct order for the words. To
do this they'll have to say the words aloud to each other to check on the
pronunciation.

   The completed lists are recorded on the cassette as a Key to the
exercise. This can be played to the class after they have completed the
task. Pause the tape for questions every so often – don't play the whole
lot remorselessly through.

There are likely to be LOTS of questions in this exercise about the meaning of the words in the lists.

Answers

æ   /bæd/   **bad**   damage   +   scandal   marry

e   /bed/   **bed**   pleasure   leisure   lent/leant   +   bury/berry weather/whether   guessed/guest   merry   check/cheque

aɪ   /baɪt/   **bite**   height   guide   eye/I   +   climb it/climate   right/ write   by/buy/'bye

ɑː   /kɑm/   **calm**   heart   +   laugh   castle   half   guard

ɔː   /bɔːd/   **bored/board**   warm   caught/court   +   wore/war shore/sure   source/sauce   walk   warn/worn   raw/roar

ɜː   /bɜːd/   **bird**   worm   +   turn   work

aʊ   /naʊ/   **now**   crowd   +   plough   allowed/aloud

ɔɪ   /bɔɪ/   **boy**   point   +   destroy   employer

eə   /ðeə/   **there/their**   scarce   where/wear   +   stares/stairs   fare/ fair   pair/pear

ɪə   /hɪə/   **here/hear**   steer   +   cleared   atmosphere   sincere

eɪ   /meɪk/   **make**   sale/sail   break/brake   +   paint   wait/weight male/mail   waste/waist

əʊ   /nəʊt/   **note**   joke   whole/hole   +   folk   soap   nose/knows

iː   /ʃiːp/   **sheep**   piece/peace   +   ceiling/sealing   sieze/seas   weak/ week   receive   meat/meet   seen/scene

ɪ   /ʃɪp/   **ship**   sink   mystery   +   guilty   business   witch/ which   mist/missed

ɒ   /pɒt/   **pot**   what   yacht   +   not/knot   knowledge quality   wander

uː   /buːt/   **boot**   truly   threw/through   +   soup   blue/blew root/route   new/knew

ʊ   /pʊt/   **put**   should   wood/would   +   cushion   butcher pull   push

ʌ   /kʌt/   **cut**   worry   money   +   blood   tongue   country one/won   thorough   wonder

(Time: 3 minutes 30 seconds)

▶ If there's time in class, or as homework, get everyone to write ten sentences each including two of the words from the lists.

C   Student's own errors are likely to be rather more subtle than these!

Corrected words

1 sure   week   to
2 truly   wait   for

3 dreadful   pours   sauce
4 their   armchair   through
5 Which   two   right
6 leant   against   climbed
7 ceiling   painting   urgently

D 🔲 Play the tape while everyone writes the missing words. This exercise should be reassuringly easy! (In the recording the missing word is spoken again after each sentence. Time: 1 minute 25 seconds)

Answers

1 *Example   Make sure everyone understands what to do.*
2 wonder   7 walking
3 wandered   8 caught
4 height   9 damage
5 guards   10 receive
6 knowledge

5.8   Finding a flat   *Listening and problem solving*

In this section, for a change, the information required for the Directed Writing exercise depends on a listening exercise.

A   This can be done as a class, or in groups. Students with more experience of finding flats (e.g. people who have recently moved to a different flat) will have more to say about this. How do the prices compare with prices in their city?
    Perhaps point out that Windsor, Sandringham and Balmoral (together with Buckingham Palace) are residences of the British Royal Family.

B   The task may work best if the class is divided into THREE groups: one group makes notes on Balmoral Way, another on Sandringham Gardens and the third on Windsor Avenue. Then, after everyone in the group has discussed their notes, rearrange everyone into new groups of three – one member from each of the original larger groups. The new groups will then discuss the features of all three flats.

🔲 Play the recording a couple of times while everyone makes notes. In this conversation one has to pay attention to the responses that the speakers give to each other (e.g. 'Mm, yeah') to find out whether they agree with each other.
    It's a matter of opinion, but the flat they probably preferred was Windsor Avenue – its garden was probably the clincher!

Model notes

BALMORAL WAY
- expensive - they could
  just about afford it
- kitchen quite well equipped
  but small and dark
- public park opposite
- nice view of park + hills
- very near station
- near town centre + shops
- freshly decorated
- spacious rooms
- extra bedroom
- noisy traffic

SANDRINGHAM GARDENS
- kitchen quite big +
  facing south
- balcony
- view over car park
- 10 mins from station
  by bike
- only newsagent's shop
  nearby
- needs redecorating
  (maybe not a problem)

WINDSOR AVENUE
- biggest kitchen but needs
  a lot doing to it: shelves,
  units, etc.
- garden - they could sit
  out in summer
- 2 miles from station (but
  John could cycle in 15
  mins)
- small shops + Co-op nearby
- needs redecorating (maybe
  not a problem)
- peaceful

Transcript

John: Well, OK, darling, we've seen 'em all, what do you think?
Jill: Well, I think we really ought to talk about the money first. I mean, well,
        the one in ... the one in Balmoral Way, now that ... that did seem ... I
        mean that was an awful lot of money compared with the others. I mean
        they were ... they were both quite reasonable, I thought. But do you
        think we could afford to pay that much?
John: Well, it's ... sure, it's more than ... than I expected to pay but it ... well
        you could do without a few things, you know. Just ... er ... so that we
        could ... Then I think we'd be able to afford it. But which of the kitchens
        did you like of all of them?
Jill: Kitchens, well the biggest one was that one in Windsor Avenue, but ... I
        mean it did need a lot doing to it, didn't it? I mean, shelves, units and
        everything. Er ... the other one I liked was the ... was Sandringham

Gardens, now that was ... that was big, wasn't it, that one and it was facing south. Um ... but the trouble with the other one [*i.e. Balmoral Way*] was that although it was ... you know ... it had ... I mean ... it was terribly well equipped, but it was very small and dark.

John: Oh, yes, yes, that's very true. You know what I liked about Windsor Avenue was the garden it had. You know, having a garden for m ... garden flat for me would ... would be *great* because it would mean we could sit out in the summer and ... and, you know, it's wonderful ...

Jill: Yes, yes, I know, but ... I mean ... but that one at Sandringham Gardens had a *lovely* big balcony an ... and that would be gorgeous too when it's lovely weather.

John: Mm ... balcony's OK, they're too small. It's a pity about Balmoral Way ... you know ... it had the park across the road. I guess that'd be all right for walks and things, having the park, but ...

Jill: Yes, and I must say the view over the park from there was lovely, wasn't it, you see? I mean, y ... you could see the hills as well, couldn't you ... well, I mean ... you know ...

John: Mm ... mm ... that's right.

Jill: ... quite far away but you could see them. And it ... much nicer than that car park, which was ... you know ... Sandringham Gardens, remember that's all you could see out of the window there?

John: Yes, unbearable. That's true. That's true. You know something else we ought to discuss is th ... the way each one of these places is positioned ... each ... where ... how ... how they are. Balmoral Way ... er ... it was close to the station. It ... it'd be quite a short walk to catch the train you know, to get into town in the morning. Windsor Avenue ... er ... must be two miles away from the station, that's too much of a walk, specially if you have to do it twice a day.

Jill: Ah, yes, but just remember that you did say you wanted to take up cycling. Yes! You see, and you could easily do that in ... in about a quarter of an hour on your bike. A ... and the ... exactly the same goes for Sandringham Gardens. Now that would only be about ten minutes to the station on your bike.

John: Yeah, but you know bicycling is fine in good weather but I'm not sure I want to bicycle in the snow or the rain and in this country that's what you've got to count on. Now, what about the shops in addition to all that? If you're close to the town centre you can get anything you want and there at Balmoral Way you're just around the corner.

Jill: Yes, but I mean there were some really sweet little shops ... er ... near Windsor Avenue, weren't there?

John: Mm.

Jill: And ... and there was the supermarket, the Co-op.

John: Oh, yes.

Jill: I mean, cer ... I mean Sandringham Gardens ... it ... I mean it just ... I mean ... the shops weren't there, were they?

John: No.

Jill: And that newsa ... opp ... that newsagent that was opposite, now that was the only shop that I saw.

John: That's true. One thing that worried me about both the Sandringham Gardens and the Windsor Avenue places was that they both needed a lot of work, you know, being done. Wallpaper and paintwork – revolting in both of them!

Jill: Yes, yes, I know but it was only a flat. I mean, it wouldn't take very long to redecorate that.

John: I don't know, it looked like a pretty big job to me. Anyway, the Balmoral Way flat ... it ... it'd just been freshly painted, it still looked ... you know ... I thought it looked pretty good.

Jill: Yes. And actually the rooms were a very good size, weren't they?

John: Mmm, yes.

Jill: I mean, they all felt quite spacious and that was ... that was the one with the extra bedroom, wasn't it? For guests. Yes.

John: That's right, that's right. And what about all the traffic going past in that road? Seemed very noisy, I think we ought to think about that. Did you notice it?

Jill: Mm, yeah, I certainly did an ... and it did seem very very peaceful, didn't it, at Windsor Avenue comparatively?

John: Yes, yes.

Jill: Still ... still, I think I've made up my mind which of them I like best.

John: I think I have too. Let's hope we decide on the same one!

(Time: 3 minutes 50 seconds)

C   In the model paragraphs below both sides of the argument are included in sentences beginning 'Although ...'. This may not be necessary as, strictly speaking, this information is somewhat irrelevant.

Model paragraphs

Jill and John might have chosen 7B Windsor Avenue because of its large kitchen and the nearby shops. But the main attraction of that flat was its garden - a place to sit on warm days and enjoy the peace and quiet of the neighbourhood. Although it was some way from the station, John could get there in a few minutes by bike. The one drawback seemed to be that it needed redecorating.

They might have decided against 44C Sandringham Gardens because it was so far from the station, though John could have cycled there in ten minutes. Although its kitchen was bright and it had a balcony, the main drawbacks were that there were no shops nearby, apart from a newsagent's, and the view of the car park was unbearable.

They might have rejected 13A Balmoral Way because it was expensive, but apart from this it had no garden and the kitchen seemed small and dark. Although it had an extra room, felt spacious, was near the shops and the station and had a good view over the park opposite, it was on a busy road and would be very noisy.

D   Depending on the aspirations and age of your students, they could design a large house, a one-room studio flat, or a bed-sitting room.

▶ There is an extended version of the 'dream house' task in *Ideas* Unit 12.

5.9   Welcome to G__!   *Reading*

The description of G__ provides a model for the composition task in 5.10.

A   These questions are quite easy, but allow time for everyone to ask questions about the vocabulary in the passage. Where do they imagine G__ to be?

Answers

1 not far	5 a short walk
2 deep	6 don't depend on tourism
3 under an hour's walk	7 not changed its atmosphere
4 sleepy	8 wants to keep it a secret

B   This discussion prepares students for the composition task in 5.10.

5.10   Starting and ending well   *Composition*

A   The suggested answers are clearly a matter of opinion and students should be encouraged to discuss how suitable they all are – some are more suitable than others.

Some of the unsuitable ones would be suitable in a different type of composition. Ask the class to suggest what kind of compositions they'd be suitable in.

Suggested answers

Suitable opening sentences: 1   3   4?   5   6?   9   10?

B   Again, students should be encouraged to discuss how suitable the various sentences are – some are more suitable than others and some would be suitable in a different type of composition. Ask the class to suggest what kind of compositions they'd be suitable in.

Suggested answers

Suitable closing sentences: 1   3?   7   8   9

C   If time is short, DON'T omit this section, get everyone to do it as homework.

D   There is no model composition in this case; the passage in 5.9 on G— can serve as a model, even though it's very long (432 words).

▶   Two alternative titles for this composition might be:
Describe your own room.
Describe your ideal home or room.

5.11   Grammar revision

This exercise can be set as homework or fitted into a spare few minutes at any stage during this unit.

Answers (Some variations are possible.)

1   *Example   Make sure everyone understands what to do.*
2   When I was a child we lived in the country.
3   We have been living in this district for eight years.
4   The furniture has to be moved from this room.
5   After we have had our summer holiday, we'll redecorate our flat.
6   Someone must have forgotten to lock the door.
7   After we had finished spring-cleaning we went out for a meal.
8   While we were having our meal, we discussed what to do at the weekend.
9   You hadn't painted this room last time I was here.
10   You shouldn't have painted the walls pink. *or* You should have painted them a different colour.

▶   For more listening and speaking activities on the topic of homes, see Unit 12 in *Ideas*.

6 Science and technology

6.1 Talking about science

Vocabulary

A   If the questions for the warm-up discussion seem to be rather highbrow get everyone to speak more generally about science by asking the class to answer these questions:
- What did/do you learn/study in science lessons at school?
- What did/do you enjoy about them?
- Are you 'interested in science'? Why/Why not?

B   This exercise may be difficult for people with no knowledge of or sympathy for science. If you find that some members of the class have never heard of Einstein or even a molecule, get the ones who do know to explain to them rather than explaining yourself.

The questions begin with theoretical science, but become more down-to-earth towards the end. In some of the later questions, several answers are possible.

Answers

1 atoms
2 element
3 compound
4 radioactive
5 chemistry   physics   biology
6 formula
7 experiments
8 laboratory
9 workshop   demonstration
10 theory   practice
11 proved
12 practical
13 technique
14 electronic
15 hardware   software
16 disk/tape/floppy disk/hard disk/magnetic tape/cassette
17 instructions
18 button/switch

19 adjust/reduce/increase
20 serviced   break down   repaired/mended/fixed/put right
21 robots
22 components/parts
23 carpenter   screwdriver/plane/drill
24 screws/nails   glue
25 whatsit/wotsit/thingumabob/thing/gadget/mechanism/device
   Pronunciation:
   whatchamacallit   thingumajig   whatnot   wotsit   thingumabob
   /wɒtʃəməkɔːlɪt/   /θɪŋəmədʒɪg/   /wɒtnɒt/   /wɒtsɪt/   /θɪŋgəmɪbɒb/

C   To start this off, demonstrate your classroom cassette player to the
class, naming all the (visible) parts and their functions.

▶ Point out that words like *watchamacallit* and *whatsit* can help you to
talk more convincingly about things you don't know the right word for
– they are used by native speakers in this way (but only in conversation,
not in writing).

   Similarly, foreign learners need a stock of 'hesitation phrases' at their
command, such as:
   *you know   well   in fact   actually   let's see   sort of   kind of
   er ...*
These phrases give you more time to think and are less embarrassing
than silence while you're working out what to say next.
And using full forms rather than contracted forms:
   I would have done it if I had known.
   If you had told them they would have come on time.
and not omitting the optional 'that' in sentences like:
   He told me that it was difficult.
   The money that I gave you was ...
can also give you more time to think during a conversation.

6.2 For a pint, just add water   *Reading*

A   Find out how many people in the class know how beer is brewed
and get the people who know to tell the ones who don't. Perhaps also get
someone to explain how wine or even spirits are produced.

   For your information, the traditional ingredients are: malted barley,
hops, yeast and water (though sugar may sometimes be added and even
various chemicals). The hops give the drink its bitter flavour. The
ingredients are mixed together and the yeast ferments, forming alcohol
from the sugar contained naturally in the malted barley. Eventually,

E

when the fermentation is complete, the liquid is filtered to remove the excess yeast and sediment and put into barrels or bottles.

B Students require no specialised knowledge to understand the article.

Answers

1 c   2 b   3 b   4 b   5 c   6 b   7 c   8 c

▶ As a follow-up ask the class to work in groups and discuss these questions.
● What do you think of this idea?
● How popular would it be in your country?
● How popular a drink is beer in your country/among your friends?

6.3 Using the passive   *Grammar*

A If the examples are studied at home before the lesson, any questions arising should be discussed in class.

B

Answers

ACTIVE	→	PASSIVE
They did it yesterday.	→	**It was done yesterday.**
They were doing it last week.	→	**It was being done last week.**
They have already done it.	→	**It has already been done.**
They will soon do it.	→	**It will soon be done.**
They will soon have done it.	→	**It will soon have been done.**
They had done it earlier.	→	**It had been done earlier.**
They have to do it at once.	→	**It has to be done at once.**
They may not have done it yet.	→	**It may not have been done yet.**

C

Answers

1 The process has been patented by Fischer.
2 The concentrate will only be sold to bottling companies.
3 Bottlers will be required to use water specified by Fischer.
4 The trade name can be chosen by the bottlers.
5 These particles can only be seen through a microscope.
6 The first laser was produced by Charles Townes in 1960.

7 Computers are being used in all kinds of work.
8 Dangerous chemicals have to be kept in a safe place.
9 The laboratory shouldn't have been left unlocked.
10 Intelligent life is unlikely to be discovered on other planets.

D   The facts and actual dates are less important than the sentences that are produced. Point out to everyone that they should use the passive.

Answers (just for the record)

bicycle 1840   computer 1943   jet engine 1937
laser 1960   margarine 1869   printing press 1455   Scotch tape 1930
telephone 1876   television 1926   thermometer 1593

▶ For more practice on using the passive, see *Use of English* Unit 29.

6.4 Serendipity
Listening

A   If playing the whole interview non-stop seems daunting, it can be paused just before Debbie says: 'And then there's . . . ' each time.

Answers

1 a   2 c   3 c   4 b   5 a   6 c   7 a   8 b   9 c   10 c   11 b
12 b

Transcript

Presenter: … good luck plays a part in scientific research too. In this case it's often referred to as **serendipity**, which according to my dictionary is 'the natural talent that some people have for finding interesting or valuable things by chance'. Debbie Charles has been looking into this for us. Debbie.

Debbie: That's right, Jenny. In fact, you know, most important discoveries in the world of science and technology came about by some sort of lucky accident. Starting with the wheel, presumably.
    Now let's just look at a few of these, starting with … er … **penicillin**. Now, Alexander Fleming found some mould growing on a laboratory dish which he'd … er … absent-mindedly left on a windowsill. Now, he found that this mould stopped the spread of bacteria, which as you know is the cause of illnesses like pneumonia. And modern antibiotic drugs based on penicillin save millions of lives every year.
    And then there's **radar**. Now, all sea and air transport depends on radar for navigation and safety – and armies depend on it for defence as well, of course. Radar was discovered during the war while British

military scientists were trying to find a death ray, which was ... er ... some sort of radio wave that could be used to kill people. They didn't find a death ray, but they did find a technique.

And then there's ... er ... **Teflon**, which is a substance which is used in non-stick frying pans. Now, this was discovered by accident in a laboratory by DuPont scientists, who were doing research into gases to use in refrigerators. Now, they discovered that a plastic coating had formed on their equipment and this was unaffected by heat and it was also very slippery. Now, no use was found for this until some time later a French researcher used it in a frying pan – and ... er ... Teflon's also used in space vehicles.

And then there's **artificial sweeteners**: now, from saccharine to the more modern sweeteners, all of these (for example ... er ... Cyclamate and Nutrasweet, etc.) were discovered by accident. The usual pattern was that scientists were ... were doing another experiment and they happened to taste one of the by-products, which they found to be sweet. Some of these sweeteners are thousands of times sweeter than sugar, you know.

And then there's **chewing gum**, which was discovered while scientists were looking for a substitute for rubber. And again there seemed at the time to be no apparent use for this product of the ... er ... Mexican Sapodilla tree! But serendipity made this product – there's no country in the world where chewing gum isn't available...

Presenter: Haha, no, but ... er ... I'm not sure that that is quite as beneficial to mankind as the others that you've talked about!

Debbie: Oh, maybe not. But here's one more very useful product. You know those ... er ... little yellow stick-on notes we use in the office and ... er ... for leaving phone messages and so on? Er ... **Post-It Notes**, they're called I think. Well, a researcher at 3M (which is the firm that makes Scotch tape) was doing research into adhesives and glue, and ... er ... he discovered a substance that seemed to be completely useless. I mean, it was ... was quite sticky but it wouldn't stick permanently to anything. You know, that's what adhesives obviously are supposed to do. And in fact, however long he left the adhesive sticking to various surfaces, it didn't make a mark on the surface and the bond became no more and no less effective. All other adhesives either get more sticky or less sticky with age, you know. Now, he was a member of a church choir and he always had to use slips of paper to mark the place where each of the hymns was in his hymn book – and the slips of paper kept falling on the floor. So he used these bits of sticky paper with this ... er ... 'useless' adhesive on to mark his place in the hymn book. And then he realised that other people could find a similar use ...

Presenter: Brilliant!

Debbie: No, just serendipity!

Presenter: Haha. Yah. Thank you, Debbie.

(Time: 3 minutes 50 seconds)

B   If the members of the class know each other *very* well, this follow-up discussion might be better as a whole-class discussion with you asking the questions.

6.5   **Helping people to understand**   *Pronunciation*

Although they will not have to read aloud in the exam, candidates' pronunciation will be marked during the Interview. These reading aloud exercises will help them to improve their pronunciation, so that people can understand them more easily.

This section emphasises the importance of PAUSES and STRESS.

A   The passage describes a simple experiment.

B   🔲 Play the first part of the recording and ask for comments.

Transcript

The text is read aloud like this with pauses in the wrong places, silly intonation and many words oddly stressed:

Quick reactions ARE imporTANT IF you're an airline
pilot. A motorist? or even a cyclist? – and OF course IN sports fast
reactions ARE especially
valuable this simple
BUT effective reaction timer makes
use of THE principle …

(Time: 35 seconds)

C   🔲 Play the second, better version of the instructions. Explain that everyone should mark the pauses that the reader makes, using a vertical line (|).

Get everyone to compare their marks with a partner.

Recording

The text is read aloud fairly slowly with a short pause between each paragraph. (Time: 2 minutes)

D   🔲 Play the recording again. This time, everyone marks the syllables that are stressed in each sentence in the text.

When they have finished and compared their version with a partner, they can see the completed version in Activity 11.

E   The reading aloud is best done in pairs. If your students are likely to find this very difficult, it can be done with each paragraph played back to students after they've read it OR maybe before they've read it.

▶ If you think your class will enjoy it, get them to carry out the Reaction Timer 'experiment' in small groups. Then the directed-writing task in 6.6 will seem much more realistic.

6.6   Reaction times   *Directed writing*

In this case there is no 'problem' to solve before the directed-writing task.

▶ If feasible, get everyone to carry out the Reaction Timer 'experiment' in small groups and record their results in a table.

A   If the class really have carried out the experiment on each other, they should use their own table.

B   If, when they come to discuss what they're going to write, everyone lacks inspiration, perhaps read out the first part of each of the model paragraphs below. (Although reports of experiments are often written in the passive, its use is avoidable in this exercise.)

Model paragraphs

1   An experiment was carried out in which we tested each other's reactions. To begin with, we cut out a piece of paper and copied a scale onto the edge of the paper. The paper was wrapped round a ruler and secured with sticky tape. Then each member of the group had to catch the ruler between their thumb and forefinger as it fell. The speed of their reaction was shown in seconds on the scale at the point they gripped it.

2   We found that there was a big difference in reaction times between members of the group and between each person's left and right hand. The person with the quickest reactions was Chris (average 0.11 seconds), though she failed to catch the ruler at all on one of her attempts. The person with the slowest reactions was Anne (average 0.17 seconds). Bill's average was 0.15 seconds and mine was 0.14 seconds, and it was surprising that my left-hand reactions were faster as I am right-handed.

3   We thought that the experiment was interesting and

surprisingly enjoyable. Before we started we were
quite doubtful, as the idea seemed rather silly and
childish, but once we got started and were
concentrating hard and trying to do our best, we
discovered we were talking English to each other in a
very natural way. The actual results of the experiment
were quite interesting, and we wondered whether one
could develop the speed of one's reactions by
exercises or more practice.

© Cambridge University Press 1990

6.7   Using prepositions – 3   *Use of English*

Answers

1 with about for	5 in for	9 for
2 of to	6 with	10 of for to
3 on with	7 from for	11 to
4 to for	8 from with	12 for from

▶ For more practice on verbs and adjectives followed by a preposition, see *Use of English* Units 27 and 28.

6.8   Chips with everything?   *Reading*

▶ To start off with, ask everyone where microchips are used nowadays (i.e. not only in computers but in luxury cars, washing machines, calculators, etc.). To what extent do they use computers themselves?

A

Answers

1 c   2 b   3 b   4 b   5 a   6 b   7 c   8 b (but this is open to other interpretations)

B

Answers

change – convert
bring advantages for – benefit
in danger – at risk

lack of differences – uniformity
simple – unsophisticated
do better than – surpass
painful – wounding
not taking part in – opting out of
intelligent – smart
feeling of not belonging – alienation

C   The discussion could lead into a paragraph-writing exercise or a composition exercise, based on one or more of the questions in the Student's Book.

6.9   I'd better explain how it works   *Listening*

[▭] This is a straightforward listening exercise.

▶ As a follow-up, the 'Listen Carefully' exercise (following instructions) in *Ideas* Unit 15 is great fun and highly recommended.

Answers

1 a   2 b   3 b   4 a   5 b   6 a

Transcript

Ted: Now, Annie, while you're here looking after the house, you may want to use the dishwasher.
Annie: Oh, that'd be lovely, yes. It'll save me a lot of bother.
Ted: Now, it's not as easy as it looks. So I'd better explain, you know, then you won't break anything.
Annie: Oh, right. Go on then.
Ted: Now listen, put all the cups and glasses in the top rack, not the bottom one, otherwise they'll all rock about and get broken. We made that mistake when we first bought it. Er ... plates and cutlery all now go in this bottom rack and you sort of slot them in.
Annie: Er ... now does it matter whether ... do the bigger ones go at the back?
Ted: You've got it!
Annie: Right?
Ted: No, actually, what ... what you do is you put the large plates on the right. Not on the left.
Annie: Oh, the right.
Ted: You know why you don't put them on the left?
Annie: No.
Ted: Be ... because if you do, the door won't close.
Annie: Ha ha. I'd have probably found that out, wouldn't I?
Ted: Now ... er ... cutlery in the two little baskets there. Oh ... handles downwards. Otherwise they don't get washed properly.

Annie: Oh really ... mm ...

Ted: Um ... now ... er ... Oh, don't try to ...

Annie: Oh, wait a minute. You know, I think I'm going to write this down, actually, because ...

Ted: Well, it's not that difficult.

Annie: Isn't it?

Ted: No, no.

Annie: All right. OK. Well, go on then.

Ted: I mean, I'll leave the manual here, just in case ...

Annie: Oh OK, yeah. Ta.

Ted: All right? And then you've got it. But anyway ... Oh, don't try to put a large plate on the ... on the far right nearest the side.

Annie: Why?

Ted: Well, if you did that, you can't slide the rack in. Well, you'd probably ...

Annie: Oh, I see, of course.

Ted: Now ... er ...

Annie: What about the powder?

Ted: Oh, yes ... ahha ... good point. Otherwise you won't ... won't be able to wash anything. Now ... er ... measure out a ... a ... full scoop of powder. You know, fill it right up ... um ... because otherwise it won't be enough powder ...

Annie: OK. One full scoop, yeah.

Ted: Full scoop.

Annie: Right.

Ted: Now, the powder container is here in the door of the dishwasher. Put the powder in there.

Annie: Uhhu ... Right.

Ted: Close the flap. And the flap'll auto ... automatically open when the ... when the programme flicks round to Wash.

Annie: Oh I see. Now ... er ... how do I actually start the whole thing going?

Ted: Dead simple.

Annie: Yeah.

Ted: Turn the control knob to three.

Annie: Three?

Ted: Number three, that's important, number three. Pull it out to start the machine going, right?

Annie: Yeah?

Ted: And the whole cycle lasts about an hour. So you just leave the things in there ... um ... and in fact it's best to leave the things longer than an hour to ... to dry completely, if you can do that.

Annie: Oh, I see. Well ...

Ted: OK?

Annie: Yeah, that's fine! Yeah, I think I've got that. Thanks!

(Time: 2 minutes 10 seconds)

6.10   How does it work?   *Communication activity*

▶ Before beginning the communication activity, demonstrate how the activity will work by telling the class how microwaves work, using this information.

Because domestically microwave cooking is a fairly new development, and because it differs so radically from conventional cooking, it tends to be regarded with some alarm. In fact, microwaving is easy to understand and a microwave oven is a most useful addition to virtually every type of household, and particularly for families who have a busy life-style.

MICROWAVES EXPLAINED

A microwave is a type of short-wavelength radiation similar in nature to radio waves. Microwaves are different from x-rays and gamma rays because they don't build up in the body.
  Microwaves are produced by a device known as a magnetron which is housed inside the oven. Metal

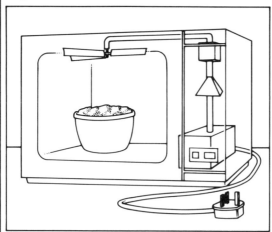

Microwaves are produced by a magnetron.

surfaces reflect microwaves, but food absorbs them; when microwaves are absorbed into food, the molecules of the food start to vibrate billions of

Food molecules vibrate, thus heating the food.

times a second. This makes the food heat up and cook, although the denser the food, the longer it takes to cook. Unlike conventional hobs and ovens, the microwaves enter the food on all its exposed surfaces. This is why it is important to arrange food in such a way that it gets the full benefit of the microwave energy.

Make sure the class is divided into an EVEN number of pairs, so that pairs of pairs can join up later. Half the pairs look at Activity 39, the other half at 47.

39 is 'Soap and washing powder'

47 is 'How a cassette works'

Although the information given in the activities is given in terms that the lay person can easily understand, some people are very non-technical, and the pairs may have to be arranged to allow for this.

When the pairs have studied the explanations, they have to explain to another pair how their thing works. They should NOT read from their information, but do this from memory, as you may have done with the microwaves explanation earlier.

6.11   Explaining a process   *Composition*

A   Ask the class to read the two paragraphs and point out what is
'good' and 'bad' about them: the first lacks detail and the second has
rather too much irrelevant detail. These faults are ones to avoid when
writing the composition in **B**.

B   Get everyone to decide what they will write about before they go
away and do it, so that they can make notes and sort out any problems
in class beforehand. Instead of writing about how something works,
some students may prefer to explain how to OPERATE something.

Perhaps point out that passives are often used in this kind of
explanation, though you can use the impersonal 'you' instead.

Emphasise the importance of checking written work afterwards and
looking systematically for mistakes in:

SPELLING: What was the affect of this? X effect

PREPOSITIONS: I'm interested for science. x in

VERB FORMS AND ENDINGS:

I was gave it. x   If I would be rich... x   She live in London. x
I was given it.   If I were rich ...   She lives in London.

ARTICLES: I'm interested in the science. x I'm interested in science.

If helpful, the model composition may be photocopied and shown to
students.

Model composition

```
MICROWAVE OVENS
Microwaves are a type of short-wave radiation, rather
like radio waves. They are produced by a device called a
magnetron which is housed inside the oven. The microwaves
are reflected by metal surfaces but absorbed by food.
They cause the molecules of the food to vibrate billions
of times a second, making the food heat up and cook.
Larger amounts of food take longer to cook, so microwaves
are especially effective when cooking small portions.
     The advantages of microwave cooking are that it is
both quicker and cleaner than conventional cooking. Food
that has already been cooked can be reheated at any time
without loss of flavour or juices, and frozen food can be
defrosted and cooked very easily.
     Microwave ovens use less energy than conventional
methods of cooking and are very safe. As soon as the door
is opened, they automatically switch off and microwaves
cannot normally leak out of the door while they are
operating - despite some frightening stories about this!
```

© Cambridge University Press 1990

▶ We return to this type of composition in 10.11 – how to make a national dish.

6.12   *Keep* and *take*   *Verbs and idioms*

A

Answers

took ...
    some photographs, a holiday together, a long time, control of the situation, action, no notice of each other, the engine to pieces, care of the children
kept ...
    calm, house for their father, quiet, their tempers, their hands in their pockets, listening, an eye on each other

B   The synonyms given below are approximate only. Refer to a dictionary for more exact definitions and further examples.

Answers

 1 keep up = continue
 2 keep on with = continue
 3 keep away from = not go close to
 4 kept on = continue
 5 keep up with = go as fast as
 6 took   in = trick/deceive
 7 take up = start an activity
 8 took to = start to like
 9 take over = be in charge
10 take off = leave the ground
11 takes up = fill
12 take   in = absorb/understand
13 take   away from = subtract
14 take after = inherit a characteristic

▶ For more listening and speaking activities on the topic of technology, see *Ideas* Unit 15.

7 Good health!

7.1 In sickness and in health   *Vocabulary*

▶ As a warm-up for the exercises, get the class to work together in groups and ask each other these questions:
- Have you ever been in hospital?
- Have you ever visited someone in hospital?
- What serious and less serious illnesses have you had?

NB Although many people enjoy talking about illnesses and accidents, some people are sensitive about revealing personal information about distressing experiences or embarrassing diseases they may have had.

A There are many variations possible in these open-ended questions.

Answers

1 thermometer
2 infectious/contagious/catching   cure/remedy/medicine
3 swollen/painful/bruised/tender/sore
4 surgery/waiting room/office (US)
5 medicine/tablets/pills
6 sneezing/sniffing/having to blow your nose
7 plaster/bandage/dressing/Band-Aid (US)/(an) Elastoplast (GB)
8 ambulance
9 operation
10 fillings
11 exercise
12 temperature/headache/stomachache
13 diet
14 stomach/tummy
15 be sick/throw up

B Discuss the meanings of the wrong answers in this exercise.

Answers

1 prescription   4 game
2 injection   5 headache
3 spots

C   Make sure everyone knows the meanings of the wrong answers and how they are used.

Answers

1 off your food   out of sorts   under the weather
2 bruise   bump   cut
3 physically fit   living a healthy life   in good shape
4 affect   damage   ruin
5 dizzy   faint   funny

D   Students should leave plenty of room around their sketch so that there is space for adding vocabulary.

Make sure there is time to discuss what can go wrong with each part (pains, aches, sprains, etc.).

▶ Instead of **D**, you might prefer to draw a body on the board and ask the whole class to tell you how to label the parts. To save embarrassment, explain that the naughty bits are often called *the private parts*.

Alternatively, pairs of pairs could do **D** with one pair starting at the toes and the other at the fingers, before forming groups of four to exchange information.

7.2   **What to do about flu**   *Reading*

A   Before reading the text, get everyone to test their previous knowledge and common sense.

Then they check if they guessed right by reading the text.

Answers

1 T
2 F   (they can't kill viruses)
3 F   (24 hours to several days)
4 T
5 F   (don't force yourself to)
6 F   (it can become serious for elderly or sick people)
7 T
8 T
9 T
10 F   (the text would say if this was advisable – but if it helps, why not?)
11 F   (they can be)
12 F   (only one year)
13 F   (winter)

14 T   (dirty plates and cutlery can spread infection)
15 T

B   This part develops into a straightforward role-play.

Some questions

Have you got a headache?
Do you feel weak or shivery?
Are you sweating a lot?
Do you feel sick?
Have you lost your appetite?
Have you got a high temperature?
etc.

Some advice

It's best to stay indoors.
You'd better keep away from other people.
etc.

C   Another role-play, but with roles reversed (the patient is now the other person).

7.3   Comparing and contrasting   *Grammar*

A   The examples should be studied at home and any problems or questions tackled in class.

B   The ten sentences can be written in pairs, or as homework. Encourage everyone to use a VARIETY of the structures shown in the examples in **A**, and not just 'more … than'. Here are two examples:
    In 1950 there were far fewer retired people in Britain than now.
    In 2025 there will be over twice as many retired people in Japan as there are now.
Make sure any mistakes are spotted and corrected.
    As this exercise is open-ended, no model answers are given.

C

Errors underlined and corrected

1 *no errors*
2 July in Cairo is far <u>more dryer as</u> Athens.   **drier than**

3 The daytime temperature in Tokyo in July is the same <u>than</u> New York. **as**
4 There are <u>much</u> differences between the weather in Cairo and Tokyo. **many**
5 The weather in Athens in July is <u>more warmer</u> than London. **warmer**
6 New York is <u>more cold</u> in winter <u>as</u> London. **colder   than**

D

Answers

1 London isn't as hot as Cairo in July.
2 There aren't as many rainy days in Buenos Aires as (there are) in New York.
3 More rain falls in Athens than in Tokyo in January.
4 Buenos Aires is cooler than New York in July, but drier.
  Buenos Aires isn't as warm as New York in July, but it's drier.
5 About the same amount of rain falls in London and New York.
6 In London summer nights are much cooler than Cairo.
7 A sprained wrist is not as serious as a broken leg.
8 AIDS is the most frightening illness you/anyone can imagine.
9 A cold is less serious than flu.
10 Not as many people die from flu as 50 years ago.

E   After the discussion, which might cover just Britain and your students' country (or several countries), make sure everyone writes down TEN sentences (probably for homework).

▶ For more exercises on comparing and contrasting, see *Use of English* Unit 18.

7.4 Sleep and dreams   *Listening*

A   [cassette] Note that the meaning of 'REM sleep' is explained in question 1.

Answers

TRUE statements: 1   3   5   6   9   12
FALSE statements: 2   4   7   8   10   11

Transcript

Interviewer: … now, sleep, like the way our brains work, is something of a mystery, but some recent research into sleep has given us a few more answers. Dr Terry Harrison has just published a book called *Sleep*. Dr Harrison, how many kinds of sleep are there?

Dr Harrison: There are three types of sleep: light sleep, deep sleep and REM sleep. Now, light sleep is 'optional' – we can do without it and yet quite a lot of our sleeping time is spent sleeping lightly. Our brains in fact require deep sleep, not REM sleep, to restore them.

Interviewer: And dreams occur when you're just about to wake up, don't they?

Dr Harrison: A lot of people think this but it … it is in fact wrong. Dreams take place during REM – and that's rapid eye movement sleep. That's every 90 minutes or so throughout the night. And they usually go on for several minutes.

Interviewer: Why do we dream?

Dr Harrison: Again, opinion is divided. One purpose of dreams seems to be to help sleepers to solve problems in their waking lives. Er … we all know the most common dreams that we experience … er … falling, flying, being chased, for instance. And in these dreams like falling or being chased, the dreamer's not usually hurt or caught, is he?

Interviewer: Now, not everyone does dream, do they?

Dr Harrison: Research has in fact shown that everyone does dream at some point, according to my research anyway. But many people can't *remember* their dreams. In fact, most people forget their dreams very quickly after waking up. Now, if I asked you to tell me about your dreams last night now, you probably couldn't remember, could you?

Interviewer: … No, no, actually I can't.

Dr Harrison: Yet, alternatively if I asked you as soon as you'd woken up you would have been able to tell me.

Interviewer: I see. And how much sleep do we really need? Er … eight hours is supposed to be what everyone requires.

Dr Harrison: Yes, in fact most people require less than eight hours' sleep a night, er … six or seven is enough for many people. And there are many successful people who need only a few hours' sleep a night. Erm … I can think of Napoleon, and there's Winston Churchill … er … Margaret Thatcher all managed … er … to manage on four hours a night – leaving them more time than their enemies to keep one step ahead!

Interviewer: Haha. Now, what about problems like er … snoring and talking in your sleep? Are there any cures?

Dr Harrison: Ah, no, no there is no cure for snoring apart from waking up. And … er … talking in your sleep is something most people do at some time in their lives, it's not a problem exactly and it occurs in all kinds of sleep, not just when you're dreaming.

Interviewer: Now what about people who have two sleeps, one sleep during the day (a siesta) and another sleep at night? Now, presumably they get more sleep than the people who only sleep at night?

Dr Harrison: It's very simple, if you ... if you split your sleep into two parts, you need less sleep. If you take a siesta and sleep for say two hours, you only need to sleep for four or five hours at night. And that's presumably why people in Mediterranean countries seem to be able to keep going until 2 a.m. or even later. But a sleep during the day has to be long enough to allow time for deep sleep. So the benefit of a ten-minute nap is only psychological, not physical. It may make you feel better, but it doesn't really do you any good at all.

Interviewer: Dr Harrison, thank you.
Dr Harrison: Thank you.

(Time: 3 minutes 5 seconds)

B   If there is no time for the discussion in the same lesson as **A**, it can be done in a later lesson. Ask everyone to make notes on their dreams as soon as they wake up the next morning.

7.5   Using suffixes – 2: Actions and people   *Word study*

This section covers the formation of verbs from adjectives and nouns, and personal nouns from verbs.

A

Answers

-**ise**   centralise   individualise   summarise   symbolise
           (Note that these can also be written **-ize**.)
-**en**   flatten   lessen   loosen   sharpen   soften   tighten
-**ify**   purify   simplify

▶   Ask everyone to write sentences using some of these words.

B

Answers

-**er**   bróadcaster   cléaner   mánager   sínger   skíer   téacher
-**or**   diréctor   inspéctor   instrúctor   vísitor
-**ant**   assístant   inhábitant
-**ist**   ártist   cýclist   scíentist   týpist

⟫⟫→

137

★ Of the words shown that end with **-ent**, only *correspondent*, *resident*, *patient* and *student* are nouns – the others are adjectives.

Ask if anyone can think of further examples of more words like the ones presented in **A** and **B**. A few more are:

   idealise   straighten   justify

   Londoner   refugee   debtor   descendant   Marxist

C

Answers

1 loosen tighten	5 sharpening
2 scientist assistant	6 sterilised heating
3 widened motorist	7 rider cyclist
4 employer employees	8 inhabitants

7.6   Welcome to the health farm!   *Listening*

A   🔊 Although the term 'health farm' is likely to be unfamiliar, its meaning can be worked out from its context.

Answers

TRUE statements: 1   2   6   7   9
FALSE statements: 3   4   5   8   10

Transcript

Dr Lawrence: Good afternoon, everybody, I'm Jane Lawrence, I'm Doctor Jane Lawrence, the administrator and medical officer. I hope you're all going to be very happy here. I must explain first that you've got to participate in all the activities we offer and no absences from the premises will be permitted. Every morning everybody has to weigh in and your progress will be monitored. Your diets are adjusted according to the progress you make – that is, how much weight you lose. Now first of all, I'd like to introduce Mr O'Hara, the sports organiser. Mr O'Hara.

Mr O'Hara: Good afternoon. Now my motto is: healthy bodies are fit bodies. And from the look of you lot, you are certainly going to need our programme of compulsory sport and exercise routines. By the way, I also organise the social activities programme, which includes dances and cross-country treasure hunts.

Dr Lawrence: Thank you, Mr O'Hara. Now I'd like to explain the rules of the house. I'm afraid no visitors are allowed; lights out at 11 p.m.;

breakfast at 7.15 a.m. Could I introduce to you Miss Burns, who is our catering manager.

Miss Burns: Good afternoon. Well, I think you'll find the food here is wholesome and well-cooked. The amount that you will receive is given in strictly controlled portions according to the amount of weight that you lose each day. However, guests on the intensive one-week course will only be served with lunch and a salad dinner, I'm afraid. There will be no cakes, sweets or bread served at all.

Dr Lawrence: Thank you, Miss Burns. Now I'd just like to point out one final thing: all post received will be opened by the reception staff to prevent smuggling of extra food. I'm afraid that's been necessary because of our bad experiences in the past. Let me wish you a pleasant stay here with us and if you have any questions about the course you are on, please come and see me in my office.

(Time: 2 minutes 10 seconds)

B   After the group discussions, get each group to report back to the rest of the class.

7.7   Suppleness, strength and stamina
Problem solving

A   Perhaps ask everyone to suggest how other sports and activities would be rated: basketball, walking, aerobics, etc.

B   With these profiles (as in the exam) some of the information given is not directly relevant to the task: the idea is to SELECT the relevant information.

C   Give everyone a chance to discuss what they'll write before they write the paragraphs for homework.

Model paragraphs

```
My advice to Anna is to take up swimming. This will help
her to develop her stamina as well as improving her
muscle power and suppleness. The best way to go about it
would be to get together with a friend and go to the
local swimming pool together two or three times a week.
Dancing would be unsuitable as she doesn't like pop
music.

If Richard wants to keep fit he should take up yoga to
improve his suppleness. This is something he can practise
```

at home on his own, or he could join a class. If he can afford the time he could walk to work every day, but this wouldn't really help him with his stiffness problem. Swimming might also be a good idea for him.

The best thing for Eric to do would be to learn to swim, then he could go for an early morning swim every day to keep fit. If this is not possible, he could become a football referee. Referees have to do a lot of running around, but they don't need to be as young as footballers. Another idea for Eric would be to take up tennis, especially if his hotel has a tennis court.

What I do to keep fit is spend ten minutes every morning doing simple keep-fit exercises: arm swinging, sit-ups, knee-bends and so on. I also run on the spot for two to three minutes, which is more energetic than running for the same amount of time. I usually swim once a week, but I don't really enjoy swimming up and down a pool. In fact, that's the trouble with most ways of keeping fit on your own: although they are necessary, they tend to be rather boring!

7.8   A pain in the neck   *Reading*

A   The pre-reading discussion can be done in groups or as a class.

B

Answers

1 c   2 b   3 c   4 d   5 c (according to the text)

C   Perhaps ask for more suggestions for suitable exercises.

7.9   *At . . .*   *Prepositional phrases*

Answers

1 at first = to begin with
2 at least = not less than
3 at last = finally
4 at first sight = when first seen
5 at a profit   at a loss

6 at war   at peace
7 at a time = not all together
8 at any rate = in any case/anyway
9 at once = immediately
10 at the same time = simultaneously

▶ For more practice on prepositional phrases, see *Use of English* Units 21 and 22.

7.10 Staying healthy   *Picture conversation*

In this 'picture conversation' exercise we look at the essential examination skill of being able to answer questions according to what you want to say about the topic, steering the conversation to your own advantage.

A   For this part the class should be divided into an EVEN number of pairs.

Discuss the questions that the pairs have produced with the whole class.

B   Now students work as pairs of pairs (each pair with another pair). Go round listening in to each group so that you can give feedback later on their performance.

A 'model conversation' between two native speakers is recorded on the cassette. This may be helpful to show students the kind of discussion they could have, before they begin the activity. Alternatively, it could be played after the pairs have finished.

Transcript

Man: ... Mm, look at these two photos here.
Woman: Mm? Oh yeah.
Man: What's your reaction to the first picture?
Woman: Which one? The woman keeping fit ... er ... jogging?
Man: Yeah. Why is she alone do you think?
Woman: Haha, well, perhaps she couldn't get anyone to go with her – or perhaps she's ahead of her companion and he's not such a fast runner.
Man: So ... um ... why do you think she's wearing headphones, then?
Woman: Oh, is she? Oh, yes. Well, I mean, jogging's not very interesting, is it? And music helps to keep you going – I mean, the rhythm ... the rhythm can help you keep you going at a steady ... steady pace.
Man: Yeah, you mean you don't fancy ... er ... swapping places with her, then?

141

Woman: Haha, it could be me. I do try to go jogging every evening after work, but I don't go on my own. No, I always go with my boyfriend, I think it's safer. Actually, it's quite good for me because he's faster than me and I have to run to keep up with him. Haha.

Man: Haha, so wh ... why do you do it, then?

Woman: Well, I don't ... don't really enjoy it but if I didn't do that, I'd have to do something else to keep fit.

Man: Well, why don't you do something different then?

Woman: Well, I think the main advantage is that you only need a good pair of running shoes.

Man: That's true.

Woman: You just go outside and start running, and it's free and you can more or less do it any time you like – even if it's raining or snowing or blowing.

Man: That's true, fair enough. OK, so ... um ... what's your reaction to the other one then, the other picture?

Woman: Let's see ... well, when I first saw it, I thought it was just a normal cigarette packet, you know with the warning on the side, but then I realised it must be from an anti-smoking campaign.

Man: Ah, now why do you say that?

Woman: Well, look, I mean there's so many warnings – your love life, your appearance, your children's future, your taste, your wage packet, your unborn baby.

Man: Yeah, but I ... I mean I don't quite understand all that. I mean, how can ... how can smoking, for instance, damage your love life?

Woman: Ah, well, makes your breath smell, doesn't it? Haha. Your mouth tastes horrid – have you ever kissed a smoker? I have. Never again!

Man: Well, all right, then, how about ... erm ... this damaging your appearance: how does smoking do that, then?

Woman: Oh, come on! I mean, look at people who smoke, look at their hands! And teeth: they're all sort of horrible yellow colour.

Man: All right, all right. H ... how can it affect your children's future?

Woman: I'm not really sure. Well, I mean, what do they call it? Passive smoking. I mean, if you smoke and your children are in the same room then they're inhaling the smoke that you're blowing out, aren't they?

Man: I see ... mm. Yeah, I remember, I ... I mean ... I worked in an office once where I was the only non-smoker – it was, it was awful.

Woman: Yes, I mean, smokers ... I mean ... they don't always realise that what they're doing doesn't just damage them but it damages the health of other people around them. I feel quite strongly about that.

Man: What about the other points, then? Um ... how can smoking damage your taste?

Woman: Ah, well, you see ...

(Time: 3 minutes 20 seconds)

7.11 Doctor's orders   *Listening*

A   Perhaps ask everyone to put crosses in pencil beside the potentially harmful items in the list.

B   [cassette] Students can assume that if an item is not forbidden, it is permitted!

Answers

Fresh fish ✓	Butter (unsalted) ✓	Tea ✓
Canned fish ✗	Tomato ketchup ✗	Grapes ✓
Fish and chips ✗	Coffee ✓	Carrots ✓
Fresh meat ✓	Apples ✓	Crisps ✗
Salt ✗	Bananas ✓	Hamburgers ✗
Bread ✓ (less)	Potatoes ✓	Beer ✓
Margarine ✗	Sausages ✗	

Transcript

Doctor: ... Fine, thank you. So, Mr Brown, you're going to have to change your diet quite considerably. Um ... let's just look at this list that you've made of the things that you normally eat. Mm, dear, well you're going to ... er ... going to have to avoid these fast foods you've been having, like ... um ... hamburgers and ... er ... fish and chips and so on. Um ... and you should try to eat rather less bread, too. And if you do eat bread, can you make sure that you don't have any margarine or salted butter – unsalted butter's all right. Um ... oh and none of this ketchup, all right?

Now, you can eat fish, but not ... not if it's in cans, it must be fresh fish. And ... um ... meat is all right but ... um ... again, only fresh meat and grilled is best, but as I said, don't eat hamburgers and sausages, they're even worse. Now ... er ... fresh fruit and ... er ... vegetables of all kinds are ... are excellent, but ... um ... make sure that you don't cook the vegetables in ... in salted water. Now, there's no harm at all in eating potatoes, even chips but definitely not crisps, OK?

Now ... er ... let's see, what else? Er ... ye ... oh yes, you can ... you can drink whatever you like, no ... no problems there and ... um ... chocolate should be OK too. Um ... but the most important thing is not to put any salt on your food. In fact, if you've got any salt in the house, just ... just throw it away. And if you do what I say then ... um ... you should start feeling better in about three to four weeks, so ... um ... come and see me in a month from now.

Patient: Yes, well, thank you, doctor. Goodbye.

(Time: 1 minute 55 seconds)

C   Mr Brown might be suffering from hypertension – a low-salt diet may help to improve his condition.

D   This is an exam-style Open Dialogue exercise. It can be done as homework or in pairs in class.

Suggested answers

Patient: Good morning, doctor.
Doctor: Hallo Mr Jones, what **seems to be the trouble?**
Patient: Well, I keep getting these headaches.
Doctor: When **do you usually get them?**
Patient: After I get home from work usually.
Doctor: What **do you take for them? / do you do about them?**
Patient: I usually take a couple of aspirins and that seems to do the trick.
Doctor: How long **have you been suffering from them?**
Patient: For the past two or three months.
Doctor: Why **haven't you been to see me before this?**
Patient: Well, it didn't really seem bad enough to be worth troubling you about.
Doctor: Have **you been working any harder than usual?**
Patient: Yes, I suppose so, Since my assistant was made redundant I've been doing his work as well as mine.
Doctor: Have **you said anything to your boss about this?**
Patient: Yes, but he says that if I can't do the work, I'll lose my job too.
Doctor: What **would you like me to do?**
Patient: Can you give me a certificate so that I can be off work for a week – then my boss will have to do my work for a week and he'll see how overworked I am.
Doctor: Would **two weeks' rest be better?**
Patient: Oh yes, *two* weeks would be even better.
Doctor: **Well, if you like I could recommend that you take a month off work, how about that?**
Patient: Thank you very much.
Doctor: **And make sure you get plenty of rest and fresh air.**
Patient: All right, doctor.

7.12   What would you say?   *Composition*

The procedure and information for this section are in the Student's Book. The model composition is 187 words, slightly longer than required in the exam.

Model composition

Good evening, everyone, and welcome! I'd just like to say
a few words about what we're going to do on this course,
in particular about our aims and methods.
     First of all, I think the one thing you all have in
common is that you think you aren't fit enough - am I
right? Good! Well, our purpose is to make you fit by
introducing you to easy exercises that you can do with us
here every week <u>and</u> at home every day. Now, none of these
exercises are going to need special equipment or skills
and you'll be able to adapt them to your own
requirements. For example, if you particularly want to
develop your strength then some of our muscle-building
exercises will be more suitable than some of the
stretching exercises, which help to develop suppleness.
     Well, that's enough from me, so let's get started.
You can ask me questions in the break later. Now, spread
out so that you don't touch anyone else and put your legs
apart. That's right. Now lift both arms up in the air and
swing them down and up again...

© Cambridge University Press 1990

E   This is optional – only do this if there is time available.

7.13 *Put*

Verbs and idioms

Answers

 1 put   on = switch on
 2 put   up = provide accommodation
 3 put   off = distract
 4 put   out/off = switch off
 5 put   off = postpone
 6 put   up = raise
 7 put on = gain
 8 put   down = write down
 9 putting   back = replace
10 put   away = remove to proper place
11 put   forward   put   back = change to later/earlier time
12 put   through = connect to phone extension (*or* put off?)
13 put up with = tolerate
14 put off = discourage

7.14   Fill the gaps   *Exam practice*

This is a revision exercise on prepositions.

Complete story (Some variations are possible.)

HAY FEVER HITS OPERA

The star $_1$ **of** the largest scale opera performance ever staged $_2$ **in** Britain pulled out $_3$ **on** its opening night $_4$ **on** Sunday. Verdi's Aïda is being performed $_5$ **at** London's Earl's Court Arena $_6$ **with** a cast of 600 singers, dancers and actors. American soprano Grace Bumbry $_7$ **in** the title role was suffering $_8$ **from** hay fever, but had promised to be 'all right on the night even if my nose drips like the Nile'. Half-way $_9$ **through** the performance she was unable to continue and was replaced $_{10}$ **in** mid-performance $_{11}$ **by** Bulgarian soprano Ghena Dimitrova who was sitting $_{12}$ **in** the audience watching the show. She was taken $_{13}$ **to** a dressing room where she put on Ms Bumbry's costume and was made up. She was ready to go $_{14}$ **onto** the stage $_{15}$ **after** a longer-than-usual interval.

Tuesday's performance $_{16}$ **in** the presence $_{17}$ **of** the Prince and Princess of Wales will go ahead $_{18}$ **without** Ms Bumbry – her role will be taken $_{19}$ **by** Martina Arroyo $_{20}$ **from** Italy.

▶ For more listening and speaking activities on the topic of health, see *Ideas* Unit 13.

8 Holidays

8.1 Getting away from it all
Vocabulary

B Make sure the wrong answers are discussed, as they contain useful vocabulary.

Answers

1 brochures	11 sign
2 view	12 excursions
3 balcony	13 cruise
4 sunbathing	14 souvenir
5 flight	15 agency
6 takes off	16 understood
7 land	17 resort
8 package	18 protect
9 fluently	19 beach
10 phrase book	20 self-catering

C Again, discuss the wrong answers too – what do they mean and how are they used?

Answers

1 day-trippers   holiday-makers   sightseers
2 bed and breakfast   full board   half board
3 active   busy   energetic
4 lazy   relaxing   restful
5 choice   range   variety

E Perhaps draw a map of your students' country on the board and ask everyone to identify the surrounding countries.

8.2   Brazilian Contrasts   *Reading*

A

Answers

the atmosphere of old Brazil – Salvador
historic buildings – Salvador
a rapidly growing city – São Paulo
a statue of Christ – Rio
one of the world's most famous
   views – Rio

a cable car ride – Rio
unusual architecture –
   Brasilia
a samba show – Rio
a magnificent waterfall –
   Iguaçu
wonderful costumes – Rio

▶ Perhaps get everyone to mark the places in the text where the information was given.

B

Answers

1 No: 'by scheduled service'
2 Early morning
3 Day 2: afternoon city tour AND Day 11–13: Carioca night tour
4 Brasilia
5 Narrow, cobbled and winding up and down the hills
6 By one million new inhabitants every year
7 The noise: 'the distant roar of the Falls increases to a deafening crescendo'
8 Evening
9 4–7 February
10 No: 'For carnival supplements see price box below'

C

Answers

1 Luxor Continental
2 Yes: '290 rooms … high rise'
3 No: '50 yards from …
   Copacabana Beach'

4 Not necessarily: 'Rooms vary in
   size and location'
5 No: 'with shower only'
6 No: 'modern accommodation'

D   Group discussion. (Some other problems of holidays in exotic places: malaria, yellow fever, snakes, sharks, jellyfish, humidity, long-haul flights, crime, terrorism, etc.)

8.3 *If* sentences   *Grammar*

A

Answers

TYPE 1:

If you **decide** / **have** to go to the USA, you **will need** / **'ll need** a visa.

TYPE 2:

If you **had** £1,000 to spend, where **would you go** on holiday?

Type 2 or Type 1:

If I **go** abroad next summer, I **'ll need** / **'ll have to get** a new passport.
If I **went** abroad next summer, I **would need** / **would have to get** a new passport.

TYPE 3:

If you **had asked** me to confirm the booking, I **would have sent** you a letter.

Types 2 and 3 in the same sentence:

If I'd been (had been) born in 1975, I'd be **XX years old** today.

'd as the short form of *had* and *would*:

1 would   had
2 would
3 would   would
4 would   had

▶ In conversation, using full forms rather than contracted forms:
I would have done it if I had known.
If you had told them they would have come on time.
can give students more time to think and many learners find full forms much easier to use than the short forms.

B

Errors underlined and corrected

1 If I <u>would have</u> known, I could have helped you.   **had**
2 If <u>it's</u> my birthday tomorrow, <u>I'll</u> invite my friends out for a meal.
   it was / it were   I would   *or*   **As** it's my birthday + no changes
3 *no errors*
4 If the weather had been better, we <u>had</u> gone to the beach
   yesterday.   **would have**

5 If you <u>will need</u> any help, please let me know.   **need**
6 *no errors*
7 If I hadn't just been on holiday, <u>I would have had</u> more money now.   **I would have**
8 Where <u>you would</u> go if you <u>can</u> go anywhere in the world?   **would you   could**

C

Answers

2 If you go to Britain, you'll be able to speak English all day long.
3 If you sunbathe all day long, you'll get sunburnt.
4 If I hadn't got a holiday job this summer, I could / would be able to go on holiday.
5 Unless you book in advance, you won't find any accommodation.
6 If I had enjoyed my holiday there, I would/might go back.
7 If you had told me where you were staying, I could have got in touch.
8 Pack a jumper to wear after dark in case the evenings are cool.
9 If you come on holiday with us, you'll enjoy it.

D   Begin the activity with students working in an even number of pairs so that they can form groups of four (pairs of pairs) later.

E   [▨] Student A looks at Activity 19, student B at 33 and C at 43.
• 19 shows an advertisement for a weekend in the country at the Springs Hotel.
• 33 shows an advertisement for English Country Cottages.
• 43 shows an advertisement for villas in romantic Italy.
This activity practises using conditionals in a conversation.

▶ For more practice on conditional sentences, see *Use of English* Units 24 and 25.

8.4   Getting away from it all?   *Picture conversation*

▶ In preparation for **B**, ask everyone to bring some photos of a recent holiday (or outing) to class.

A   Before the pairs start asking each other the questions about the photos, remind them of ways of encouraging a partner to give more information and to keep talking (see 3.11 **B**).

B   Your own holiday snaps could be used to demonstrate to everyone what kinds of things you might say about such photos.

C   The ads for Yugoslavia and Cyprus could be complemented by using ads for some other countries or regions, taken from magazines.

▶   After discussing the attractions of Yugoslavia and Cyprus, ask everyone to work in groups and compose a similar advertisement for their own country or region. First, they should discuss what points they'll make, then make notes, before writing their ads, and then showing them to another group.

8.5   Island-hopping   *Listening*

A   [cassette icon] Before they hear the recording make sure everyone familiarises themselves with the Greek Islands on the chart and map.
   Allow time for everyone to compare notes between listenings.

(The capital of Santorini is actually called *Fira* or *Phira* and the island itself is known also as *Thira*. Moreover it's an active volcano. Ferry sailings for the islands leave from *Piraeus*. Even travel agents make mistakes!)

Answers

	Attractions	Drawbacks
Athens	Museums, classical sights	Noisy, hot in summer
Corfu	Night life, direct flights	Touristy
Rhodes	Quiet outside town, good hotels in town, cheap villas and rooms in Lindos, direct flights	Busy in main town
Paros	Pretty, good beaches, unspoilt outside town, clear water	Six hours on ferry from Athens
Santorini	Beautiful scenery, direct flights, black sand beaches	Climb to capital, 10 hours on ferry, a bit frightening
Zante	Green, unspoilt, wild flowers, friendly people, direct flights, small beaches(?)	

F

Transcript

Travel agent:	Good afternoon. Can I help you, sir?
Client:	Oh yes, good afternoon. Well, I hope you can, yes. Um ... I'm thinking of going off to Greece this summer ...
Travel agent:	Yes.
Client:	... and really I need some advice. I mean, if you've got any maps or whatever.
Travel agent:	I see, yes certainly, sir, yes, of course I can help because in fact I've been to Greece several times myself on holiday there. I think it's a marvellous place ...
Client:	Oh, good.
Travel agent:	... and I did see quite a lot of the islands as well as the mainland. Now ... er ... let's get a couple of facts sorted out first: how long do you actually want to go for?
Client:	Well, I've got two weeks free. Um ... and ideally, of course, I want ... er ... to have time to see the sights and so forth but ... er ... I want to relax as well, you know ...
Travel agent:	I see.
Client:	... so if we could manage a bit of both.
Travel agent:	Yes, yes, certainly. Um ... well, we'll talk about the ... er ... sightseeing first, shall we? Um ... of course the most obvious place is Athens.
Client:	I was going to say, yeah.
Travel agent:	Right, er ... now if you want to have a look at this map here ...
Client:	Ah, yes.
Travel agent:	So ... now you can see exactly where Athens is.
Client:	Yes.
Travel agent:	It's very noisy, I have to tell you that, very hot in the summer, but there are marvellous museums and the classical sites are quite fantastic. It's very best ... er ... c ... to combine ... this with a quite ... a quiet island, so you spend one week in Athens and one week on an island.
Client:	Oh, I see. Oh, how about Corfu? I mean, that's ... er ... is that all right?
Travel agent:	Y ... yes it is. Um ... I hesitate to recommend it because it's terribly touristy. I mean, it actually depends what you want and what you like. There's certainly plenty of night-life and things to do.
Client:	Mmm.
Travel agent:	But in fact more tourists visit this island than the whole of the rest of Greece put together ...
Client:	Oh, good gracious!
Travel agent:	The one advantage about Corfu is that there are direct flights ... Um ... in fact, I think the place I'd recommend most is Rhodes.
Client:	Oh, yes, yes. Somebody told me about Rhodes.
Travel agent:	It's very busy near the town itself but elsewhere it's very quiet, even in the summer. The best way to see the rest of the island is to hire a car and if I were you I'd probably stay in Rhodes Town itself or in Lindos.

Client:	Oh, I see.
Travel agent:	There are good luxury hotels in Rhodes Town and there are very reasonable villas and rooms in Lindos. And again there are direct flights there.
Client:	Oh, that's useful to know. But ... er ... what about the places that aren't quite so well-known? I mean, some of these little islands.
Travel agent:	Mmm. Well, as you can see, there are a lot to choose from. Um ... I'll tell you a little about my favourite islands.
Client:	Mmm.
Travel agent:	Er ... Paros ...
Client:	Oh now ...
Travel agent:	Now can we find that there?
Client:	There's Poros here.
Travel agent:	No, we mustn't confuse the two. This is Paros there, which is just south of Mykonos.
Client:	Yes, I see.
Travel agent:	Now, to get there you fly to Athens and take the ferry, which takes six hours to get across. But it's a very pretty island, there are good beaches and it's quite unspoiled outside the main town. The best way of exploring the island is either by hiring a moped or a motorbike. And the swimming's marvellous because the water's very clear.
Client:	Oh smashing ... Great, where else?
Travel agent:	Er ... Santorini, now that's ...
Client:	Oh, that's down the bottom there.
Travel agent:	... one of the southern ones there. That's unbelievably beautiful. Very impressive scenery. The island's actually an extinct volcano and in fact you can still see it smoking in the bay.
Client:	Oh, gracious!
Travel agent:	The town itself is built on top of the edge of the crater and the cliffs plunge into the sea below, so you can imagine how the scenery really is very impressive.
Client:	Fantastic ... yeah.
Travel agent:	Er ... there's one slight problem about this place is that to ... to get from the ferry up to the capital, which is called Thira, you have to climb up the track or ride on a donkey. So, you know, that's something to take into account. The ferry from Athens takes longer, it takes about ten hours, but in fact you can now fly there direct as well. Oh and ... and the other marvellous thing about this place is that the beaches are black sand ...
Client:	Good gracious me!
Travel agent:	... which is breath-taking, but I also found it a little bit frightening at first. Um ...
Client:	Where else?
Travel agent:	Yes, the other island I'd recommend to you is Zante. Er ... it's a very very sweet island, very green, completely unspoiled. There's amazing wild flowers, the beaches are small and the people are very very friendly.
Client:	Oh, that sounds really my sort of thing.
Travel agent:	Oh, does it? Yes, it's lovely. You can fly there direct or you can

fly to Athens and take the ferry or a plane from there.
Um … if you, you know, wanted to ignore the city centres
altogether, you could do what we did last year, which was
'island-hopping' – going from one island to another by ferry,
spending a day or two on each.

Client: Oh super!

Travel agent: That way, you see, that way you don't get a chance to get fed up
with them and we had a marvellous time.

Client: Mmm!

(Time: 4 minutes)

B   Even the most untouristy places have their attractions – encourage
everyone to think positively about their region, if necessary!

▶ This and the follow-up role-play could develop into a mini-
presentation or short talk by groups of students (or even individuals)
about their own country or region: 'My country and why you'd enjoy
going there on holiday'.

8.6   Three more islands!   *Problem solving*

A   Remind everyone that they can find out what weather to expect on
each island in August, April or October by looking at the holiday
weather chart.

▶ Get each group to list the ten most important articles (clothes,
walking boots, etc.) they'd take to all three places. Which of them would
they pack in an overnight bag?

Then, when the lists are complete, ask:
   If most of your luggage went to Cairo/Bangkok/Beirut, which four
   articles would you choose NOT to lose?

B   For this role-play, the groups should consist of three or four
members. Perhaps get everyone to imagine they're sitting together in a
café, talking about holidays.

▶ Instead of the 'If I could go to one of the islands … ' paragraph in C,
perhaps substitute this more expansive introductory phrase: 'If I could
go anywhere in the world on holiday, the place I'd go to is …'

C   Make sure everyone makes notes before they write their four
paragraphs. Each paragraph should be about 50 words, though the
following model paragraphs are nearer 100 each.

   As usual with these problem-solving activities, the models are not 'definitive' – the reasons why Kim would like Madeira are given, for example, but there may also be good reasons why another island would be suitable.

Model paragraphs (The fourth is on the alternative topic suggested above.)

```
I'd advise Gerry to go to Kos. Even if he goes in the
middle of the summer, he'll discover that it's peaceful
and quiet. It's quite a large island, so there will be
plenty to do and the beaches won't be over-crowded. He
can explore the island by hiring a bicycle. The main
problem would be the heat. In the middle of summer the
sun shines all the time and the temperature is 30° or
more. If he doesn't like hot weather, perhaps he could go
there during the Easter holidays.
```

```
If I were Kim I'd go to Madeira. In the autumn the
weather is pleasantly warm but not too hot. Kim would
enjoy walking in the mountains and seeing the wild
flowers, for which the island is famous and which flower
all year round. Kim would enjoy the fantastic scenery and
visiting the little villages, and the lack of beaches
wouldn't worry her. I think Madeira would suit Kim very
well - much better than the other islands, in fact.
```

```
My advice to Sandy would be to go to Majorca. There's
plenty to do there and it has wonderful scenery and great
beaches as well as places to go for a good night out.
There's a wide range of different things to do, which
would make it ideal for an active person like Sandy. The
one problem about going in April or May is that it won't
be very hot at that time of year, so from that point of
view perhaps Kos might be better.
```

```
If I could go anywhere in the world on holiday, the place
I'd go to is the west coast of Scotland - not for
sunbathing and discos, but for the scenery, which is
magnificent. Even in summer it can be cool and may rain a
lot and be windy, but between the showers when the sun
shines it is gorgeous. In summer the days are incredibly
long too, and it doesn't get dark till quite late in the
evening. The best way to see the country is by hiring a
car and driving up the coast road.
```

8.7   By . . .   *Prepositional phrases*

Answers

 1 by far = far more popular than anywhere else
 2 by sight = recognise   by name = know their names
 3 by plane   by ship
 4 by heart = memorise
 5 by accident
 6 by train   by car
 7 by day   by night = during the day/night
 8 by surprise
 9 by chance
10 by all means = certainly
11 by mistake
12 by post   by hand = deliver personally
13 by yourself = alone/on your own

8.8   An excursion programme   *Listening*

A [cassette] If you can get hold of a large map of Scotland or the British
Isles to show where the places mentioned actually are, this will make the
task more realistic – or draw a map on the board.

Answers

	Depart		Return
Sunday	*14.00*	Edinburgh city sightseeing *(no need to book)*	*16.30*
Monday	9.00	(Braemar Castle) and (Aberdeen)	17.30
Tuesday	*7.45* ~~8.30~~	Glencoe and Fort William	17.30
Wednesday	8.00	Inverness and Loch Ness	*18.30* ~~17.30~~
Thursday	14.00	Edinburgh city sightseeing tour	16.30
Friday	~~9.15~~ *cancelled* ~~Galashiels and the Borders~~		~~16.00~~
	7.00	*Glasgow and River Clyde steamer trip*	*17.45*

Transcript

Tour leader: Good morning, everyone. Er ... ha ... sorry to ... er ... interrupt breakfast. I've got here a few changes to the excursion ... er ... programme, which I think you've all got. Um ... I might as well go through them all and then you'll know where you are. In fact, they make absolutely no difference to the tours: in fact they ... they improve them, which is basically why we've made the changes. Now, your Monday 9 o'clock ... um ... where you've got the Braemar Castle ... er ... Aberdeen: what we're going to do is we're going to swop round there and we're going to go to Aberdeen first and then on to Braemar, returning here at 17.30. Now we move to Tuesday. Ah ... the only difference there ... I'm going to make an earlier start for Glencoe and Fort William: ah ... 7.45 instead of 8.30. Ah ... Wednesday: yes, the ... the Inverness and Loch Ness – one of my personal favourites, I think ... um ... everyone – um ... instead of returning at ... er ... 17.30, we'll come back a ... a ... a little bit later there on that one ... er ... 18.30 ... give us a bit more time actually at Loch Ness. Hope we spot the monster, eh? Ha! Well ... er ... Thursday ... um ... now this is ... this is our ... our big day in Edinburgh, where we're doing the city sightseeing. Um ... also ... er ... we're going to do an Edinburgh this afternoon – that's today, Sunday, we're going to do an Edinburgh ... um ... because ... er ... we ... we had nothing planned for today, but we're going to do an Edinburgh as well. Er ... same time, no need to book. Er ... now unfortunately on Friday we've had to cancel your Galashiels and your Borders. Er ... but instead we're substituting Glasgow, leaving at 7 for Glasgow and then I think a fitting end to your holiday, one I think you're going to go for: the River Clyde Steamer Trip. Yes, on an actual River Clyde steamer. Re ... returning at ... at 17 ... 17.45. Er ... I hope those are all satisfactory. Sorry we've had to make these changes, but I think you'll find that they'll improve the holiday and make it even better than it already is. Oh, now I ... can I remind you that the ... the excursions are of course optional, you know, but I'm sure you'll all want to go on them. Er ... and would you decide which ones you want to go on by lunchtime today. Thanks very much, everyone, enjoy the rest of your breakfasts.

(Time: 2 minutes 25 seconds)

B   This could also be done as a class: draw an outline map of the area on the board and ask everyone to suggest which places of interest you should add. Then work out a nice excursion route.

8.9   Spelling and pronunciation: Consonants
Word study

A   Remind everyone that in 5.7 we looked at different spellings of vowel sounds. Perhaps ask everyone to suggest a few more words that can be added to the lists.

B 🔲 Pause the tape between each group of twelve words so that everyone can catch their breath and, if necessary, discuss what they've written so far. The correct spellings are in Activity 25, but students shouldn't look there until they've done all three parts of the exercise.

Answers

These are in Activity 25 of the Student's Book.

Transcript

Narrator: Add the words you hear to the lists in your book. Here are the first twelve. Ready?

slipping	He kept slipping on the ice.
sleeping	She was still sleeping at 10 o'clock.
trouble	Don't worry, it's no trouble.
robber	The robber stole the money.
total	What's the total amount?
putting	You're putting on weight.
address	What's your name and address?
doubled	Their speed doubled.
request	I agreed to his request.
Christian	Is he a Christian or a Moslem?
angle	90° is a right angle.
ignorant	They are very ignorant.

Narrator: And now here are the next twelve.

engine	This car has a petrol engine.
average	The average is 50%.
adventure	We had an exciting adventure.
butcher	You get meat from the butcher.
careful	Please be very careful.
million	The population of Britain is 50 million.
often	How often have you seen her?
sudden	There was a sudden noise.
immense	The problems are immense.
coming	Are you coming to see us?
worry	It's all right, don't worry!
railway	I'll meet you at the railway station

Narrator: And now here are the last fourteen.

please	Please don't smoke.
assistant	My assistant will help you.
pleasure	It was a pleasure to meet you.
insurance	Don't drive without insurance.
laughing	He kept on laughing.
rough	The surface isn't smooth, it's rough.
convince	They tried to convince me.
live	Where do you live?

theory   In theory that sounds like a good idea.
themselves They did all the work themselves.
twelve   Six plus six is twelve.
while   I'll wash up while you dry.
university She's a student at the university.
yawning   I'm very tired, I can't help yawning.

(Time: 3 minutes 10 seconds)

C   Some more examples of 'silent letters' that don't come up in **D** below:
through   straight
crumb   thumb
postman   fasten
know   knock   knit   knickers
stalk   talk   would
far   father   farther   confirm   (only in R.P.)
honour   dishonest   exhausted

D   [symbol] Activities 5 and 22 contain more words that students dictate to each other, but in case of confusion – i.e. frequently – the words should be spelt out.

Activity 5 contains these words:
hopeless   abbreviation   butter   lucky   juice   charming   ready surprise   social   telephone   half
Silent letters: thorough   debt   soften   knot   chalk   scared vehicle

Activity 22 contains these words:
approximately   beauty   matter   quickly   edge   cheerful   wreck lazy   information   cough   halve
Silent letters: height   doubt   whistle   knowledge   calm   heart exhibition

▶ For more practice on spelling and pronunciation, see *Use of English* Unit 6.

8.10   Writing letters   *Composition*

A   Get everyone to find the faults in the two 'students' compositions' – there are no spelling mistakes or grammatical errors.

B Activity 41 contains improved versions of the two compositions. Get everyone to underline the improvements that have been made.

C You might prefer to ask all your students to write on the same topic, rather than choose. There are no model compositions in this case, as the improved compositions in Activity 41 can serve as models.

  Insist that everyone makes notes before they start – perhaps ask to see the notes as well as the completed compositions.

D Perhaps allow a few silent minutes in class for everyone to check their work through before they show it to a partner.

▶ We return to writing letters in 11.11.

8.11 **Duty-free goods**   *Listening*

  Give everyone a chance to compare answers with a partner before going through the correct answers. The recording can be conveniently paused after question 1, as shown in the transcript.

Answers

1

Airports		Airlines	
Amsterdam	£8.50	British Airways	£10.50
Athens	£7.50	Air France	£10
Gatwick	£10	Alitalia	£10
Heathrow	£10	Iberia	£9.50
Madrid	£9	JAL	£10.50
Manchester	£10.50	KLM	£9.50
New York	£9.50	Olympic	£8.50
Paris	£9	Swissair	£10.50
Rome	£10	Varig	£8
Tokyo	£12		
Zurich	£10		

2 they don't carry such a large stock   5 Do I really need this?
3 a local supermarket   Is it really cheaper?
4 souvenir   6 higher   normal

Transcript

Presenter: If you're going abroad this year and you're going by air, you'll
            probably do what every air traveller does – stop at the duty-free shop

or buy duty-free goods on the plane. But not all duty-free shops offer the same value, as Jonathan Harris now explains.

Jonathan: That's right, Stella. I've been ... er ... I've been looking at prices in ... er ... duty-free shops and on airlines in various countries. Now, I've taken the average shopping basket that most travellers would buy ... er ... the most common purchase is one bottle of whisky and ... er ... 200 cigarettes and I've found out the prices vary enormously depending on where you shop. Now, let's say you buy £10 worth of goods at the airport in London – it's the same at both Gatwick or at Heathrow. Now, if you bought exactly the same things at Amsterdam Airport those goods would cost you £8.50 and if you bought them at the airport in Athens they'd only cost you £7.50. In Madrid they'd cost £9, and in Paris they'd be £9 too. In New York they'd be £9½ [*Note: the speaker is an American*] and in Zurich and in Rome exactly the same price as you'd pay for them in London. Now, the only airports more expensive than London are Manchester, where that £10 basket of goods would cost you £10.50, and in Tokyo where you'd pay £12.

Presenter: Mmm, that's quite a variation, isn't it? Well, is it any cheaper actually on the plane?

Jonathan: Well, there is just as much variation from airline to airline there, too. Er ... most expensive I found were British Airways, Swissair and JAL (that's the Japanese airline). Here the £10 worth of goods at Heathrow would cost you £10.50. Now, Air France and Alitalia charged just the same as Heathrow prices. Um ... Iberia and KLM were £9.50 and ... er ... cheapest of all were the Greek airline Olympic at £8.50 and Varig (that's a ... a Brazilian airline) at £8.

(*Questions 2 to 6* ↓)

But there is a problem with airlines and that's they just can't carry the stock that a shop on the ground can – so if you ... er ... smoke a particular brand of cigarettes or you prefer a particular brand of Scotch, you can't depend on them to have it. And ... er ... then again, if you're at the far end of the cabin from where they start down with the trolley, by the time they get down to you they may have nothing left.

Presenter: Right, so is there any advice that you'd like to offer?

Jonathan: Ah ... yes, there are a couple of things. In some countries you may find that it's cheaper to look around the local supermarket before you leave, because very often prices locally are cheaper than here anyway and that's got to do a lot with their tax structures. Um ... in addition to that, surely a bottle of the ... er ... local drink ... er ... whatever it is, is a nicer souvenir to take back home than the same old bottle of Scotch whisky that you'd get back in the United Kingdom anyway.

Presenter: Er ... what about other duty-free purchases?

Jonathan: Well, there I'd say: Think before you buy – think twice in fact and ask yourself two questions:

The first one is this: Do I really need this? Things like perfume, after-shave, silk ties and so on are things you can do without and in fact if you weren't at the airport or on the plane you probably wouldn't buy them anyway.

Second question is this: Is it really cheaper? Many of the ... er ... electronic goods ... er ... tape recorders, calculators, Walkmans – and I've got caught on this one – on display at 'duty-free prices' are probably cheaper i ... in a normal shop where the prices are discounted. You'll be saving VAT by buying at the airport but you're probably also paying a higher price anyway.

Presenter: Thanks very much, Jonathan.

(Time: 4 minutes)

8.12   *Break, bring, call, cut*   *Verbs and idioms*

A

Answers

Kit broke ... a window   Jan's heart   the ice   the news to us
Lee called ... a doctor   the dog Rover   to see Sandy
Chris brought ... Lee to the party   the book to Sandy (+ possibly: a
    doctor, a piece of paper, the ice, the news to us)
Sandy cut ... a piece of paper   the grass   himself/herself

B

Answers

1 broken down	6 bring them down	11 call for
2 broke off	7 bring them back	12 call me back
3 broke up	8 called off	13 cut down
4 brought about	9 call in	14 cut out
5 brought up	10 call it off	15 cut off

8.13   **Fill the gaps**   *Use of English*

A   If students are in doubt about the words that are missing in an exam-type 'modified cloze' exercise, it often helps to work out what part of speech is missing, as this exercise shows.

Possible answers

1 *Adjective:* splitting, bad, terrible   4 *Adverb:* eventually, finally
2 *Noun:* night   5 *Articles:* a   the
3 *Verb:* cross

B

Complete story (Some variations are possible.)

We were late as ₁ **usual**. My husband had insisted on doing his packing by ₂ **himself**, and when he discovered that he couldn't manage he'd asked me for help at the last ₃ **moment**. So now we had an hour to get to the ₄ **airport**. Luckily, there wasn't much traffic on the ₅ **road** and we were able to get there just in ₆ **time**. We checked in and went straight to the departure ₇ **lounge** to wait for our ₈ **flight** to be called. We waited and waited but no announcement was ₉ **made**. We asked at the information ₁₀ **desk** and the girl there told us that the plane hadn't even arrived yet. In the ₁₁ **end** there was another announcement telling us that passengers waiting for Flight LJ 108 could collect a ₁₂ **free** meal voucher and that the plane hadn't left Spain because of ₁₃ **technical** problems. We thought that meant that it wasn't safe for the plane to ₁₄ **fly**. We waited again for ₁₅ **ages** until late evening when we were asked to report to the ₁₆ **information** desk again. They told us we would be spending the ₁₇ **night** in a hotel at the airline's ₁₈ **expense**.

The next morning after a sleepless ₁₉ **night** because of all the planes taking off and landing, we reported back to the airport. Guess what had ₂₀ **happened** while we were ₂₁ **asleep**! Our plane had arrived and taken off again leaving us ₂₂ **stranded**. All the other ₂₃ **passengers** had been woken up in the night to catch the plane, but for some ₂₄ **reason** or other we had been forgotten. You can imagine how we felt!

▶ For more speaking and listening activities on the topic of holidays, see *Ideas* Unit 14.

9 Books and reading

▶ If your students are NOT studying one of the prescribed books for the exam, the exercises in this unit are certainly still relevant, though you might decide to omit a few parts of some sections.

Note that the questions and discussion in this unit are 'general' and they may not suit every type of book. You should work out your own questions that apply to the particular book your class is reading.

9.1   A good read   *Vocabulary*

A   Warm-up discussion: to get things started perhaps suggest your own answers to the questions in the Student's Book.

B

Answers

1 library   bookshop/bookstore
2 author
3 paperback

4 title   cover
5 biography (*or* an autobiography)

C   Note that it is the BEST alternative that has to be chosen – as in the exam. In some questions other answers may not be quite as good as the 'best' one.

Make sure the meanings and uses of the other alternatives are discussed.

Answers

1 literature
2 characters
3 verse
4 rhymes
5 table of contents
6 index
7 chapters
8 publisher

9 message
10 well-written
11 favourite
12 put it down
13 get into
14 minor
15 borrow

D

Answers

1 central   main   principal
2 entertaining   readable   true-to-life
3 amusing   believable   likeable
4 convincing   realistic   true-to-life
5 about real life   non-fiction   textbooks
6 appreciate   bear   stand

E   Follow-up discussion. Again you might answer the questions yourself first, referring to the UK or the USA.

▶ Even if you and your class aren't doing a prescribed book together, perhaps tell them what is on offer this year, so that they can choose one to read on their own.

For a complete list of this year's books, consult the current Regulations obtainable from your Local Examinations Secretary.

9.2   Call for the Dead *Reading*

A   Note that the simplified version omits a great deal of detail and some difficult words, but there are also some additions:
An anonymous letter
clear him **of the accusation**
Communist Party

B   The main events in the story are given in both versions – only questions 1 and 2 cover information that's only in the unsimplified version.

Answers

2 He had been woken up in the middle of the night by a phone call – version B.
3 He had learned the skill years before/long ago – both A and B.
4 An anonymous letter had been received accusing Fennan of being a (Communist) Party member – both A and B.
5 Friendly – both A and B.
6 Because he was anxious/in a bit of a state – both A and B.
7 No – both A and B.
8 Suicide – both A and B.

⟫→

C   Encourage everyone to explain why they don't enjoy or avoid reading certain kinds of books.

9.3   **Joining sentences**   *Grammar*

A   **IDENTIFYING RELATIVE CLAUSES:**

Perhaps point out that *that* and *which* tend to be interchangeable when referring to things, *that* and *who* are interchangeable when referring to people.

B   **NON-IDENTIFYING RELATIVE CLAUSES:**

Answers

> *Hamlet* , **which** is a famous play by Shakespeare , is a tragedy.
> Hamlet's father , **who** dies before the play begins , appears to Hamlet as a ghost.
> Hamlet's mother , **whose** husband has died , marries her husband's brother.

C

Answers (Some variations are possible.)

2   New York, which I'd love to visit one day, is a wonderful city.
   or New York is a wonderful city, which I'd love to visit one day.
3   Ms Fortune, whose body was found in the cellar, was a writer.
4   I met an old friend, who told me all about a book he'd just read.
5   The car that/which was found at the airport was / had been stolen.
6   Science fiction books, which some people love and others hate, are about the future and space travel.
7   The book (that) you recommended to me was very good.
8   A simplified edition, which is shorter than the original, is (also) easier to read.

D   **CONJUNCTIONS AND PREPOSITIONS:**

Perhaps draw attention to possible confusions between *as* as a time conjunction and as a reason conjunction.

E

Answers

1   In spite of the (enormous) difficulties she managed to escape.

2 It is such a wonderful story that I'd recommend it to anyone.
3 As I wanted my friends to know when I'd be arriving, I phoned them.
4 While I was sitting in bed reading, my friends were dancing.
5 Although the book is over 500 pages long, I'm going to try to read it before next week.
6 Before I go and see the film, I'm going to read the book.
7 After the heroine had escaped from the villain, she rescued the hero. *or* After escaping from the villain, the heroine rescued the hero.
8 During my summer holiday / my holiday in the summer I read a lot of books.

F

Complete story (Some variations are possible.)

The Captain and the Enemy is a novel ₁ **which** was written by Graham Greene in 1988. It is a story ₂ **about** a boy, Victor Baxter, ₃ **whose** father (₄ **who/whom** he calls 'The Devil') loses him in a game of backgammon to a man ₅ **who** is only known as the Captain. The Captain, ₆ **whose** real name is never revealed, appears to be some sort ₇ **of** criminal. ₈ **After** the boy has been taken away from his boarding school, he is brought ₉ **up** by a woman called Lisa, ₁₀ **who** is the Captain's mistress. From time to ₁₁ **time** the Captain returns ₁₂ **to** visit them, ₁₃ **but** for months on end they are alone together. ₁₄ **During** this time a close relationship develops ₁₅ **between** them, and Lisa treats Victor as if he is her son. Eventually, the Captain goes to live in Panama, ₁₆ **but** tells them that they cannot join him there ₁₇ **until** he has made enough money. ₁₈ **When** he is eighteen, Victor leaves Lisa and gets his own flat, but ₁₉ **after** her death in a road accident he flies to Panama ₂₀ **to** meet the Captain ...

▶ For more practice in using relative pronouns, see *Use of English* Unit 26. For more practice in joining sentences using conjunctions and prepositions, see *Use of English* Units 35 to 37.

9.4 Reading habits   *Listening*

A [▭] The recording can be played in two parts with a break before question 6.

As we hear only part of the broadcast, the speaker's opinions on the questions posed in **B** are not given.

Answers

1 85%   electronic noise
2 inexpensive/cheap   portable
3 bookmark
4 one   airport   plane   beach
5 established authors/best-selling authors
6 Plot A is *Savages*
   Plot B is *Zoya*
   Plot C is *Alaska*
   Plot D is *Glamorous Powers*
   Plot E is *To Be The Best*

Transcript

Presenter: According to a recent survey, 85% of American adolescents, quote 'can no longer take in a printed page if their act of reading does not have an accompanying background of electronic noise' end of quote. And many students nowadays seem to need a background noise of headphone music to cut out outside distractions. But are we reading less these days? Will the days of books soon be over? Mike Osborne reports.

Mike: Well, there are two questions really. Er ... first, will other entertainments – er ... computer games, videos, TV and so on – stop people reading? And second, will the new technology – that's electronic publishing, information on computers and books recorded on cassettes and so on – will these things provide substitutes for the printed page?

Well, the main advantage that books have over all these media is that they're relatively inexpensive and they're very portable. I mean, you can take a book with you wherever you go, it doesn't ... it doesn't break down if you get sand inside it, and you don't need batteries ... you can put it down and pick it up whenever you like – the only equipment you need is a bookmark.

Now, according to the survey, many people only buy one book a year – as holiday reading. Er ... they probably buy it at the airport on their way to the sun and they ... they read it in the airport (while their flight is delayed) on the plane and on the beach, of course.

Nevertheless, books by best-selling authors are selling more and more copies every year, not fewer. All the signs are that people are spending more and more money on books. Now, the most popular books are books by established authors – that's writers who've developed a product that their readers know they'll enjoy and whose books they'll 'collect'.

(*Question 6 ↓*)

So I thought I'd give you a few examples of some recent best-selling paperbacks by authors who sell hundreds of thousands of copies of every book they write:

First, there's *To Be The Best* by Barbara Taylor Bradford. Now, this book centres around a wealthy family and the action switches between Hong Kong, Australia, America and Yorkshire. It's basically about a woman who has to become more ruthless than her grandmother.

The second book is *Zoya* by Danielle Steel. This is about a Russian countess who escapes from the Russian Revolution in St Petersburg and becomes a ballerina in Paris. The book follows her career to America where she faces her toughest struggle yet in the business world of present-day New York.

Then there's *Alaska* by James A. Michener. This is a story of Eskimos and of Russian and American explorers and colonists struggling to survive in a hostile environment. The action spans thousands of years and is a blend of historical fact and fictional narrative.

Savages by Shirley Conran is about five women on a tropical island who see their husbands killed in front of their eyes. They escape into the jungle and eventually find that they're involved in a mysterious international plot.

And lastly, *Glamorous Powers* by Susan Howatch is about a man who becomes a priest after playing many different roles in life. He falls in love with a woman and they have to struggle to find their happiness.

Of course, the one thing that all these books have in common is that they're all over 500 pages long, which is fine if you're used to reading. But the problem is that many people aren't. Reading tends to be something you enjoy more as you get older – but if you don't develop a taste for it when you're young, you may never discover the pleasures of getting involved in a good book. Now, technology and its influence on reading is, as I said, another question. Will people who study need to buy textbooks in the future? Or will they just sit in front of computer screens and get all the information they need ...

(Time: 4 minutes)

B   The discussion questions take up the issue of technology and books that the speaker was about to tackle in the broadcast in **A**.

9.5   Using suffixes – 3: Abstract nouns *Word study*

A   Nouns from verbs:

Answers

–ation	association demonstration starvation translation
–ion	connection objection reflection
–ment	astonishment embarrassment encouragement improvement

–al	approval proposal removal survival
–ance	acceptance assistance disappearance

▶ Some nouns can be formed from verbs by adding **-ing** as in these examples:
painting   sailing   skating   learning English

B   Nouns from adjectives and nouns:

Answers

–ness	blindness carelessness cheerfulness sadness selfishness shyness weakness
–ence	confidence intelligence patience silence
–ity	availability probability reality suitability
–y	accuracy efficiency fluency photography
–ship	leadership membership ownership sportsmanship
–hood	motherhood parenthood

▶ Another way of forming nouns is by adding **–ism** as in these examples:
Buddhism   Catholicism   Communism   Marxism   Socialism
vegetarianism   sexism

C

Answers

2 translation	5 description childhood
3 violence	6 kindness honesty
4 weakness	

▶ For more practice on forming abstract nouns, see *Use of English* Unit 32.

9.6   Holiday reading   *Problem solving*

A   Make sure everyone gives reasons for their decisions. Be prepared for questions on the vocabulary in the blurbs, but by no means all of the words need to be understood to do the exercise and many are not really worth memorising (e.g. 'Mesmerizing, hypnotically compelling') as long as their function is clear (i.e. 'praise').

B   Everyone should make notes in this part of the discussion.

C Each paragraph should be about 50 words long. As usual, the model paragraphs below are not definitive.

In the exam, students should be discouraged from quoting from the text. It might be worth considering how the quotes in the model paragraphs could be 'avoided'.

Model paragraphs

Anna may be rather too young to have appreciated Jupiter's Travels, in particular the 'journey to the centre of the author's soul'. However, the author's adventures were probably quite exciting for her to read about. A better choice for her might have been Hills of Kalamata: its Greek setting and romantic plot might have been just right for her to read on the beach.

The Human Factor sounds as if it is the kind of book that needs a fair amount of concentration to appreciate. If Bob is the sort of person who reads a lot, I think he might have enjoyed it during his walking holiday. On the other hand, even though the plot is exciting, a more conventional thriller like Send No More Roses might have been a better choice.

Colin's choice of holiday reading was unfortunate because Send No More Roses is a thriller and, for a student of literature, a book like Empire of the Sun might have been a better choice as it is both exciting and well-written. According to the blurb on the cover it is one of the major novels of the twentieth century.

I'm sorry I took Hills of Kalamata with me because I really hate romantic novels. Generally they're badly written and the plot is unbelievable. Although I was interested in its descriptions of 'the most primitive part of Greece', I found the characters lifeless and the plot predictable. It was a complete waste of time. I wish I'd taken Empire of the Sun instead.

9.7 *In . . .*   *Prepositional phrases*

Answers

1 in common = share qualities
2 in danger
3 in a hurry
4 in all = total
5 In general = in most cases
6 in particular = especially
7 in secret
8 in debt = owe money

9 in difficulties
10 in public   in private

11 in a way = partly   in other words
12 in tears = crying/weeping   in prison

9.8   The Captain and the Enemy   *Reading*

A   Make sure everyone realises why their wrong answers were wrong. Some of these questions are deliberately 'nasty' as a foretaste of the exam!

Answers

1 b   2 c   3 c   4 c   5 c   6 b   7 d   8 c

B

Answers

2 gym shoes	6 in a bit of a quandary	10 from hearsay
3 recklessly	7 reluctant	11 ajar
4 slithered	8 conceal	12 trim
5 abrupt	9 obscure	

9.9   Talking about books   *Listening and speaking*

A

Answers

Title	*Author*
A Taste for Death	P. D. James
Boy	Roald Dahl
Catch 22	Joseph Heller
Cider with Rosie	Laurie Lee
I Know Why the Caged Bird Sings	Maya Angelou
Surfacing	Margaret Atwood

B

Answers

TRUE statements: 1   5   6   7   8   10   11   12   15   16
FALSE statements: 2   3   4   9   13   14

Transcript

Narrator: David, what kind of books do you like?

David: I must admit, I ... there's nothing I enjoy more than a good thriller. I mean, there are some marvellous writers around like Agatha Christie and of course her marvellous creations of Miss Marple and Hercule Poirot, but in fact my favourite writer is P. D. James. She is, I believe, one of the finest thriller writers that we've got in England at the moment. And certainly my favourite book of hers is *A Taste for Death*. Er ... it comes ... the title of the book comes from a saying 'There's this to say for blood and breath, it gives a man a taste for death'. And I love the way she uses language and doesn't talk down, I believe, to the reader. And you get this marvellous story in *A Taste for Death*: an MP found dead in a church together with a tramp, and apparently the two are unconnected but as the story moves on, you realise that their lives become closer and closer ... interweaved. And it's just a gripping read from start to finish. I think that's what I enjoy most in a book: the fact that you can pick it up and just be gripped by it from beginning to end.

Narrator: Jocelyn, What sort of books do you enjoy?

Jocelyn: Well, I suppose I like novels and biographies best. And if I was pressed, my favourite author would be Margaret Atwood, who's a Canadian author. She's ... er ... an award-winning author, she ... she's won awards from all over the world and my favourite book would be *Surfacing*, which is her second book, and it's about a woman who returns to an island in the Canadian wilderness and she undergoes a ... a sort of a personal transformation. I suppose I like Margaret Atwood because she's ... er ... she's very witty and she makes very sharp observations from a woman's standpoint – she makes me laugh. But there's always ... um ... a meaningful edge to her writing: the laugh catches in your throat, if you like.

Narrator: Ken?

Ken: I suppose the kind of reading I enjoy most are travel books and autobiographies and I think my favourite author for this particular genre is Laurie Lee. Er ... but I think the book I enjoyed most with ... was *Cider with Rosie*. It's about his childhood in a Gloucestershire village, and I enjoyed this because it's very evocative of an era which now seems totally lost to us. Um ... he writes about the seasons which seemed to be more clearly defined than they are now, you know, very hot summers and cold winters and there are some wonderful descriptions of the countryside and it's often very funny and ... er ... there are some extraordinary characters in the village, often very eccentric ... um ... like neighbours, and er ... his brothers and sisters. And I think ... er ... the reason I like it so much is because it has a very nostalgic appeal to me.

Narrator: Jill, what do you enjoy?

Jill: I enjoy reading autobiography and ... er ... my favourite writer at the moment is ... Maya Angelou. Um ... the first book in the series of her life is called *I Know Why the Caged Bird Sings*. Um ... she's a black American writer and ... er ... the book is about her life as a child in the Deep South. Um ... I enjoyed it because ... er ... she has a very simple way of writing about a very complicated and exciting life.

Narrator: How about you, Blain?

Blain: Well, I like reading comedy books. Basically I like to laugh when I'm reading and I've enjoyed a lot of good American authors – Salinger, Thurber – but I think probably the greatest author of the twentieth century, and I think his greatness is based on one book is Joseph Heller. I think *Catch 22* is probably the finest, the funniest book I've ever read. And one of the things I like about it is because it says so much as well, it's a great satire and it ... er ... has a lot to say about modern life and particularly about the reasons why people go to war. Um ... it's probably the book I've enjoyed most and the most often. I've read it several times and I read parts of it a lot.

Narrator: And finally, Judy, it's your turn.

Judy: Um ... I like reading lots of different sorts of books, I like ... um ... thrillers and spy stories and so on, I like biographies very much. I read ... um ... Roald Dahl's biography, the two ... it comes in two parts – the first one's called *Boy* and the second one I think is called ... um ... *Flying Solo*. But *Boy* in particular I ... I liked enormously. He's written it for children as well as for grown-ups and ... um ... the style appears to be very simple – I don't mean by that that he writes down to children, 'cause he certainly doesn't, but this simplicity makes it very very direct and ... and some of the ... the memories that he ... that he brings back are ... um ... are amazingly vivid. There's ... there's one I remember and was amazed that the publishers allowed it to go through. It's a description of a headmaster who was a particularly savage sort of man who in fact became an Archbishop of Canterbury eventually, but it is one of the most frightening childhood ... er ... remembrances I think I've ... um ... I've ever come across and ... um ... that's why I like Roald Dahl's writing so much. It's ... it's very honest.

(Time: 5 minutes 35 seconds)

C   This could be set as homework or done in pairs in class.

Completed dialogue (Many variations are possible.)

YOU: What **kinds of books do you enjoy reading?**

Friend: Books that are easy to read and exciting.

YOU: Who **are your favourite authors?**

Friend: Oh, John Le Carré, Len Deighton – writers like that.

YOU: Do **you only read spy stories, then?**

Friend: No, not only spy stories. I do read other kinds of books too.

YOU: And what **are you reading at the moment?**

Friend: At the moment? Well, I'm on the very last chapter of a book by J. G. Ballard.

YOU: What's **the title of the book?**

Friend: 'Empire of the Sun'.
YOU: What's **it about?**
Friend: It's about a boy who is separated from his parents during the war.
YOU: Where **does the action of the book take place?**
Friend: In Shanghai.
YOU: What **happens to the boy in the story?**
Friend: He learns how to survive in spite of all the suffering and starvation.
YOU: Is **it a depressing book?** It sounds as if it is.
Friend: Yes, parts of it are depressing and even horrifying, I suppose.
YOU: Then **what are you enjoying / have you enjoyed about it?**
Friend: Well, it's very exciting and it's really well-written too.
YOU: Would **you recommend it to me?**
Friend: Yes, I certainly would. I think you'd enjoy it.
YOU: Will **you lend it to me when you've finished it?**
Friend: Yes, sure. I'll try to remember to bring it along tomorrow.

D   The groups find out about each other's tastes. Stronger students will not need to refer to the questions in C for inspiration. Omit this part if it has already been discussed in 9.1 **A**.

E   Omit this part if your students are not studying a prescribed book. If the questions here don't cover any important aspects of the book they are studying, further questions will be required, especially if it's non-fiction.

▶ Prepare a list of possible questions about the particular book you've chosen.

▶ If you haven't already chosen a book, perhaps let your students participate in the decision of which book to choose, by showing them the first pages of each one that is on this year's list.

9.10   Writing about a book   *Composition*

Go through the advice given in the Student's Book on allocating time when writing compositions. Ask everyone what 'system or routine' they prefer to use.

A   The questions in this part are a basis for discussion – there are no 'correct answers'. Allow time for the pairs to report back to the class about what they have decided or found out.

Suggested answers

1 In the extract from *The Captain and the Enemy*, most of the paragraphs show that a different speaker is talking.
   'I slid ... ' marks a return to the main stream of the narrative.
   The only possible breaking point in the first paragraph might be after '... for the first time.'
2 In the two versions of *Call for the Dead*, each line of dialogue (or Smiley's thoughts in brackets) is a new paragraph. The second paragraph in each version ('The taxi turned ...' 'The cab turned ...') marks a resumption of the main stream of the narrative after the digression in the previous paragraph.

▶ It is unnecessary at FCE level to explain in detail how different kinds of paragraphs are structured or built up. There are no fixed rules. Students should be encouraged to develop their 'feelings' for what seems right – the tasks in **A** will help them to cultivate these feelings.

Point out that normally a new paragraph begins when a new idea is introduced.

Perhaps point out that the main advantage of paragraphs is that they 'break up' the text and make it easier to read.

B   Students who aren't studying a prescribed book should answer question 8, which is the one that is the model composition in this case. The main text of this is about 140 words, not counting the address, date, etc.

Model composition

Imagine that you're recommending a book you've read to an English-speaking friend. Write a letter explaining what it's about and why your friend will enjoy it.

```
                                13 Richmond Avenue
                                Cambridge CB2 2RU

                                15 May 19##

Dear Peter,

        I felt I simply had to write to you about the
enclosed book which I'm sure you'll enjoy reading.
        As you'll see from the cover it's by David Lodge
and it's called "Nice Work". It's all about two people
who live close to each other in the same city. One is a
female university teacher who lectures about English
literature, the other is the male managing director of a
factory. They have nothing in common but they are thrown
```

together when the teacher becomes the industrialist's 'shadow' and spends one day each week with him as part of a scheme to increase cooperation between the university and local companies. I won't spoil it by telling you what happens in the end!!

You'll enjoy the humour of the relationship and the contrast between the world of the university and real life in the factory.

When you've read it, let me know what you think.
Best wishes,

© Cambridge University Press 1990

9.11   You know that book I borrowed . . . *Listening*

A 🔲

Answers

2 a month
3 garden
4 radiator
5 bath
6 out of print
7 replace the book (Peter ignores what Jean has told him!)
8 damaging them
9 returned it with a flat tyre
10 she won't lend anything to him

Transcript

Peter: Hi, Jean!
Jean: Oh, hallo, Peter.
Peter: I've brought that book back you lent me. You remember the ... er ... the Eric Ambler.
Jean: About time, isn't it? I lent you that book two months ago.
Peter: Oh, it was only a month, wasn't it? Last month ...
Jean: No, it wasn't, it was longer than that.
Peter: Look, before you get ... er ...
Jean: Wh ... what's this?
Peter: I knew you were going to say that. What happened was ... what happened was, I was reading it in the garden, right? And I ... I just left it out. And it rained. But I've dried it out over the radiator. I think it's ...
Jean: Peter! It looks as if you've dropped it in the bath and then dried it out on the radiator!
Peter: Look, you can turn all the pages. It's fine. Anyway ...
Jean: When I gave it to you, it was as good as new!

Peter: Yeah, I know, I know. Look, I … I'm really really sorry …
Jean: Peter, do you realise that this book's out of print? I can't get hold of another copy, you know.
Peter: I'm really sorry. I mean, I do feel a bit guilty about it …
Jean: I should think so! I mean, I know I've read it but I like to keep all the books I've read and I never throw them away.
Peter: Yeah, well it's only a paperback. I mean, if you … if you feel like that, I mean, I … Look, I'll tell you what: I'll buy you a new one. OK?
Jean: Oh, that's not the point. You're always losing things and damaging them. Do you remember when you borrowed my bike? You brought it back with a flat tyre.
Peter: Oh, come on! I think you're being a bit …
Jean: Well, it's true!
Peter: … unreasonable. It's only a paperback book.
Jean: I'm not being unreasonable. It's you who's being unreasonable. You've got the most casual attitude of anyone I know …
Peter: I've offered to buy you a new one!
Jean: You never take anything seriously … Listen, it's the last time I'm going to lend you anything and that's final!

(Time: 1 minute 15 seconds)

B   Perhaps find out if everyone would react differently if other possessions were returned damaged:
    cassette   lecture notes   Walkman   calculator   computer

---

9.12   *Fall* and *hold*   *Verbs and idioms*

Answers

  1 falls for = be attracted to
  2 fell out with = quarrel
  3 fell over = fall on the ground
  4 fall in with = agree to
  5 fallen through = fail before completion
  6 held up = rob
  7 holding on to = grasp
  8 hold on = wait
  9 held up = delay
 10 hold out = continue in spite of difficulties

10 Food and drink

10.1 Talking about food   *Vocabulary*

A   This is a warm-up discussion, but you may prefer to return to this after doing exercises **B** to **D**. Supply vocabulary as necessary during the discussion.

B

Answers (Many variations are possible.)

1 cooks
2 raw
3 food processor/electric mixer/maid/husband, etc.
4 chopped/sliced
5 stirred
6 bread and cakes: baked
   vegetables: steamed/boiled/microwaved/eaten raw
   meat: fried/roasted/stewed/grilled/boiled
7 vegetarian
8 kettle/saucepan/pan/electric kettle
9 peel/cut/slice
10 bowl
11 oven
12 sour
13 washing-up/clearing-up
14 beef/veal/chicken/lamb/pork/ham/bacon/turkey
15 sour, salty, bitter (*All flavours are a combination of the four tastes.*)

C   Make sure the 'wrong' answers are discussed:
• Why are they wrong in each context?
• What do they mean?
• How are they used?

Answers (In some cases these are 'best' answers and others may be just possible, especially if you're being facetious.)

1 hot	3 recipe
2 dishes	4 rare

»»→

5 additives   8 helping
6 wine list   9 avoid
7 greedy   10 gone off

D   This can be done using dictionaries in class. To save time, different groups could make different lists, but do make sure that all ideas are pooled at the end.

Some suggested answers

FRUIT
strawberry, raspberry, pineapple, apple, pear, apricot, peach, melon, blackcurrant, blackberry, banana, grape, grapefruit, plum, greengage, orange, lemon, lime, kiwi

VEGETABLES
potato, pea, cauliflower, cucumber, cabbage, carrot, onion, celery, broccoli, asparagus, artichoke, mushroom, tomato, lettuce, spinach, aubergine, courgette, garlic

DRINKS
tea, coffee, beer, lager, bitter, wine, whisky, brandy, lemonade, orangeade, orange juice, tonic water, mineral water, vermouth, cider, milk

▶ Perhaps also discuss what kinds of food can be eaten at different times of day and what kinds of food would only be eaten on special occasions – these vary from country to country, as do eating habits generally.

10.2   Eating out   *Reading*

A   This pre-reading exercise allows everyone to apply their previous knowledge to the content of the passage and answer the questions from their own experience of eating out in their own country, where conventions may be slightly or significantly different from the UK, where the *Good Food Guide* is published.

B

Answers (According to the *Good Food Guide*)

1 The restaurant may be turning customers away and it's a legal requirement.

2 Your table may be given to somebody else and it's good manners.
3 So that the restaurant can prepare for the child's requirements.
4 To see whether the prices include cover charges, service and VAT.
5 In case you regret a hasty choice later.
6 To benefit from their expert knowledge.*
7 Because it's polite and they may object to your smoking, for example.
8 Because the restaurant can try to improve.*
9 Because the bad food was probably not his fault.
10 So that good restaurants can gain customers and bad ones lose them.

* This is implied but not stated explicitly in the article.

C   The first three questions may have already been discussed when going through the answers to the questions above. If so, concentrate on the three last questions on national eating habits. For example, is it polite in your students' country to eat in the street, cut up all your meat and then eat it with a fork, mop up sauce with bread, etc.?

10.3   *–ing* and *to* __   *Grammar*

A

Suggested answers

–ing as the subject of a sentence:
  Travelling/Going abroad is interesting.
  Washing up/Clearing up after a meal is boring.

–ing after prepositions:
  I'm looking forward to **going** to Spain on holiday.
  I can't get used to **having/drinking** tea without milk.
  I've got an upset stomach after **eating too much**.

Verbs + –ing:
  I avoid **eating/dining/staying** in expensive hotels.
  I couldn't help **laughing** when he fell over.
  I dislike **washing up/doing the dishes** after a meal.
  I always enjoy **trying/tasting** new dishes.

Verbs + to__:
  I can't afford **to stay/to eat** at the Ritz.
  We managed **to get/to find/to reserve** a table by the window.
  We decided **to have/to stop for** a drink in the pub.
  He tried **to open/to unscrew** the lid.

Verbs + *–ing* OR + *to___* with no difference in meaning:

I don't like **eating/dining** alone in restaurants.
After the meal we continued **talking/chatting**.
Which dessert do you intend **to have/to choose**?
I **hate/like/prefer** to drink/drinking black coffee.

Verbs + *–ing* OR + *to___* with a difference in meaning:

stop –ing and *stop to___*
Their mother told them to stop **talking/shouting/being rude**.
I was half-way through my meal but I had to stop **to answer** the
phone.
remember to___ and *remember –ing*
You should have remembered **to send/to give** Jill an invitation to the
party.
I remember **posting** the letter yesterday evening after work.

▶ A more advanced point (for students who won't be baffled or
confused) is that *try* can be followed by *to___* or *–ing* with a slight
difference in meaning:
try to___ and *try –ing*:
I'm trying to open this jar but the lid just won't unscrew.
Try using this new gadget, it'll open anything. (= try this method …)
We tried to reach you on the phone but you weren't available.
Why didn't you try calling me at home? You know my number.

to___ after adjectives:

I was glad **to meet/to see** my old school friends again after so many
years.
We were surprised **to get/to receive** a bill for £45.
It's easier **to get** from here to the centre by bus than **to go** by car.

too … to___ AND *… enough to___*

The tray was too heavy for me **to carry/to manage/to lift**.
Boiled eggs are easy enough **to cook**.

B

Answers

1 I'm looking forward to seeing my friends on Friday.
2 It's essential to phone the restaurant if you want a table for ten.
3 I'm not used to eating at restaurants.
4 Would you prefer to sit by the window or outside on the terrace?
5 They didn't stop smoking all through the meal.
6 I didn't remember to bring my wallet with me, have you got / did
   you remember to bring yours?

7 It's easy to boil an egg.
8 I'd like you to get me some water, please.
9 I can't afford to eat in expensive restaurants.
10 I don't mind you sharing my pizza.

C In this kind of exercise in the exam, this symbol: / denotes a missing word – though this is not always consistent. Point out to everyone that other words may have to be changed too, especially verbs.

Answers (Some variations are possible.)

2 I always look forward to going to see them and enjoy spending the day with them.
3 My grandmother likes to grow / growing all her own vegetables.
4 She never prepares a meal without using fresh vegetables and refuses to use any ingredients which have artificial additives.
5 When we arrived we decided to go for a short walk before sitting down to lunch.
6 I love walking in the country, even though I dislike walking when I'm in the city.
7 When we got back, the table was laid in the garden for lunch and we all began to eat and talk and we went on eating and drinking all afternoon!
8 I'm not used to eating a lot, but everything was so delicious that I just couldn't stop eating!
9 I managed to eat a great deal more than I (had) intended to eat.
10 When we had all finished eating, we sat round the table and went on talking till it got dark.

▶ For more practice in using verbs followed by *to__* and *–ing*, see *Use of English* Units 13, 14 and 15.

10.4 A memorable meal
Listening

A 🔲 The tape can be paused between each of the speakers to make the task easier. As usual, there is no need to worry about understanding every word they say, as long as students can get the gist and answer the questions.

As the recording is quite long in this case, perhaps ask the class to answer all the questions on ONE listening only and see how they get on.

B To start off this follow-up discussion, perhaps tell the class about a meal YOU remember well.

▶ Ask everyone to work out their ideal menu – including all their favourite dishes.

Answers

TRUE statements: 1   3   7   8   9   12   13
FALSE statements: 2   4   5   6   10   11   14   15

Transcript

Narrator: Judy, tell us about a meal you remember.
Judy: Um ... last ... last Boxing Day, I'd invited ... er ... my parents, my sister, my aunt and my brother and his family for lunch and I was really looking forward to this because it was having all the family together and I love the idea of lots of people round a table, but ... er ... I think I'd gone a bit far. There were twelve of us as it turned out with ... um ... my children and husband as well and so it was a bit of a squash round the table. But the main problem was my brother's children, who were aged about two and four, and they were awful. They screamed the whole time, they didn't like the food that I'd produced, they knocked the glasses over, they ate with their fingers – they were awful. And what I had planned as a lovely, happy family meal turned out to be ... um ... I think one of the most disastrous meals I've ever produced.
Narrator: Anne.
Anne: Er ... my most memorable meal ... er ... was ... um ... takes place in the West Indies in a tiny island called Nevis. I went out there to stay with some friends who were running a hotel and I'd had a very long, arduous journey to get there from Heathrow and the last lap had been quite frightening in a very tiny rickety plane and I didn't get there till very late at night and ... er ... they'd saved some food for me and we sat out on the terrace with the tree-frogs croaking in the palm trees and these wonderful, exotic smells coming from the countryside around us. Er ... I don't remember what we ate but it was like suddenly arriving in paradise, it was really wonderful, and I won't ... will never forget it.
Narrator: Blain.
Blain: This summer I spent two weeks holidaying on Crete for the first time. I hated the food in Crete: the meat was tough all the time, the salads were identical no matter wherever you had them and everything, whether it was meat, potatoes or salads, were covered in huge lashings of oil and grease. My most memorable meal happened on the first day, the first two hours back in the UK, when I sped straight from the airport to the nearest McDonalds. I got in, and crunched into a juicy Big Mac with the mayonnaise squirting out, the tomato sauce squirting out, I had handfuls of great chips, I loved it.
Narrator: Jill.
Jill: Well, my most memorable meal was in Greece. We used to go to a little taverna for lunch every day and then on our very last night we went to the same taverna in the evening for an evening meal. And it

184

was very beautiful, it was on a deserted beach ... um ... there were hens and cats and cockerels wandering about, we sat under olive trees ... um ... with little lights in them and the whole atmosphere was wonderful. The owner's name was Harry. Um ... we had a delicious meal and then we asked him to ... um ... order a taxi for us, but instead of a taxi he ... um ... brought wine, more wine, and ... er ... about an hour later more wine came. And we kept asking for a taxi but no taxi came, just more wine and more food. And at the end of the meal, we were all pretty drunk and he said it was all on the house because he 'enjoyed us all so much'.

Narrator: Ishia.

Ishia: I think I've had my most memorable meals in Italy but possibly my most memorable meal in Italy was in the South. And I was working there and I went to an extraordinarily marvellous ... um ... restaurant and had ten courses, something I've never done before or since. Er ... four or five of them were pasta courses and included ... er ... pasta and raspberries, pasta and champagne with mushrooms, and pasta and smoked salmon and caviar. It was absolutely wonderful and the most remarkably good part about the meal was that I didn't have to pay for it.

Narrator: Coralyn.

Coralyn: Er ... a very memorable meal that I had recently was memorable, not so much for the food ... um ... but for the situation which again ... was ... um ... rather comic ... er ... not funny at the time. Um ... I'd cooked this meal ... mm ... my boyfriend and I had cooked a meal and invited two other couples, it was a Sunday lunch and we'd cooked a cassoulet, which had got various bits of spicy meat and sausages in it, and we knew one of the couples very well and the other couple less well and we sat down and had our starter, can't even remember what that was, we got ready to bring the cassoulet to the table and I remember making a joke about ... um ... 'That's good ... lucky ... it's a very meaty dish, I hope nobody's a vegetarian!' Two mouths opposite dropped open and of course this couple we didn't knew ... know very well were vegetarians. But they hadn't told us that they were vegetarians, so I don't know quite how they expected us to know. Um ... it got very embarrassing at this point because I made a ... another joke about fishing the meat out of the cassoulet, which instead of meeting with laughs in response, got stony looks. The husband said, 'No, actually that won't do at all, anything cooked with ... er ...' I said, 'Oh no, absolutely, no, I'll think of something.' Went in the kitchen and there was nothing really to come up with. It all got more and more embarrassing because this couple were not laughing or sort of getting into the spirit of things. I felt like throwing the cassoulet over their heads ... um ... but all was saved at the end of the day by my very good-natured boyfriend who went in the kitchen and improvised with a risotto containing I don't quite know what, but ... um ... good for him, he came up with something and it all ended happily ever after.

(Time: 6 minutes)

10.5   *On . . .* and *out of . . .*   *Prepositional phrases*

Answers

1 on time   on business
2 out of order
3 on holiday/on vacation   out of doors
4 on your own
5 on the house
6 on purpose
7 out of date
8 on the telephone
9 on the other hand
    or on the whole
10 out of work
11 out of reach
12 out of stock
13 on duty
14 on the whole

▶ For more practice in using prepositional phrases, see *Use of English* Units 21 and 22.

10.6   **The humble spud**   *Reading*

A   This brief discussion may give students studying in Britain a chance to express their feelings about the ubiquitous potato! Perhaps suggest some useful expressions for degrees of liking/disliking:

I don't care for ...
I don't like ... very much.
I can't stand ...
I quite like ...
I'm not very keen on ...

B

Answers

1 b   2 d   3 c   4 c   5 a

C

Answers

1 After boiling or steaming them.
2 While they're still warm.
3 When they're crisp and brown.
4 After you've preheated the oven, washed the potatoes and rubbed oil on them.

5 When they're tender (after about 1 or 1½ hours).
6 When they're on the table (the guests can do it themselves).

D   In a multi-national class, make sure the groups are mixed so that they can find out about each other's countries.

10.7   **In a restaurant**   *Listening and Interview exercises*

A   A sophisticated, cosmopolitan class may be able to answer quite a lot of the questions before hearing the recording – if so, encourage a discussion of the ingredients in the dishes mentioned.

Reassure everyone, if necessary, that they won't have to understand or be able to spell French or Italian in the exam!

[▭▭] Play the recording, pausing occasionally if necessary. The more sophisticated class may find Philip and Anne's ignorance amusing.

▶   Before going on to **B**, students could role-play the same situation.

Answers

1 a gin and tonic   sparkling water
2 tomatoes   olives
3 veal   breadcrumbs
4 chopped potatoes   onions
5 layers   pasta   meat   oven   cheese
6 wine   cream   starter   main course
7 grated   bacon   fried eggs
8 moules marinière   Spanish omelette   green
9 Greek salad   lasagne
10 fresh orange juice   a half bottle of the house red wine

Transcript

Waitress: Good evening. Would you like to see the menu?
Anne: Oh, yes, please.
Waitress: Er ... do you want a drink before you start?
Philip: Oh, I think so, yes. Um ... I'll have a gin and tonic, how about you?
Anne: I think I'll just have a sparkling water.
Waitress: Right, thank you.
Anne: Mmm, let's have a look. Oh, I see they've got pizzas.
Philip: Mm, yeah, I think I fancy some fish tonight actually.
Anne: Do you? Hey, Philip, what does a Greek salad consist of?
Philip: Greek salad? Um ... it's got cucumber, tomato, olives and ... um ... you know, that *feta* ... er ... goat's cheese.

Anne: Oh, I don't like goat's cheese. Er ... oh, what about 'Vienna Schnitzel' what is that?

Philip: Oh ... er ... I don't know. We could ask the waitress. Oh, hold on, do you know what ... er ... Spanish omelette is?

Anne: Oh yes, it's an omelette made with eggs, of course, and then it's got chopped potatoes and onions in it.

Philip: Mm, sounds good.

Anne: It is.

Philip: What about ... er ... 'Lasagne al forno'?

Anne: Oh, well, I know it's some sort of pasta, but I'm not quite sure what ... well, we'll have to ask the waitress ...

Waitress: ... Are you ready to order?

Anne: Oh ... er ... yes. Could you just tell me something? What is 'Wiener Schnitzel'?

Waitress: Er ... yes, it's a thin piece of veal coated in egg and breadcrumbs and then it's fried in oil.

Philip: And ... er ... what's ... um ... 'moules marinière'?

Waitress: That's ... um ... mussels cooked in wine with onions and a little cream. You can have it as a starter or as a main course.

Philip: Mussels, mm. Er ... and what's ... er ... 'Rost ... Rösti'?

Waitress: 'Rösti', yes, that's grated potatoes, bacon and onions fried together. You can have it with two fried eggs on top as a main course, you can have it with your main course instead of French fries, if you like.

Philip: Oh, right.

Anne: And ... er ... just one thing. What's 'Lasagne al forno'?

Waitress: Yes, that's thin layers of pasta and meat sauce with a béchamel sauce, baked in the oven with cheese on top.

Anne: Oh. Oh, well ... gosh ... Yes, all right. I'll have ... um ... moules marinière as a starter, please, and then I'd like the Spanish omelette with a mixed salad ... um ... no, no. Could you make that a green salad?

Waitress: Yes.

Philip: And ... er ... I won't have a starter. If I could have the lasagne as a main course and a ... um ... mixed salad to go with it.

Waitress: Right. So that's one moules marinière as a starter, a Spanish omelette, a lasagne and two mixed salads.

Anne: Er ... no mine was a ... a green salad, actually.

Waitress: Oh, right ... OK.

Philip: Yes, and ... and could I ... sorry ... could I have a Greek salad instead of a mixed salad. But as a starter, is that all right?

Waitress: Right, yes, that's fine. Anything to drink?

Philip: Er ... what do you fancy, red wine?

Anne: Oh, no, I won't have any wine, I'm driving. Have you got apple juice?

Waitress: Oh, I'm afraid not, but we have fresh orange juice.

Anne: Oh, that'll be fine, thank you.

Philip: Mm, and could we j ... er ... a half bottle of the ... er ... house red?

Waitress: Right, fine.

Philip: Thanks.

(Time: 2 minutes 55 seconds)

B [cassette] Don't explain any items on the menu: these are all explained in the information given in the communication activities. Student A looks at Activity 7, student B at 35 and C at 48. They should spend a few minutes studying the information before beginning the conversation, so that they don't read the explanations out word-for-word but try to remember them.

While they are doing the activity, explaining unknown dishes to each other, you could yourself play the role of (head) waiter, answering any other queries they may have.

[cassette] There is a 'model conversation' on the cassette, which can be played to the class before they take part in the activity in **B** to give an idea of how their conversation might go. Alternatively, the model conversation could be played afterwards.

Transcript

Narrator:	This model conversation gives you an idea of how the conversation about the menu might develop.
First woman:	Shall we have a look at the menu? I'm so hungry.
Man:	Yeah, OK. Boy, there are a few things here that I don't understand.
Second woman:	There's a lot of this stuff I don't understand. What's all this then?
First woman:	Well, what about the starters? Hey, do you know what 'prawns' …
Man:	The appetisers.
First woman:	Appetisers, oh. 'Prawns' are what?
Man:	They're like large shrimps.
Second woman:	Oh, they're delicious with avocado.
First woman:	Really? Mind you, I like the sound of 'melon and orange salad'.
Man:	Hey, hey, look at the main courses. What is 'Lancashire hotpot'?
Second woman:	I've heard of that. That's … um a … sort of lamb and vegetables cooked in the oven, sort of broiled and the potatoes are sliced on top and put in a layer. It's delicious.
First woman:	It sounds good. And what's this one: 'steak and kidney pie', do you know what that is?
Man:	Yeah, that now is a typical English dish – it's made of beef which is cut up into pieces along with pieces of kidney in a rich brown sauce. It is lovely. And that is traditionally English.
First woman:	Sounds delicious!
Second woman:	The one I don't understand is 'cottage pie'.
First woman:	Er … I've come across that before. That's minced beef in gravy and it's got mashed potato on top. I don't know if that's going to be that good, although this does look like a good restaurant, don't you think?

Second woman:	Yeah … OK. Now, do either of you know what's this: what's 'nut and mushroom roast'?
Man:	Well, it's a vegetarian dish … er … hasn't got any meat in it – made of nuts, mushrooms and baked in the oven like a cake. Might be quite nice. Er … but the other one I don't know here is 'chicken Madras'. Anyone know that?
First woman:	No.
Second woman:	Yes, that's an Indian dish. I can tell you that's … um … it's, I think it's pieces of chicken …

(Time: 1 minute 50 seconds)

10.8   Compound words

Word study

A

Further examples

long-haired   curly-haired
super-   power   store
multi-   purpose   storey   national   coloured
mini-   bus   lecture
wine waiter   football pitch   racing circuit   athletics track
tennis racket

B

Answers

first	first floor first name first course
high	high-class high-level
home	home-grown home-produced
middle	middle-aged middle-sized
second	second-best second-hand second cousin
self	self-discipline self-respect self-service
well	well-known well-off

★ The advice given in the Student's Book is intended as a rule of thumb – there are no fixed rules about using hyphens in English. The examples with *self-* do normally have a hyphen even though they are nouns.

C

Answers

coffee beans   exercise book   food processor   instant coffee
intelligence test   railway station   recipe book   restaurant owner
salad dressing   savings account   sports ground   story telling
tea bag   television set   tennis court   tomato soup   wholemeal bread
yogurt carton

D

Answers

breadcrumbs   chairman   dishwasher   headache   housekeeping
playground   postman   seafood   taxpayer   teapot   toothache
toothbrush   toothpaste

E

Answers

1 high-speed/high-powered
   or maybe even: high-class/high-pressure/high-level?
2 coffee cups
3 toothpaste
4 stomachache
5 first cousin
6 well-done
7 girlfriend
8 home-grown
9 old-fashioned
10 salad dressing

10.9   A nice cake   *Listening*

A   Perhaps team up students who know a little about cookery with
ones who claim to know nothing.

B   ▭ Play the recording, perhaps pausing the tape occasionally.

Answers

RICH DUNDEE CAKE

220g flour	300g mixed dried fruit
1½ teaspoons of mixed spice	(raisins, currants, sultanas)
(ground cinammon, nutmeg, cloves)	50g glace cherries
150g butter	1 tablespoon of sherry
150g sugar	1 tablespoon of rum
3 eggs	50g ground almonds
	50g split almonds

12	**A**	Remove cake from tin.
10	**B**	Test after 2 hours with knitting needle.
3	**C**	Beat eggs and add to creamed butter and sugar.
8	**D**	Arrange split almonds on top.
5	**E**	Add remaining ingredients.
4	**F**	Fold in flour and mixed spice.
1	**G**	Measure out all ingredients.
13	**H**	Allow to cool completely before cutting.
9	**I**	Cook in preheated oven (160°C) for 2½ hours.
11	**J**	If ready, remove from oven and allow to cool for 15 mins.
6	**K**	Grease a medium-size cake tin.
7	**L**	Pour mixture into cake tin.
2	**M**	Cream butter and sugar in large mixing bowl until light and fluffy.

Transcript

Harry: Jill, that wonderful cake ... um ... we had last time we met. You promised to give me the recipe for it. Have you got it?

Jill: Mm, I haven't forgotten. I've written it all out for you – well, at least I've written out the ingredients for you ... Have you ever made a cake before?

Harry: Yes, yes ...

Jill: Oh good.

Harry: ... on occasions, yes.

Jill: On occasions? So this is going to be quite an adventure, then?

Harry: Oh yeah, yeah. I can't wait to do it, actually.

Jill: Well, have you got a largish mixing bowl? It needs to be quite big ...

Harry: Yeah.

Jill: ... because it's quite a big cake. Er ... so you just need a mixing bowl, wooden spoon and a medium size cake tin.

Harry: Right, no problem, yes.

Jill: Right ... so, well, you measure out the ingredients and the ... I've put all the measurements on here.

Harry: Right.

Jill: So, first of all, you put the butter and the sugar into the bowl. And that's the hard work because you have to sort of cream it all together with a spoon and keep beating and beating and beating until it's really light and fluffy.

Harry: Yes.

Jill: Then you beat the eggs ... and pour them in.

Harry: How many eggs is it? Oh yes ...

Jill: Three.

Harry: Three.

Jill: Three eggs, yes. Pour them in and beat them into the creamed sugar and butter.

Harry: Yep.

Jill: Now, when it comes to actually putting in the flour and the mixed spice, dispense with the wooden spoon and get an ordinary ... er ... table spoon ...

Harry: Why do you do that?

Jill: Well, the ... the secret is to fold in the flour, you see ... You don't beat it in, you fold it in ... Er ... so you fold in the flour very carefully ...

Harry: Right.

Jill: ... rather than beating and then add your sherry, rum, fruit and the ground almonds. I usually grind mine up in a ... in a coffee grinder. They're nicer if you buy them whole and grind them yourself.

Harry: OK, right.

Jill: And then again you sort of fold in all that and you ... you grease very very well the bake ... the bake ... the ... er ... the cake tin.

Harry: Sure.

Jill: Er ... you can actually line it with greaseproof paper if you want but I usually ...

Harry: That's to stop it sticking?

Jill: To stop it sticking, yes. And if you're really lucky and you've got one of those with a bottom lifts up, it helps it when you want to take it out at the end of all the cooking time. Anyway, you pour it in – but do make sure it's very very very greasy. Pour the mixture in and arrange your split almonds on the top ... Cook it in a slow oven – preheat the oven by the way ...

Harry: Ah, right.

Jill: ... to about 160 degrees Centigrade. And cook the cake for about two ... two and a half hours. But after two hours, take it out of the oven and test it with a knitting needle or a skewer or something by just putting the needle into the top of the cake, pulling it out and if there's any cake on it, it's not cooked. So put it back again and test it every 15 minutes thereafter until it's cooked.

Harry: Right, OK.

Jill: Let it stand for about 15 minutes and remove it from the tin.

Harry: Yes.

Jill: And then wait until it's completely cooled before ... trying it. Well, that's if you can ... you can manage to wait!

Harry: Well, that's great, thanks very much. I can hardly ... er ... hardly wait to get home and try it myself. Thanks very much!

(Time: 2 minutes 50 seconds)

C ▐▜▌ Divide the class into an even number of pairs, so that later they can work as groups of four (pairs of pairs) – some 'pairs' may have to be groups of three to achieve this. Half the pairs look at Activity 6, the other half at 29.

⋙→

Activity 6 contains a recipe for LASSI – a refreshing Eastern yoghurt drink.

Activity 29 contains a recipe for OLD-FASHIONED LEMONADE.

After they have studied and discussed the instructions, rearrange the class as pairs of pairs. Remind everyone not to read out their recipes word-for-word, but to explain them in their own words.

10.10   Revision exercise   *Grammar*

Answers

1 A meal is being prepared for us now.
2 As the table has been laid, you can sit down now.
3 White bread is not supposed to be as good for you as brown.
4 I've never had a worse meal than the one I had at my brother's flat. / I've never had such a bad meal as the one I had at my brother's flat.
5 If you hadn't arrived so early, the meal might/would have been ready.
6 If we get there early, we'll be able to get a table.
7 If there had been any coffee left, we wouldn't have had to have tea / we could have had coffee instead of tea.
8 Although I'm on a diet, I love chocolates so much that I'll just have one.
9 During dinner there was a power cut.
10 When they arrive, I'll make some tea.

▶ There are more exercises of this type in *Cambridge First Certificate Examination Practice 1, 2* and *3*.

10.11   How to make a national dish   *Composition*

Discuss the advice given in the Student's Book before starting **A**.

A   Here we're looking at STYLE – and the way that the style of a composition should suit the imagined reader. No hard and fast rules can be given about this, but students should be encouraged to develop a 'feeling' for what seems appropriate in different situations.

Answers (These are debatable.)

1 Spoken by an adult to a child (suitable style for 'Write what you would say to a child.')

2 Spoken to a group of adults
3 Spoken to a friend
4 Spoken to a stranger – rather formal style
5 Written in a magazine or newspaper
6 Written in a recipe book
(5 blended with 6 would be suitable style for 'Write instructions for a friend.')

B   A very complicated dish may be too ambitious. Perhaps encourage students to choose something that is relatively straightforward. Remind them that ingredients and processes they take for granted may be completely alien to a foreigner.

▶   In a multi-national class, take advantage of the different cuisines represented to get students to share recipes with each other.

C   In this case the 150-word limit may well be exceeded – as in the model composition below. The model composition might be clearer if each step was numbered.

Model composition

44 Arcadia Ave
Greenwood

2 April 19##

Dear Les,

You asked me to send you the recipe for a typical national dish. The one I've chosen is something I'm sure you'll enjoy cooking and eating, but it's one you've probably never tried before. It's called:

Blackberry Fool

To make it you need:
  ½ kilo fresh blackberries (frozen ones will do)
  200 g sugar
  3 eggs
  ½ litre milk
  ¼ litre cream

Cook the fruit on a low heat with half of the sugar until soft (about 15 mins).
  Meanwhile, beat the eggs with the rest of the sugar in a bowl. Heat the milk to just below boiling point and pour it slowly onto the eggs and sugar, stirring all the time. Then put the bowl into a pan of almost boiling water and keep stirring until the mixture thickens (about

195

```
5 mins). Then remove the bowl and put the custard you
have made in the fridge.
    Rub the cooked fruit through a sieve and put the purée
you have made in the fridge.
    When everything is cold, whip the cream. Then fold the
cold custard into the purée and then fold in the cream
too.
    Serve in a large glass bowl or individual glass
dishes.

It's quite tricky to make but you'll find it's absolutely
delicious!

Best wishes,
```

10.12   *Leave, let, pull* and *run*   *Verbs and idioms*

A

Answers

1 let	4 leave	7 leave	10 run
2 pulling	5 leave	8 runs/ran	11 let
3 pull	6 let	9 left	12 runs

B

Answers

1 let   in = allow to enter
2 let   down = disappoint
3 leave   out = omit
4 let   off = allow to explode
5 pulls up = stop
6 pulled out = extract
7 pulled down = demolish
8 running over = kill or injure   ran into = collide with
9 run out of = have no more
10 run after = chase
11 ran into = meet unexpectedly
12 run away with = leave secretly or illegally

▶ For more speaking and listening activities on the topic of food, see
Ideas Units 8 and 10.

11 Work and business

11.1 Earning a living

Vocabulary

A You may think that part of this preliminary discussion may 'invade' people's privacy. If so, get everyone to ignore the second question.

B Young students may find this exercise particularly difficult, but even they will be workers one day!

Note that, among the wrong answers, the words *applicate* and *overhours* don't exist. There are not normally such distractors in the exam.

Answers (Some of these are open to discussion, but these are the 'best alternatives'.)

1	qualifications	11	permanent
2	firm	12	promoted
3	profession	13	training
4	career	14	earn
5	apply	15	pension
6	fill in	16	department
7	referees	17	routine
8	staff	18	a salary
9	employee	19	profit
10	overtime	20	goods

C Again, discuss the wrong answers.

Answers

1 makes   manufactures   produces
2 dismissed   fired   sacked
3 became unemployed   lost their jobs   were made redundant
4 experience   personality   qualifications
5 computer   typewriter   word processor

D Get each group to report back to the class at the end of their discussion.

11.2   How to create a good impression ... *Reading*

▶ Begin by finding out how many members of the class have been interviewed.

A

Answers

DOS – all items except 6 and 11, which are DON'TS.
(7 and 10 are things you should not forget.)

B   Note in the first question that a *score* is 20.

Answers

2 c   3 c   4 b   5 a   6 b   7 c   8 c   9 a   10 b   11 c   12 a
13 c

▶ Suggest that everyone chooses the five most useful expressions to learn.

C   Perhaps begin by making it clear what the differences are between a job interview and the FCE Interview:
• Normally candidates and examiner don't shake hands.
• There's no need to take your certificates with you.
etc.

11.3   Reported speech   *Grammar*

A   Reporting Statements

Answers

3 She said that **she hadn't found a job that suited her yet.**
4 She told me that **she would telephone them and ask them to send her an application form.**
5 I found out **that she hadn't got the job she had applied for.**
6 She admitted **that she had done very badly at the interview.**
Note: *that* can be omitted in all the above sentences.

B Reporting Orders, Promises, Offers, Requests and Advice

Answers

3 He wanted me **to type the letter out for him.**
4 I offered **to do it on my word processor.**
5 I reminded him **to send it by first-class post.**
6 He persuaded **me to make a photocopy of it for him.**

C Reporting Questions

Answers

3 I asked her if it **was her first interview.**
4 She asked me what the **most important thing to remember at an interview was.**
5 I wanted to know **what she was going to wear for the interview.**
6 I wondered **how she would feel before the interview.**
7 I asked her if **she had got the job when I saw her after the interview.**
8 I tried to find out **why she didn't look pleased.**
9 She said she was disappointed because **it wasn't really the kind of work she wanted to do.**

D

Answers (Some variations are possible.)

1 He said that he wasn't enjoying his work.
2 He told me (that) he hadn't remembered to post the letter the night before.
3 She said (that) she wanted me to get there early the next day.
4 She asked me if I had already phoned our clients or if I would / was going to do it later.
5 She reminded me to order the supplies she needed.
6 He wanted to know when the delivery van would arrive.
7 She persuaded me/us to phone them.
8 He admitted (that) it was / had been his fault.
9 She threatened to scream if we didn't stop laughing.
10 He promised to make the phone call first thing tomorrow/the next day.

▶ For more practice on reported speech, see *Use of English* Units 19 and 20.

11.4   Four candidates   *Listening*

A   Perhaps also ask everyone to say what the qualities are of a good teacher and a good student too?

B   [cassette] Possibly pause the tape between the descriptions of each candidate. (A *short list* is a list of the candidates who are interviewed, once the unlikely applicants have been weeded out.)

Answers

	GOOD POINTS	BAD POINTS
Mr Anderson	Well-qualified, experienced, reliable	Unimaginative, lacking in drive, too long in present job
Miss Ballantyne	Recommended, hard-working	Aggressive?? (or nervous)
Mr Collins	Good sense of humour, did well at school, asked good questions, would learn quickly	No experience, too well-qualified?
Miss Davis	Serious, imaginative, intelligent	Unreliable? 5 jobs in 2 years

C   There are no 'correct answers' to these questions – they are a basis for discussion only.

Transcript

Dennis: Well, then, Margaret. Four quite interesting people. What's your verdict?

Margaret: Well, I think before we make any decision, we should compare notes, you know, see what ... we think.

Dennis: Yes, fine, fair enough, let's ... er ... take them in alphabetical order, shall we?

Margaret: All right. What do you think?

Dennis: Well, that is ... er ... Mr Anderson, isn't it? Well, he seems pretty well-qualified, don't you think?

Margaret: Yes, yes, qualified, well-qualified ... and pleasant, I thought.

Dennis: Yes, oh, exceedingly so, yes. Plenty of experience in ... in our field too, that's very very important.

Margaret: And he seemed a reliable sort of chap.

Dennis: Yes. Do you think perhaps he's been a little too long in his present job?

Margaret: Could be ... I mean, he ... he didn't come over as very imaginative ... Perhaps he's lacking in drive.

Dennis: Yes, I think ... er ... I think possibly so.

Margaret: What about Miss Ballantyne?
Dennis: Ah, Miss Ballantyne, now the ... she's very interesting, I think. She
            was ... er ... after all recommended to us by Mr Fowler of Acme
            Engineering.
Margaret: Mm. I liked her. She seemed a hard-working sort of person, you
            know the type. Oh yeah, I liked her.
Dennis: Mm. What did you think about her ... er ... her personality at ... at
            the interview? I ... I didn't think that was too good, did you?
Margaret: Oh, what worried you?
Dennis: Well, she seemed a ... a little ... little aggressive.
Margaret: Oh, you thought she seemed aggressive?
Dennis: Yes. That didn't come over to you?
Margaret: No, no, not at all.
Dennis: That ... that's very interesting.
Margaret: Maybe that's a male point of view. I thought she seemed rather
            nervous, not at all aggressive.
Dennis: Ah, yes, I ... it just ... I don't know, I ... I was just thinking that,
            well, you know, she's not giving a very good interview. Therefore
            probably not giving ... doing herself justice. And then I ... Sorry, go
            on.
Margaret: Mm, I was going to say, what about Mr Collins?
Dennis: Mr Collins, ah yes, now that's a very nice sense of humour. I ... I
            liked him very much ... Mm ... The on ... the only thing against him
            of course is that he ... he has no experience in our line of work. I
            don't know, do you think there's any value in that?
Margaret: I don't know. He seemed intelligent and ... and would learn very
            quickly.
Dennis: Yes ... yes. Of course, he did very well at school and ... and ... and
            then college, of course.
Margaret: Yes, and he asked us some very good questions.
Dennis: Yes, that's true.
Margaret: You know, one thing bothered me.
Dennis: Yes?
Margaret: I think he's too well-qualified.
Dennis: Too well-qualified? Do you think so?
Margaret: Yes, could be.
Dennis: Yes, even ... despite the fact that he has no experience? I would have
            thought that the one might have balanced the other, no?
Margaret: I don't know, we could try. What about Mr Dav ... Miss ... Miss
            Davis?
Dennis: Miss Davis ... yes. Yes, very very pleasant ... Um ... she worries me
            a little bit. Er ... that ... point, I mean she was very honest about it
            but she's after all had five jobs in the past two years ... Makes me
            feel a little cautious, you know.
Margaret: Yes, she could be a bit unreliable, but then ... She ... she seemed to
            have a serious sort of nature. She seemed ... seemed serious about us
            too. Seemed interested in our kind of work.
Dennis: Yes ... yes and she was very intelligent ... very intelligent ideas. And
            a very good imagination. I thought some of her points were very
            imaginative.

Margaret: Right, well ... So of the four, yes, what do you think?
Dennis: Well, it seems to me that of the four ... given what we've taken and thinking about it, that the best for the job is probably ...

(Time: 3 minutes)

11.5   Fill the gaps   *Use of English*

Complete story

One of ₁ **the** most enjoyable jobs I've ₂ **ever** done was when I ₃ **was** a student. When you ₄ **hear** what it was you may be a ₅ **bit** shocked, but ₆ **although** I know it sounds unpleasant I can assure you that it was ₇ **in** fact delightful. Believe it or ₈ **not**, I was a grave-digger for a ₉ **whole** summer. It was one of ₁₀ **those** hot, dry summers which made the ₁₁ **ground** as hard as rock and it needed a great deal of ₁₂ **effort** to dig the graves. Now, a grave-digger doesn't have ₁₃ **anything** to do with dead bodies. All he has to do is dig two-metre deep holes and fill them in ₁₄ **again** when the coffin has been put in. As I ₁₅ **said**, it was a marvellous summer and I'm glad to say ₁₆ **that** I didn't have to work on my ₁₇ **own**. I had a workmate who had been digging graves ₁₈ **since** 1950. In ₁₉ **spite** of his depressing trade he was a cheerful character, always laughing and ₂₀ **telling** jokes. He used to tell me ₂₁ **all** about his experiences and I ₂₂ **listened** to him for hours on end. Mind you, we had to work quite ₂₃ **hard** and usually there were two or three graves to dig every day. By the ₂₄ **time** I had to go ₂₅ **back** to college I was fitter, browner and in some ₂₆ **ways** a wiser person.

▶   It might be interesting for your students to describe any unusual part-time or full-time jobs they have ever had. Perhaps there's one that *you* have done which they could ask you about. Are there any jobs which they would refuse to do in any circumstances?

11.6   Situations vacant   *Problem solving*

A   In case your students have difficulty understanding the advertisements, here are a few notes of explanation:
1   INN ON THE PARK: *beverage* = drinks
2   ATTENTION: *the Services* = army, navy, air force   *commission* = money paid as a percentage of sales   *incentives* = extra money for higher sales   *advancement* = promotion

3 TWO YEARS AGO: *broke* = had no money, bankrupt   *five-figure income* = £10,000 per year or more
4 THE SELFRIDGE HOTEL: *rota* = changing regularly
6 STEWARDESSES: *sailboat* = yacht   *will train* = training will be given   *resumé* = CV (curriculum vitae, career history)

▶ If the class is divided into four groups, each one could concentrate on finding a job for a different one of the people. Then rearrange the class into groups of four, consisting of one member of each of the original groups.

B   Point out that the opening words require the use of certain structures – as the model paragraphs show.

Model paragraphs

```
The best job for Anne would be to find out more about the
part-time job in number 7. She has all the right
qualifications and, assuming she has no objection to
using her car and working on Sundays, the job might be
very interesting. The pay is reasonable but she should
find out how much she would have to spend on petrol and
other expenses. The work itself is not described and she
should find out exactly what is involved.

Bob would perhaps enjoy the job of Room Service Order
Taker at the Inn on the Park. He seems to have no
previous experience, but he is well-educated and no doubt
he could cope easily with the work. The danger is that he
might quickly get bored with the work and lose patience
with guests who are too fussy.

Cherry might like to apply for the job of secretary at
the language school. She is perhaps over-qualified for
the job but it sounds like an interesting job with a
chance to meet people from all over the world. However,
she may not speak German well enough to get the job. But
a person with Cherry's experience should have no
difficulty in finding a suitable job.

Doris should write a letter and send her photo to T.W.
Charters in Miami. As a stewardess she could have a real
break from the monotony of working in an office and enjoy
the excitement of cruising in a sailing yacht. She might
meet all sorts of fascinating people on board and ashore.
On the other hand, there may be unexpected risks involved
in living on board a boat.
```

11.7   Word stress +   *Pronunciation*
Joining up words

▶ 🔲 A and B are recorded on the cassette. If you don't intend to use them, wind the cassette forward to the next 'beep' to find C on the tape.

The purpose of these exercises is to increase awareness of stress and catenation (joining up words) – these features of pronunciation are assessed in the Interview.

A   Both the examples and the correct pronunciations are recorded on the cassette. Perhaps play the examples before the exercise is done and then use the rest of the recording as a kind of aural key at the end.

Answers

Verbs and -ing forms	*Nouns and adjectives*
These bananas are impórted.	Ímports have risen this month.
He insúlted me.	That was a terrible ínsult.
I objéct to being insulted.	Unidentified Flying Óbject.
They perfécted a new method.	Your work is not quite pérfect.
Smoking is not permítted.	You need a pérmit to fish in the river.
His work is progréssing well.	Prógress to First Certificate*
(*This could be the imperative form of a verb, if so it's Progréss!)	
They protésted about the situation.	They held a prótest meeting.
Listen to the recórding.	Have you heard their new récord?
He is suspécted of the crime.	He is the main súspect.

(Time: 1 minute 15 seconds)

B   Both the examples and the correct pronunciations are recorded on the cassette. Perhaps play the examples before the exercise is done and then use the rest of the recording as a kind of aural key at the end.

Answers

ádvertising   advértisement   attráction   certíficate   cómfortable communicátion   députy   désert   dessért   desírable   détails devélopment   expérience   gírlfriend   himsélf   informátion intélligence   machíne   pérmanent   phótograph   photógraphy qualificátion   recéptionist   reservátion   secretárial   sécretary télephone   teléphonist   témporary   themsélves   tóothache végetable   yoursélf

(Time: 1 minute 15 seconds)

▶ The stress in multi-syllable words is usually on the third syllable from the end, except in **-ion** words and **-ing** forms.

C ⌑ Play the tape, pausing after each sentence.

Suggested answers (These are not definitive.)

1 Stréss is just as impórtant in a conversátion as whén you're réading sómething alóud.
2 Knówledge of at léast óne fóreign lánguage is requíred in this jób.
3 The unemplóyment fígures are hígher agáin this month, it sáys in the páper.
4 I heárd on the néws that éxports are úp agáin this yéar.
5 Mále sécretaries were replácèd by wómen in the Fírst Wórld Wár.
6 Fínd óut as múch as póssible abóut the jób befórehand.
7 Shów some enthúsiasm when the jób is expláined to you.
8 Nó one is góing to emplóy you if you lóok as if you've wándered óut of a dísco.
9 The wáy you ánswer will shów what kínd of pérson you áre and if your educátion, skílls and expérience mátch whát they're lóoking fór.
10 It tákes móst péople a lóng tíme to perféct their pronunciátion in Énglish.

(Time: 1 minute 15 seconds)

D First get the pairs to mark the catenation in the sentences.

⌑ Play the recording again whilst everyone compares their marks with the voices on the tape.
   Finally they should take it in turns to read each of the sentences aloud.

▶ More advanced points:
Not only consonant-vowel catenation takes place, but many consonants can be catenated with other consonants. For example:
t‿s 'last‿sound'   t‿w 'next‿word'   t‿p 'that‿people'
t‿f 'unemployment‿figures'   etc.

▶ Although reading aloud is NOT a skill required in the FCE exam, it is the best way of concentrating on pronunciation and practising it.

Suggested answers (These are not definitive.)

1 Stress‿is just‿as‿important‿in‿a conversation as when you're reading something‿aloud.
2 Knowledge‿of‿at least‿one foreign language‿is required‿in this job.

3 The unemployment figures are higher again this month, it says in the paper.
4 I heard on the news that exports are up again this year.
5 Male secretaries were replaced by women in the First World War.
6 Find out as much as possible about the job beforehand.
7 Show some enthusiasm when the job is explained to you.
8 No one is going to employ you if you look as if you've wandered out of a disco.
9 The way you answer will show what kind of person you are and if your education, skills and experience match what they're looking for.
10 It takes most people a long time to perfect their pronunciation in English.

E   This gives everyone a chance to put what they have been doing so far in this section into practice.

11.8   First jobs

Listening

A   ▣ There are two separate conversations. Note that students have to choose the 'best alternative', as in the exam.

Answers

1 c   2 a   3 a   4 b   5 b   6 c   7 c   8 a   9 a   10 c

Transcript

David: Do you remember the ... er ... the very first job you ever had?
Jill: Yes, I certainly do. I wasn't very good at it, actually. Um ... it was as a secretary, I was supposed to be a secretary but I hadn't done very much secretarial training, and I went along – it was a design studio – and in fact I wanted to be a designer, so I used to sit around doing drawings all the time where I should have been typing letters, shorthand and typing. And ... er ... my boss went away for three weeks' holiday and there was ... um ... a horrible woman put in charge and ... er ... she was very very nasty and got me into terrible trouble with my boss, who came back and gave me a big lecture and I ran home in tears and then I didn't go back and then several ... several weeks later I had a letter from him, saying: 'Please come back because the ... ' – now what did he call her? Something horrible, anyway – 'She's gone' he said.
David: So you went back?
Jill: 'And would you like to come back?' – No, I didn't. Tell me about yours.

David: Oh mine, oh, straight out of school I worked in a library for six
           months, which was so boring it was untrue and the ... the only
           excitement we got out of the day was seeing people come in the door
           which was at the far end and we would all decide between ourselves
           what sort of book they were going to take out, right? So they'd come
           up to the desk and you'd ... you'd sort of say: 'Oh, she's going to get
           an Agatha Christie.' 'No, no, no she's into cars', you know. And then
           of course it would turn out to be something totally different. We ...
           we used to have a point system, you know, you'd score points
           according to ... Apart from that I would never ever go back to work
           for a library, but what I do know now is how to get ... how to find my
           way round in a library. So if you find yourself in a library you don't
           know, you can find your way around. That's the only part I enjoyed
           about it.

Richard: Well, the first job I had and certainly one of the best was straight after
           school and before I went to university, I had some months off, and I
           was fixed up with a job in Berlin as a postman in ... in a ... a quarter
           of Berlin called Spandau ... Spandau. Er ... and it was a lovely job. I
           find postmen the world over tend to be very friendly sort of people
           and the ... there were a group of us Englishmen in there and the
           German postmen were wonderful, they sorted all our mail for us and
           everything, and took us round, and got drunk with us after the round
           and ... And ... er ... it was strange for me 'cause I'm not used to
           getting up quite that early but I lived about an hour and a half away,
           the other side of the city, I had to get up at five in order to be there for
           half past six, do the round and I was back in bed by about one o'clock
           in the afternoon.
Jocelyn: Was it well paid?
Richard: Well, it ... for someone who'd just left school it was quite well paid,
           yes. Er ... it was ... um ... and a German postman has to do far more
           than an English postman. They have to take the old-age pensions
           round and hand them out and collect various moneys and things, so
           it's a much more responsible job and I was amazed that they were
           giving me all this responsibility – an English schoolkid, basically,
           carrying thousands of pounds around with me, accountable for it in
           theory. But it was great fun.
Jocelyn: Well, my first job was about the same time really, I suppose, I was
           leaving school, but I ... made a lot of money but it was an awful job
           ... it was selling encyclopedias door-to-door in the United States and
           the pressure to sell was incredible. I mean, you had to go back every
           night and ... and ... and produce the goods and I found that I just
           used to burst into tears. I mean, they would drive you into an area
           that ... where you didn't know the streets, you didn't know where
           you were, and they said: 'Well, we'll pick you up in four or five
           hours', and there was no sort of steady wage, you had to sell in order
           to make any kind of money at all. And at first I was so timid I'd, you
           know, I'd ring the doorbell and I'd expect them to slam the door in
           my face and of course they did. And after a while I thought: 'The only
           thing that's going to save me is a sense of humour here'. So I would
           make jokes, I would run through the sprinklers on the lawn and this

seemed to ... um ... interest them. So I found myself getting asked in and I would spend the evening talking about everything else other than encyclopedias and then sort of towards the end I'd sort of say: 'Oh by the way ... ' And they'd buy them. It would be ... yeah ...

Richard: So you made a living out of it?
Jocelyn: Yeah, I did. Well, I put myself through college on it.
Richard: Fantastic!

(Time: 4 minutes)

B   If anyone in the class has worked (even only holiday work) get them to describe their first job.

11.9   The secretary   *Reading*

A   Make sure everyone realises why their mistakes are mistakes.

Answers

1 d   2 a   3 a   4 c   5 b   6 d   7 b   8 a   9 c   10 a

B   A chance for people to air their prejudices – and be made to justify them!

11.10   A typical working day   *Listening*

A   🔲 If your students are 'good at listening' you could omit this part. (Albert Wilson is an underground train driver; Gordon Spencer is an author.)

B   🔲 Pause the tape before the interview with Gordon Spencer begins.

Answers

TRUE statements: 2   4   6   7   10
FALSE statements: 1   3   5   8   9

C   🔲

Answers

TRUE statements: 2   4   6   9
FALSE statements: 1   3   5   7   8   10

▶ In the exam the questions are likely to be harder, BUT candidates don't have to get 100% right.

Transcript

Interviewer: Albert, tell us about a typical working day in your job.

Albert: Well, if you're on the morning shift, er ... you might have to get up as early as four to be at work by five, you know, which is when the first train leaves. But, you know, not all the trains start that early ... er ... they leave every ten minutes or so up to about seven. So, if you're driving a later train, you wouldn't report for work until ... oh ... you know, six forty-five ... er ... in the case of driving at seven o'clock. But ... er ... it all depends, you know. Er ... you know, I find the work itself is quite tiring. Even though you're sitting down all the time, you have to remain alert the whole time and it's a big responsibility because there are only two or three minutes between each station. This means you're always starting and stopping or accelerating and slowing down. I ... er ... I wouldn't say it's a very healthy job, really, you know, because ... er ... you know, the lack of air and lack of ventilation. You know, although the line I'm on at the moment, it runs as much above ground as it does below ground. You know, it's quite nice out in the country there sometimes. But ... er ... more because of ... er ... th ... you know ... because of the strain on the nerves is the health thing really. It's the strain on the nerves. You get ... er ... headaches quite often. On the whole, though, I don't mind the work. Though I don't suppose I ... I don't really enjoy it. Er ... I don't mind being on my own most of the time, you know. You get a chance to chat to your mates in the refreshments breaks you get between journeys. But ... er ... I suppose the advantage of the work is that you ... you don't have to answer to anyone. You know, you're your own boss, there's no one telling you what to do the whole time.

Interviewer: What ... what's the pay like?

Albert: Oh, the pay is very good. I think it's very fair for what ... for what we do. Um ... and the other advantage is if you're on a morning shift you're free the whole afternoon, you know ... you know with my hobbies and ... er ... all that kind of thing, and helping the wife out with the shopping, it's great. But if you're on the evening work it can be a real problem.

Interviewer: Why ... why is that?

Albert: Well ... you know, because you're too tired, er ... you know, working and this means you can't spend ... er ... time with your mates except on your days off, as well, that's another thing. I ... I suppose I get about two days off a week, sometimes three. And four weeks holiday. You ... you try to take the ... er ... the family to the seaside on one of those weeks, really. Because, you know, I get ... er ... I get free travel anywhere in London for myself and my family, that's another thing. So on rest days we try to go out for the day with the family if the weather's nice and we take a picnic to the park or something like that.

Interviewer: Well, thank you very much, Albert.

Next we have Gordon Spencer. Gordon, would you tell us how you spend a typical working day?

Gordon: Yes, indeed, the ... er ... I suppose the only time I ever stick to a really strict routine is when I'm actually writing a book. I suppose I get up at six, yes, it's always fairly early, have breakfast, swim and then off I go to my writing hut which is about five miles from home.

Interviewer: A writing hut?

Gordon: Yes, it's marvellous, you see, it's a little place where I can actually shut myself away, be absolutely private and quiet. There's no telephone there or anything like that and I can really concentrate on writing.

Interviewer: Oh, I see.

Gordon: Er ... work, yes, well, I suppose it starts round about ... about seven. Um ... I make rough drafts in longhand and ... er ... type up these drafts every day immediately afterwards. You see, I don't leave anything over until the next day. I always sort of complete what I'm doing on the day. Now the books, as you'll know if you've read them, are always based very carefully on the research that I do.

Interviewer: I think that's quite evident from the sort of stories that you write.

Gordon: Well, I have notebooks absolutely chock full of information about people and places kept locked away in the writing hut. I keep them all in a big safe there. Now, I work through the day for about eight hours and I stop only to make tea or have some biscuits or something like that. And then I stop at three o'clock. Dead stop at three o'clock and home I go, home I go, cycle home and I have a swim and a ... and a sauna.

Interviewer: I expect you need it after that, don't you?

Gordon: Well, it's ... er ... it's not a doddle, writing a book. At ... er ... five o'clock, you see, I then eat. My wife's got the meal ready. And ... er ... well, after that we settle down and relax a bit.

Interviewer: And what sort of time do you go to bed? What time does your day actually finish?

Gordon: Oh, I suppose, not too late, about ten o'clock if I've got to be up at ... er ... six the next morning.

Interviewer: Mm. How long on average would you say it takes you to write a book?

Gordon: Well now, the actual writing of a book takes, what, about five or six weeks, I suppose if you ... if I work seven days a week. Er ... my output is one book a year and that's always in July and August. And the rest of the year I spend ... well, well, what do I spend ... er ... yes, I spend it relaxing at home or travelling abroad doing research for the next one.

Interviewer: I see, well thank you very much, Gordon Spencer.

Gordon: A pleasure.

(Time: 5 minutes)

11.11   Writing a formal letter   *Composition*

A   Once the pairs have discussed what kind of information would be relevant and irrelevant, ask them to report back to the class.

B   The first writer has made the following 'mistakes':
- The name and address of the recipient don't appear on the left-hand side.
- The writer has started 'Dear Sir' when the name of the recipient is Ms Brown. (If one knows the name of the person, one should use it.)
- 'Yours sincerely' isn't suitable as an ending if the opening is 'Dear Sir' or 'Dear Madam'.
- The writer isn't 'selling' him/herself hard enough and a little more personal detail about previous experience would be a good idea.
- It is shorter than an exam composition should be (though in real life this is not a fault, of course!).

The second person seems more suitable for the job, though the details of the time he/she is available are probably unnecessary. This letter can serve as a model for the task in C.

C   There is no model composition in this case: refer back to the second letter in **B** if necessary.

Make sure everyone times themselves, makes notes and checks their work through afterwards – as instructed in the Student's Book.

11.12   *Set, stand* and *turn*   *Verbs and idioms*

A

Answers

1 stands	8 set
2 turned	9 stand
3 stands	10 set
4 stands	11 turned
5 set	12 set
6 turned	13 turn
7 stand	14 turned

»→

B

Answers

1 set out = start a journey
2 set up = found/start
3 sets out = explain
4 standing in for = be a substitute
5 stands for = tolerate
6 stand up to = resist
7 stood for = be a candidate for
8 stand by = support
9 stood up = rise to one's feet
10 turn up = arrive
11 turn over = go to the next page
12 turned down = reject

▶ For more work on phrasal verbs, see *Use of English* Units 38 and 39.

11.13 Different kinds of jobs *Interview exercises*

A This is a straightforward picture conversation. Notice, however, that the photos have been chosen to provoke discussion about stereotypes and prejudices. In the 1990s, do any of your students still maintain that certain jobs are 'women's work' whilst others are 'men's work'?

▶ Remind everyone that they aren't expected to know everything about an unfamiliar topic for the exam. There are ways of dealing with unknown items, like saying to the examiner:

'I haven't **come across** this word/tool/profession before.' And this may be safer than pretending they know something they don't.

B The class is divided into groups of three to discuss these jobs:

author carpenter government minister nurse postman/woman sales representative secretary shop assistant taxi driver

After discussing the jobs and their attractions and drawbacks, student A looks at Activity 26, student B at 30 and C at 45. There they find more ideas on the pros and cons of the jobs which will help to inform their discussion – knowledgeable students may not need to see this information.

▶ If your class are doing the Interview some time before the written papers of the exam, make sure they look at the final exam advice for the Interview at the end of Unit 14 on page 208.

▶ For more listening and speaking activities on the topic of work and employment, see *Ideas* Unit 17.

12 In the news

12.1 The press, politics and crime *Vocabulary*

▶ For this section it would be a good idea to bring some copies of English-language newspapers into class, so that the discussion in **A** and **C** can refer to real events that are in the news. This will help the whole topic to come alive.

A In this discussion, remember that many people hardly ever keep up to date with the news – give them a chance to say why.

B Don't forget to discuss any useful words among the wrong answers.

Answers

1 article	11 election
2 headlines	12 government
3 editorial	13 Prime Minister
4 newsreader	14 arrested
5 hostages	15 stolen
6 revolution	16 lawyer
7 earthquake	17 jail
8 weapons	18 guilty
9 support	19 jury
10 democracy	20 socialist

C At the end of the discussion, ask each group to report to the whole class. Do the members of the class agree what the most awful and amusing events were? Perhaps ask:
• Why is so little good news reported – can you remember any from the past week?

12.2 The robber gendarme *Reading*

A In case of difficulty, perhaps explain to the class that: *gendarme* is a French word for policeman; *bingo* is a kind of gambling game; a *home loan* is money borrowed from a bank to buy a home (i.e. a mortgage).

B

Correct sequence

1 Played bingo
2 Found himself in debt
3 Decided to rob bank
4 Was afraid to rob bank
5 Robbed bank

6 Alarm raised by manager
7 Paid part of his debts
8 Reported for duty
9 Arrested

C

Answers

1 d   2 c   3 c   4 b   5 d   6 a

D   Once the groups have discussed the questions, perhaps rearrange them into pairs from different groups. Then each partner can find out about another group's opinions.

12.3   Word order   *Grammar*

▶   The points covered in parts **A** to **D** are a very tricky area. There are no firm rules, and concepts like 'frequency adverbs' tend to be confusing. Hopefully, by now, students will have developed a 'feeling' for the position where adverbial phrases can be placed in sentences. Some places feel 'just right' or 'comfortable', others feel 'not quite right' and others feel 'wrong'.

Students who are mystified in **A** and **B** may find that the work they do in **C** and **D** will make everything clearer and help them to realise that, in fact, they do already have this 'feeling'.

A   ADVERBS and adverbial phrases
The gaps (—) in the chart are the positions where the adverbs are not normally placed in the example sentence, as explained in **B**.

B   If you read to the class these sentences that were 'missing' from the chart in **A**, they'll probably agree that they sound 'wrong':
He was arrested never. ×
He yesterday was arrested. ×
He by the police was arrested. ×
Tell everyone to rely on this feeling for what sounds right, not to depend on rules to follow.

C   There are three possible ways of dealing with this exercise – the one you choose will depend on the level of your students and the time you have available.

The first group of adverbs in the Student's Book (*almost* to *seldom*) are all mid-position adverbs. The rest can be placed in various positions. In some cases the adverbs simply don't make sense in the context – so there is no 'comfortable position' in these cases.

Three possible procedures:

a) As homework, get everyone to decide on just one position where each adjective can be placed in each sentence. Go through this in class later, accepting any positions that seem 'comfortable'. Point out how the emphasis may change, according to where the adverbs are placed.

b) In class, write up the sentences on the board, perhaps with numbers as shown below. Ask everyone to call out the positions where each adjective can be placed in each sentence. Point out how the emphasis changes, according to where the adverbs are placed.

c) In class, divide the class into pairs and get each pair to decide on just one position where each adjective can be placed in each sentence. Go through this as a class later, accepting any positions that seem 'comfortable'. Point out how the emphasis may change, according to where the adverbs are placed.

▶ IMPORTANT: DO NOT point out any possible positions that the class have missed – only any they have got wrong. The whole topic is confusing enough as it is, without adding further details!

1 **They** *2* **didn't** *3* **arrive on time** *4* .
5 **She** *6* **was** *7* **able to finish her meal** *8* .
9 **We** *10* **knew** *11* **that the work** *12* **would** *13* **be very difficult** *14* .

Suggested answers (Some of these may be debatable: don't point out the ones that students have missed.)

almost   2   7
always   3   4   6   7   10   11   13
hardly ever   7   10   13
just   2   7   10   13
nearly   2   7
never   6   7   10   12   13
rarely   2   6   7   10   12   13
seldom   2   6   7   10   12   13

as usual   1   4   5   7   8   9   11   12   13   14
certainly   1   2   5   6   7   9   10   12   13

H

definitely   1   2   6   7   10   11   12   13
frequently   not 3
maybe   1   5   9   11
normally   all
obviously   all
often   all
one day   1   4   5   8   9   11   13   14
on Friday   1   4   5   8   9   11   14
perhaps   all
possibly   not 3
probably   not 3
really   all
still   1   2   5   6   7   9   10   11   12   13
usually   all
yesterday   1   4   5   8   9   11   14

D

Answers (With variations given, though others may be possible.)

1 She worked hard to finish the essay.
2 You hardly ever read about my country in the newspapers.
3 Unexpectedly, it was a hard task that took a long time to finish.
    It was a hard task that took an unexpectedly long time to finish.
    It was an unexpectedly hard task that took a long time to finish.
    It was a hard task that unexpectedly took a long time to finish.
    It was a hard task that took a long time to finish, unexpectedly.
4 He walked slowly into the room and clapped his hands.
    Slowly he walked into the room and clapped his hands.
5 They did the work very well on their own.
    They did the work on their own very well.
6 There is normally not much news in the paper on Saturday.
    Normally, there is not much news in the paper on Saturday.
    On Saturday there is normally not much news in the paper.
7 We will definitely hear the election results on TV on Sunday.
    On Sunday we will definitely hear the election results on TV.
8 We always listen to the evening news on the radio during dinner.
    During dinner we always listen to the evening news on the radio.
    We always listen during dinner to the evening news on the radio.

▶ E and F are a different aspect of word order, which could be covered in a later lesson.

E   IT and THERE:

Answers

There was (loud) **applause at the end.**
It wasn't me who **broke the window.**
It was **the tall man who started the fight.**
It's also **interesting to read good news.**
It is said **that crime is increasing.**

▶ Ask the class to suggest further examples of the structures shown in the examples:

There is/are …	… twenty people in this class.
There has been …	… a lot of rain recently.
It was/wasn't me who …	… forgot to post the letter.
It was (someone else) who …	… finished all the biscuits, not me.
It was interesting/amusing/ depressing to …	… read about the air disaster/ Belgian gendarme
It is said/believed that …	… $1 million was stolen.

F

Answers (Some variations are possible.)

1 It isn't as easy as it looks to rewrite sentences.
2 It was the right-wing party who/that won the election.
3 It was kind of you to help me.
4 There's no need to read the paper unless you want to.
5 There isn't much difference between the policies of the two parties.
6 It was the left-wing candidate who was unexpectedly elected.
7 There were unfortunately no survivors of/from the air disaster.
8 It was George Bush who was elected President in 1988.
9 It is believed that 100 people have been killed.
10 There will probably be no change in the weather.

▶ For more practice on word order, see *Use of English* Unit 40.

12.4   What happened?   *Composition*

There are two Composition sections in this unit.

A   After the pair work, perhaps get each pair to explain their story to another pair.

B   This composition could be written in class under exam-like conditions.

Model composition

```
I was just crossing the road the other morning on my
way to take part in a demonstration when a man on a
bike nearly ran into me - I was astonished to see
that he was wearing a bowler hat and had a big
rucksack on his back. He didn't apologise but just
waved his umbrella at me and rode on. 'That looks
pretty dangerous, I hope he doesn't fall off,' I
thought. Well, two blocks further on I discovered
that he hadn't fallen off, but that the sight of him
must have distracted two motorists who had lost
control of their cars and collided. Although both
cars were damaged, I was glad to see that no one was
hurt. I overheard the drivers explaining to a
policeman about the cyclist but I could tell from
his expression that he didn't believe a word of it.
However, I couldn't stop because I didn't want to be
late for the demo. Luckily I got there just as the
march was starting and took my place among the other
students as we all started marching.
```

▶ Make sure every member of the class knows what his or her 'typical mistakes' are – the ones he or she persistently makes.

▶ These are the marking scales that are used by the examiners. As you can see, an 'impression mark' is given according to rather vague criteria. (What do they mean by 'reasonably correct', for example?)

The Teacher's Book of *Cambridge First Certificate Practice 3* contains some authentic candidates' compositions with the marks that were awarded. Perhaps award your students marks according to these scales from now on.

18–20	Excellent	Natural English with minimal errors and complete realisation of the task set.
16–17	Very good	More than a collection of simple sentences, with good vocabulary and structures. Some non-basic errors.
12–15	Good	Simple but accurate realisation of the task set with sufficient naturalness of English and not many errors.
8–11	Pass	Reasonably correct but awkward and non-communicating OR fair and natural treatment of subject, with some serious errors.
5–7	Weak	Original vocabulary and grammar both inadequate to the subject.
0–4	Very poor	Incoherent. Errors show lack of basic knowledge of English.

12.5   Better safe than sorry!   *Listening*

A   [cassette] Point out that some of the answers may be guessable before hearing the recording, but one still needs to hear the talk to confirm that one has guessed right.

The advice given about locking windows may sound strange to people who live in a tenth-floor flat!

B   This discussion leads on from what the crime prevention officer was going to say next in his talk about personal safety.

Answers

1 95%
2 60%
3 two thirds
4 a) locks
   b) front door   key
   c) chain
   d) insured
5 1½ million

6 25%
7 a) doors   boot
   b) valuables   boot
   c) windows
   d) well-lit
8 a) forget the number
   b) two to three

219

Transcript

Man: Erm ... er ... good evening, everyone. My name's Matthew Jackson, I'm the area crime prevention officer. I ... I'd just like to talk to you for a few minutes. Er ... we hear a lot on the television and in the papers about the increase in violent crime. Now, it's true that it is increasing, but the facts are that about 95% of crimes are against property, not against people. Now you can reduce the risk of losing your property by taking simple precautions in your home and when away from your home. For example, according to a recent survey, 60% of homes do not have window locks. Now, this means that a thief can just break a window, open the catch, climb in. Two thirds of all burglars get in through a window. So to increase the security of your home, make sure you have locks on all your windows. Have a lock on the front door that can only be opened and closed with a key. Have a chain on the front door and make sure your property is insured.

Now, i ... in Britain over 1.5 million cars are broken into or stolen each year. That ... that's six cars every two minutes. Now, if you regularly park your car in a city street, there is a one in four chance it will be stolen or broken into. So, when you leave your car you should always lock all the doors and the boot and take your valuables with you or lock them in the boot. And if the car's empty, close the windows completely – don't even leave them open a fraction. And if you can, make sure you park in a well-lit street at night.

Now i ... if you have a bicycle it must be locked up securely with a good lock whenever you leave it unattended. N ... not a combination lock, you know, where you have to remember a number, because ... well ... you may forget the number and they're absolutely useless because it ... it only takes a thief two to three minutes to open one.

Now, as for making sure of your own personal safety; first of all, remember that criminals are looking for easy opportunities and again there are simple precautions you can take, for instance, always go out ...

(Time: 2 minutes 30 seconds)

12.6 Opposites   *Word study*

A   This is revision of previous word study sections on negative prefixes and suffixes (3.5 and 4.5).

Answers

disagree   disapprove   uncomfortable   harmful   dishonest   unkind
illegal   unlucky   impolite   irregular   irrelevant   unsafe   unwilling

B   The opposites in this exercise are all different words. Note that in some cases there are a number of opposites to the word.

Answers

modest   ugly   expensive   kind   victory/beat   succeed   lead
melt/thaw   love/adore/like   well/healthy   win   quiet/silent   polite
fresh   loose   fast asleep

C   This exercise contains a mixture of words, some of which have
opposites formed with a suffix and others with opposites that are
different words.

Answers

raw/uncooked   safe   similar/identical   truth/non-fiction   solid
immature   unnecessary   support   impersonal   unpleasant/nasty
impolite/rude   smooth   untrue/false   invisible   loser   correct/right

▶ For more practice on opposites, see *Use of English* Unit 33.

12.7   Hurricane Gilbert   *Reading*

A   The map is for reference only, so that everyone has an idea of where
the places referred to in the article are.

Answers

1 b   2 b   3 d   4 b   5 b   6 b   7 d   8 b   9 b   10 c

B

Answers

refused to take seriously – brushed aside
attack – onslaught
poor – impoverished
number of people killed – death toll
reach the coast – make a landfall
make more extreme – intensify
serious – grave

▶ As a follow-up, ask the class:
• What similar natural disasters have there been recently (hurricanes,
  floods, storms, earthquakes, etc.)?
• What can be / is being done to help the survivors?

12.8   Exam practice

Answers

2 Have you heard the story of Edwin Chambers Dodson?
3 He was an antique dealer in Hollywood whose customers included many famous film stars.
4 He led a secret life as a bank robber.
5 He robbed more banks than any other man in American history.
6 He held up more banks than Jesse James and Bonnie and Clyde.
7 He took part in 64 robberies in California and made $300,000.
8 He was known as the 'Yankee Bandit' because he wore a blue New York Yankees baseball cap during most of his robberies.
9 He was sent to prison for fifteen years after he had pleaded guilty to eight robberies.
10 He is still in prison now.

(*This is a true story, by the way.*)

12.9   Here is the news ...   *Listening*

▶ If you have time to work out some true/false questions, perhaps use an authentic news broadcast (preferably from the BBC World Service) instead of this.

The broadcast is occasionally distorted slightly and there is some static noise, as listeners have to cope with this kind of noise when really hearing the news on short or medium wave. In the exam, too, there may sometimes be distracting noises (e.g. traffic noise) on the tape.
    The tape could be paused after each news item, but in this case it might be better to simulate exam conditions:
1 Allow 15–20 seconds for everyone to read the questions.
2 Play the tape for the first time.
3 15–20 seconds silence between playings.
4 Play the tape for the second time.
5 15–20 seconds more silence.

Answers

TRUE statements: 2   6   8   10   13   15
FALSE statements: 1   3   4   5   7   9   11   12   14

Transcript

Woman: Nine hours Greenwich Mean Time. The news read by Wendy
Gordon. A hundred and twenty-five people involved in drug
manufacture and smuggling have been arrested in Bolivia. The Greek
airliner hijacked to Algeria is on its way back to Athens.

In an attempt to stop the flow of cocaine and other drugs from
Bolivia to the USA, a series of arrests have been made in Santa Cruz in
the east of the country. Among the 125 people arrested are Miguel
Castro, believed to be the leading figure in the manufacture and
export of cocaine to the USA. According to the US Drug Enforcement
Agency, who have been working in close cooperation with the United
Nations and the Bolivian army, three planes loaded with drugs have
been destroyed in a raid on an airfield and more than 2.5 tons of pure
cocaine has been seized in other raids.

The worst of the heavy rains and thunderstorms that have been
sweeping parts of Europe during the past week appears to be over.
Exceptionally heavy rainfall brought flooding to many parts of
Germany, Switzerland, Northern Italy and France and chaos to rail
and road transport. Air traffic too has been affected with flight delays
at airports. Although most flights are expected to be back to normal
by this time tomorrow, there are expected to be serious delays on the
German and Italian motorways over the forthcoming holiday
weekend and train services are unlikely to be normalised for several
days. A government spokeswoman in France announced that the
damage to homes and property is expected to be at least four
thousand million francs. It is reported that at least five people have
lost their lives. Experts agree that casualty figures are low because
emergency warnings were issued on the day before the storms began.
The federal government in Switzerland has urged motorists and rail
travellers not to travel during the next few days and no international
traffic will be allowed on the main north—south motorway routes
across the country until next Tuesday.

The Greek airliner that was hijacked and flown to Algeria on
Tuesday is now on its way back to Athens. After nearly 48 hours on
the tarmac at Algiers airport, the five hijackers were persuaded to
leave the plane in the early hours of this morning and the relief crew
who have been standing by took over from Captain Georgiou and his
crew. The Olympic Airways Airbus A310 airliner is due to land in
Athens in an hour from now. Our correspondent who has been
following the hijacking reports that the six members of the crew and
the 123 passengers on the airliner, which was on an internal flight
from Athens to Crete, are all well. There is no information about the
hijackers, but it is believed that they will be allowed to leave the
country though their proposed destination is unknown.

Share prices in Tokyo rose sharply after the government's
announcement that import restrictions are to be lifted. In brisk
trading the Nikkei share index was up 25 points at the end of today's
trading. The value of the dollar against the yen rose by 2.3 cents to

133.6 yen to the dollar. Sterling rates remained unchanged at 1.78 dollars to the pound.

And now to end the news, here again are the main points: 125 drug manufacturers and smugglers have been arrested in Bolivia. Storms and flooding in Europe appear to be over. Despite widespread damage to property and transport facilities, relatively few lives have been lost. The Greek airliner hijacked to Algeria is on its way back to Athens. All the passengers and crew are safe. Share prices have risen sharply in Tokyo.

And that's the end of the news from London.

(Time: 4 minutes)

12.10   Giving your opinions *Composition*

A   Perhaps reassure everyone that, in the exam, they don't need to write a brilliantly logical essay – all that's required is that they communicate their ideas and justify them to some extent.

Students who find this kind of topic beyond them should, perhaps, avoid the opinion-giving topic in the exam.

Suggested answers (These do not necessarily reflect the author's views!)

2 It would be a better world if there were no nuclear weapons because the entire world could be destroyed if someone pressed the wrong button or if a world leader went crazy.
3 Nuclear power stations are a good thing because, unlike coal-fired power stations, they do not add carbon dioxide into the environment. On the other hand, ...
4 The government should change the law on drugs so that people are afraid to use them as well as sell them, because, at the moment, it's only the dealers who are likely to be punished, not the users.
5 If a criminal has committed a very serious crime such as murder he should be sent to prison for the rest of his life with no possibility of being released on parole.
6 The only solution to terrorism is to call for world action against terrorists so that there is nowhere they can be safe. If this is done, and every government enforces this law, terrorists will become outlaws in every country.

▶ Perhaps warn everyone against using *According to me* ... and over-using *In my opinion* ... . If several reasons will be given, they might want to use *For two/three reasons:* ...

B   Remind the class that there is no need to start with number 1, unless they want to. Perhaps, if you need to save time, get different pairs to make notes on different questions.

C   This could be done under exam conditions in class – or make sure everyone does this task at home under similar conditions, with no interruptions and no dictionary.

As the choice is so wide, there is no model composition here.

12.11   Exam practice   *Interview exercises*

📼 All three parts of this section are recorded on the cassette as a 'model mock interview'. The speakers are playing the roles of 'Candidates' and 'Examiner', but as they are all native speakers this is not really what would happen in the exam – however, it may give everyone an idea of the kind of conversation they could have with the examiner.

In the recording the Examiner does NOT encourage Candidates B and C to justify their ideas and seems satisfied with receiving very brief answers – consequently, the interviews don't develop into conversations. Ask the members of your class to suggest how Candidates B and C should have expanded on their replies.

There is a transcript of this recording on pages 228–231.

▶ If your students are going to take the Interview as a pair (some centres offer this option, where the examiner feeds the pair with questions and then listens in to their conversation), these exercises can be done in groups of three with one member playing the role of examiner.

A   At the end, ask for feedback:
• Which questions led to very short answers?
• Which questions led you to ideas you found it difficult/impossible to explain?
• How could you have avoided answering any of the difficult questions, or steered the conversation towards easier ideas?

▶ Further points to mention:
One problem in the exam, of course, is that candidates don't know what they're going to be asked. However, examiners don't try to catch candidates out or make them feel uncomfortable – what they do is encourage candidates to speak and put them at their ease.

B   This exercise is intended to give students a chance to speak about the kinds of things they like to read about in the paper and explain why. Each headline suggests a different field of interest. Students are not expected to provide the 'right answers'.

C   If this is being done by pairs, with one partner playing the role of examiner, make sure that the 'candidate' isn't silent for too long pondering the problem.

▶   In the exam, the examiner will be assessing the following aspects of each candidate's spoken English:

Fluency, grammatical accuracy, pronunciation of sentences, pronunciation of individual sounds, interactive communication and vocabulary resource.

These are the marking scales that are used by the examiners.

1   Fluency

5 Virtually native-speaker speed and rhythm in everyday contexts though there may be some hesitation when speaking on more abstract topics.
4 In everyday contexts speaks with minimal hesitation. Hesitation when discussing abstract topics does not demand unreasonable patience of the listener.
3 Does not hesitate unreasonably in everyday contexts though may experience some difficulty with more abstract topics.
2 Unacceptable hesitation even in everyday contexts.
1 Speech very disconnected.
0 Not capable of connected speech.

2   Grammatical accuracy

5 Few if any errors over a wide range of structures, including tenses, prepositions etc. Completely sufficient to deal with everyday contexts and more than adequate for abstract topics.
4 Basic structures sound though more difficult structures may sometimes be inaccurate.
3 Basic structures sufficiently controlled to deal adequately with everyday contexts though difficulty experienced with more complex structures.
2 Basic structures often inaccurate in everyday contexts. More complex structures rarely attempted or grossly inaccurate.
1 Gross distortion of basic structures.
0 No awareness of basic grammatical functions.

3   Pronunciation: Sentences

5 Near-native stress-timing, rhythm, and placing of stress, intonation patterns and range of pitch within sentence, natural linking of phrases.

4 Good stress-timing, rhythm, placing of stress, intonation etc. so that in spite of sounding foreign, speech is easily understood.

3 Stress-timing, rhythm, placing of stress, intonation etc. noticeably foreign but can mostly be understood.

2 Unacceptably foreign speech patterns predominate, with incorrect phrasing impeding interpretation. Often difficult to understand.

1 Stress and intonation so foreign that little is comprehensible.

0 Not intelligible, through faulty stress and intonation.

4   Pronunciation: Individual sounds

5 All individual sounds virtually as a native-speaker.

4 Individual sounds sufficiently well pronounced for clear and easy understanding.

3 Sounds sufficiently correct for broad understanding.

2 Poor pronunciation of individual sounds.

1 Pronunciation so poor that it represents only a crude approximation to English sounds.

0 Unintelligible.

5   Interactive communication

5 Wholly effective at communicating in everyday contexts. Largely effective in communicating on more abstract topics.

4 Communicates effectively in everyday contexts but lapses sometimes when dealing with more abstract topics.

3 Communicates adequately in everyday contexts but experiences some difficulty in discussing more abstract topics.

2 Experiences difficulty in communicating even in everyday contexts.

1 Rarely able to communicate even at a basic level.

0 Communicates nothing.

227

6 Vocabulary resource

5 Wide and appropriate range of vocabulary for everyday tasks and rarely searching for vocabulary when discussing more abstract topics.

4 Shows few gaps in vocabulary for everyday tasks though more abstract topics reveal weaknesses.

3 Vocabulary adequate for everyday tasks though may experience difficulty when discussing more abstract topics.

2 Vocabulary often insufficient to accomplish even everyday tasks.

1 Severe lack of vocabulary makes it almost impossible to communicate.

0 Vocabulary too slight for even minimal communication.

Transcript

Narrator: These model conversations give you an idea of the form that the examination interview takes. A: Picture Conversation.

A

Examiner: What do you think's happening in these pictures?

Candidate A: Um ... yes ... in the first picture ... er ...

Woman: I see a guy in a car. He looks like he's arguing maybe with a policewoman, who perhaps is giving him ... um ... a ticket or ...

Examiner: Why ... I mean ... what do you think's happened?

Candidate A: Erm ... perhaps he's just been caught driving too fast – speeding ...

Examiner: Mmm, good.

Candidate A: Or parking somewhere where he shouldn't. Um ...

Examiner: And the other one?

Candidate A: Ah, the other picture. Um ... this boy looks as though he's sad or guilty about something ... um ...

Examiner: Can you think of why perhaps?

Candidate A: Yeah ... er ... well, the conductor of the train ... um ... is either giving him or asking him for his ticket. Um ... perhaps he didn't buy one – perhaps he's breaking the law.

Examiner: So what do you think will happen next in that case?

Candidate A: In the case of the second picture ... um ... I should think the conductor would take the man's name and address and ... er ... perhaps ask him to buy a ticket.

Examiner: Right. And in the first one?

Candidate A: Er ... the first one ... um ... looks as though the argument's going to go on for some time.

Examiner: How do you think each of the ... each of the people in the photograph is feeling at this time?

Candidate A: Er ... well, I think in the first picture ... the guy is very angry. I think he feels the situation is unjust. Um ... second picture, it's hard to say – you see the man might be a traveller ... um ... a foreigner who just isn't used to being in the country so he might feel unsure ... guilty ...

Examiner: Right ... OK, so ... and which of these ... of these people in these pictures do you feel that you could support in ... in such a situation?

Candidate A: Um ... I think I'd ... I'd be able to support ... er ... the guy in the first picture ... um ... because I've been given a parking ticket many times when I've felt that it wasn't necessary to do so. Because sometimes you just cannot park anywhere ...

Examiner: So you know how he feels?

Candidate A: ... and you have to park there, yeah ...

Examiner: You've been there?

Candidate A: Yes, I have.

Examiner: And what could you say to ... to each of them if you were actually there with them in that situation?

Candidate A: Um ... I'd say, 'Try to put your case over as calmly and as sensibly as possible. Um ... don't argue too much with ... um ... people in authority because it can get them angry and then it could go against you. Um ... but try to work out the best way to solve the situation.'

Examiner: Good. And ... er ... do these ... er ... sort of things happen very often in your country?

Candidate A: Oh yes, yes, a lot of the time. Um ... I've been asked ... um ... sometimes for instance, I'm travelling on the subway in Toronto and ... er ... there's so many people travelling you can't buy a ticket, so you have to just get on the train otherwise you'll miss it, and then the conductor comes along and says, you know, 'Hey, where's your ticket?' And you have to try and explain and they just have to believe you, I suppose, that you're an honest person.

Examiner: Sounds as though it's the same the whole world over! Thank you very much.

Candidate A: I think so! Thank you.

(Time: 4 minutes)

B

Examiner: Can you tell me which of the articles here you'd be interested in reading?

Candidate B: Yes, I'd ... read first of all the ... um ... the one about the prime minister dying in an air disaster.

Examiner: Right.

Candidate B: And the one about the peace talks breaking down. And possibly the one about the hurricane hitting Mexico.

Examiner: Yeah ... OK, that first one about the prime minister dying in an air disaster: why would you particularly be interested in reading that?

Candidate B: Well ... I think, first of all I'd want to know who the prime minister was and then, whoever it was, I think it ... it would obviously be ... be very important news ... um ... for a prime minister to be killed – very serious news.

Examiner: Right, second choice: 'Peace talks break down'.

Candidate B: Um ... well, I ... I'm a member of the Peace Movement and interested in that area of things so ... er ... obviously that would be ... um ... something of interest to me immediately, of ... of great concern.

Examiner: Mm. And now which was your third choice?

Candidate B: The hurricane hitting Mexico.

Examiner: Oh, yes, and why are you so interested about that?

Candidate B: Well, that's really only because I ... I went on holiday to Mexico once for a couple of weeks so ... um ... I know it a little bit and ... er ... I'd like to know whether that part of Mexico was affected so ... Maybe a ... a silly reason but that ... that would have been the ...

Examiner: No, understandable. If we look at the ... the list of headlines here, perhaps you could just briefly tell me what you think each article is about? Now, the 'Royal baby shock'.

Candidate B: Um ... I would think that was ... um ... someone who found out that the ... one of the royal babies had developed some disease, something like that, some illness.

Examiner: Yes. Second one: 'Film star's guilty secret'.

Candidate B: I should imagine that's ... um the discovery that a film star ... or a confession that a film star has had an affair or a relationship.

Examiner: Good. '800 metre record broken'.

Candidate B: Um ... that must be a ... a sprinter or a runner who's broken ... a sprinting record.

Examiner: Now we'll leave the next one because you've already told me about that one. Er ... 'Jumbo crashes in Mediterranean'.

Candidate B: Mm ... that must be ... er ... an aeroplane disaster.

Examiner: I think so. And lastly: 'The holiday s ... holiday sunshine traps drivers in nationwide traffic jams'.

Candidate B: Yes, well, that must be all the people driving out to enjoy the ... the good weather and ... er ... spending most of their time in the car.

Examiner: Mm, thanks very much.

Candidate B: Thank you.

(Time: 2 minutes 20 seconds)

C

Examiner: Could you just look at this list of cases and tell me which one ... which cases you think are more serious than others?

Candidate C: Yes, right. Um ... well, I think a motorist driving after dr ... after drinking a whole bottle of wine is ... is more serious than a motorist driving after drinking a couple of glasses of wine.

Examiner: Right.

Candidate C: And I think that a motorist parking – sorry, a motorist driving faster than the permitted maximum speed is more serious than a motorist parking on a double yellow line.

Examiner:	OK. One ... one other comparison.
Candidate C:	Um ... a gang of youths attacking an old lady and taking her purse is more serious than someone keeping your wallet which ... which fell from your pocket.
Examiner:	Good, now ... um ... why do you think ... er ... a motorist driving faster than the permitted maximum speed is more serious than a motorist who parks on a double yellow line?
Candidate C:	Well, a motorist who drives faster than the permitted maximum speed could cause an accident in which somebody could be killed, whereas if he parks on a double yellow line it's going to cause an obstruction, and not a death.
Examiner:	Mm ... OK. Can you tell me, if you look at that list, um ... which are the most serious cases of all there?
Candidate C:	Well, I would say a group of terrorists killing one of their hostages was serious and I would say a husband killing his wife's lover was serious.
Examiner:	Good. And which are the most trivial ones there, do you think?
Candidate C:	Perhaps the motorist not wearing a seat belt ... um ... or ... Let me see ... Again, one I mentioned before, someone keeping a wallet which fell from your pocket.
Examiner:	Right. Now, finally, I'm going to ... er ... ask you four of these cases, and I'm going to ask you what punishment you think should be given to ... er ... to someone who breaks the law in each of these cases. Now, first of all, a motorist who parks on a double yellow line, what punishment should he receive?
Candidate C:	I would say ... a small fine.
Examiner:	Right ... um ... what about someone who keeps your wallet which fell from your pocket?
Candidate C:	Um ... I would say a small fine again.
Examiner:	Mm ... and a company that doesn't declare all its income from ... for income tax?
Candidate C:	I would say a large fine.
Examiner:	And finally, what about a husband who kills his wife's lover?
Candidate C:	I'd say imprisonment, depending on the case, possibly for life.
Examiner:	Mm ... er ... what would this depend on?
Candidate C:	Well, we don't know the reason he killed the wife's lover: it might have been self-defence, there might have been reasons that would mean that you would give him a lower sentence.
Examiner:	OK, thank you very much.

(Time: 3 minutes 15 seconds)

12.12   *Have* and *give*   *Verbs and idioms*

▶ As the exam is approaching, both parts of this section contain several rather tricky points.

A   Note that if more words are added, some different answers are also possible (e.g. Carol gave the information *to her friend*).

Answers

Alex had ...
a quarrel with Tim   a good time   permission   a meal   a drink
a headache   his/her hair cut   a chance   a look   an interview
a good idea   the information   never been abroad   an accident   a rest
a swim   the details   a newspaper   no imagination   better be careful
Barry was having ...
a quarrel with Tim   a good time   a meal   a drink   his/her hair cut
a look   an interview   a rest   a swim
Charlie gave us ...
a good time   permission   a meal   a drink   a headache   a chance
a look   a good idea   the information   the details   a newspaper
Carol gave ...
a sigh   a good performance   his/her opinion
− AND, if an indirect object (e.g. *to her friend*) is added:
   an order   permission   the information   the details

B

Answers

 1 gave   back = return
 2 had given up = quit, stop
 3 giving out = distribute
 4 give   away = reveal
 5 gave   up = surrender
 6 giving   in = hand in
 7 gave in = surrender
 8 had   on = wear
 9 have   back = have returned
10 having   round = have as a guest/visitor

▶ For more speaking and listening activities on the topic of the news and current affairs, see *Ideas* Unit 18.

13 People

13.1   It takes all sorts . . . *Vocabulary*

A   Be prepared to intervene with suitable vocabulary. If your students will be interested, perhaps look up what the characteristics of people with different birth signs are supposed to be.

B   Note that in this exercise more than one answer may appear to be right – students should choose the 'best' one, as in the exam.

Answers

1 cheerful
2 bad-tempered
3 sensitive
4 likeable (but all the others are just about possible)
5 sympathetic (but all the others are just about possible)
6 smartly
7 jealous
8 naughty
9 generous
10 forgetful (or possibly: preoccupied?)
11 self-confident (or possibly: self-satisfied?)
12 spoilt

13 stand
14 handsome (or possibly: beautiful?)
15 lonely
16 anxious
17 going out
18 sight
19 engaged
20 get married
21 best man
22 relations
23 anniversary
24 rows
25 step-father
26 tree

▶ Remind everyone that they should make sure that the answers they choose fit the context grammatically.

C and D   Be prepared to answer questions about vocabulary during these activities.

E   You might possibly want to change the question here to:
What qualities do you admire most in people of the opposite sex?

▶ For more practice in describing yourself and other people, see *Ideas* Units 1 and 16 and the Teacher's Book for *Ideas*.

233

13.2   **What is Dateline?**   *Reading*

A   Some of these questions are tricky, to give students a little foretaste of what they may have to cope with in the exam.

Answers (With quotes from the passage, where relevant.)

 1 B ('just as there are stars in the universe')
 2 B
 3 A ('only by our own experts')
 4 D ('The old 'school-work-early marriage' syndrome is disappearing')
 5 D ('the opportunities for widening your circle were still restricted')
 6 B ('making the most of the world's opportunities')
 7 D ('plenty of their own friends')
 8 D ('Yes, it does happen: so frequently you shouldn't be surprised')
 9 D ('every week … scores of letters')
10 C ('very thorough')

B   Perhaps your students might like to fill in the form, or just discuss it as suggested in the Student's Book.

13.3   **Difficult questions**   *Grammar*

▶ This section focusses on some tricky points of grammar that haven't been covered so far in the course.

A

Answers

1 You'd better be careful.
2 I wish I was happier / wasn't so unhappy.
3 I'd like you to use a dictionary.
4 It was you who told me to do that.
5 I suggest (that) you arrive a few minutes early.
6 It's time you did the work.

B

Suggested answers

better AND best
You'd **better take** several pens to the exam, not just one.
It's **better to guess** the answer than to leave a blank space if you don't know.
It's **best to arrive/get there** early on the day of the exam.

I'd rather / prefer / like
Would you rather I **did it** today or tomorrow?
Would you like me **to carry it** for you?

wish, if only AND hope
She wishes she **were/was** on holiday.
I wish **there were/was** more time before the exam, but there isn't.
If only we **knew** in advance what questions would be asked!
I hope we all **pass / get through / do well.**

It's time
It's time **to do / we did** some revision.
It's time **to have / we had** a break.

suggest
They suggested **that we did/should** not worry about the exam.
What do you suggest **doing / we do / we should do** after it's all over?

C

Answers

1 I'd rather you didn't interrupt me when I'm speaking.
2 We suggest you phone and ask for information.
3 It's much better to be tactful than frank.
4 I'd prefer you to let me know your decision today, not tomorrow.
5 I'd rather stay at home than go out tonight.
6 I'd like you to fill in this questionnaire.
7 It's time we found out how much it's going to cost.
8 They'd better book early if they want tickets for the concert.
9 I wish I didn't have/hadn't got so much to do today.
10 If only you had told me earlier!

13.4   **Synonyms**   *Word study*

▶ Part C deals with hyponyms (words like *vehicle*, which includes the meanings *bus, car, tram*, etc. or *flower*, which includes the meanings *rose, dandelion, chrysanthemum*, etc.).

B

Some suggested answers

nice: pleasant, attractive, satisfying, friendly, likeable, agreeable
good: splendid, excellent, terrific, perfect, fine, great, marvellous,
    wonderful
bad: terrible, dreadful, awful
thing: object, topic, article, item, subject
like: love, appreciate, enjoy, value
dislike: hate, loathe, detest, dread, despise

large: big, enormous, huge, immense, great
small: little, tiny, unimportant
important: serious, vital, essential
intelligent: clever, bright, brainy, brilliant
interesting: exciting, entertaining, fascinating
strange: unusual, unfamiliar, odd
unpleasant: disgusting, annoying, terrible, frightening, nasty
beautiful: attractive, good-looking, pretty

C

Answers

sister, etc.	relations/relatives
bread, etc.	food
grass, etc.	plants
rabbit, etc.	animals/mammals
lamb, etc.	meat
bus, etc.	vehicles
house, etc.	buildings/dwellings
parrot, etc.	birds
copper, etc.	metals
breakfast, etc.	meals
autumn, etc.	seasons
suit, etc.	clothes/garments
dollar, etc.	currencies

rugby, etc.	sports/games
photography, etc.	hobbies
medicine, etc.	professions
parrot, etc.	pets
wheat, etc.	cereals
rose, etc.	flowers
ant, etc.	insects
book, etc.	publications

13.5 'Due to a computer error . . .' *Problem solving*

▶ This section could be done under exam conditions, leaving out the discussion in **A**. Allow 30 to 40 minutes for this, but point out that in the Use of English paper (total length 2 hours) they should allow enough time to answer and check all the other questions.

▶ Many students find that it's a good idea to read the information for the Directed Writing question first of all in the exam (even though it's usually the last question) and make notes on it. Then they do all the earlier questions, before writing the paragraphs. Others prefer to leave the Directed Writing question to the end, when they know how much time they have left.
  Discuss with the class which approach they prefer, and which you recommend.

▶ The Directed Writing task is worth 20–25% of the total marks in the Use of English paper, so if too much time is spent on it at the expense of the other questions, marks may be lost on the other questions.

A Remind everyone that, in the Interview, they may have to take part in a problem-solving discussion of this kind.

B Make sure everyone makes notes before they write their paragraphs.

Model paragraphs

```
On their first date, Andrew and Anne may have got on
reasonably well. There isn't too great an age gap between
them and they both describe themselves as outdoor types.
The problem may have been what to talk about. The only
interest they have in common is travel and Anne wouldn't
have enjoyed it if Andrew talked about politics. I hope
they didn't go to a pub or a disco, for Andrew's sake.
```

Although Bill and Brenda are both extroverts, there's a
ten year difference in their ages and they don't have
much in common. They may have enjoyed talking about
travel but Brenda doesn't share Bill's interest in sport.
Their mutual dislike of poetry is unlikely to have
improved their conversation much.

Colin and Carole probably got on quite well. Of course,
they don't share exactly the same interests but they both
like reading and pop music. Carole dislikes classical
music, though, which is a pity. They are both shy people.
Perhaps Colin is a bit old for Carole, though. They
probably found something to say to each other about
Carole's course and Colin's job on their first date.

Of the people described, the one I'd most like to meet
myself is Colin, though not as a marriage partner of
course! He's quite a lot younger/older than me but he
seems a pleasant sort of person. I'm interested in all
kinds of music and reading, as he is, but not sport and
although I dislike poetry, I quite like watching
television and going to pubs sometimes.

13.6   Using your brain   *Listening*

⌷▭▭⌷   This could be done under exam conditions, with a 20-second
break between the two playings. In the exam itself candidates would not
normally have to write down so much as here, though.

Answers

1 right-hand
2 LEFT (rational side)   RIGHT (irrational side)

LEFT (rational side)	RIGHT (irrational side)
language	rhythm
numbers	**colour**
linearity	**imagination**
analysis	**daydreaming**
logic	space: three dimensions
lists	seeing **collections** of things as a whole
sequencing	

3 reversed
4 corpus callosum   successful thinking
5 12 multiplied by 137
6 directly above this chair in the room upstairs
7 look to the right   visual information

8 close their eyes
9 do not get worse
10 stimulation   exercise
11 fresh air/oxygen   lifestyle
12 Three Golden Rules:
    1 in an abstract, rational way   visually
    2 both halves
    3 you can't solve a problem   just as good as

Transcript

Man: ... you see the human brain weighs about 1½ kilos. It contains ten to fifteen thousand million nerve cells. Now, each nerve cell can connect with any number or combination of other neurons – that's what you call a nerve cell, a neuron – the total number of possible connections, of course, is enormous. Now, if you want to type that number so you'd have ... get an idea of how many combinations there are, you'd have to start by typing a one, then follow that with ten million kilometres of zeros.

Every human brain has an unlimited potential – only a small fraction of neurons are used for ... er ... everyday routine tasks like eating, moving, routine work, etc. The rest are constantly available for *thought*.

Now, our brains consist of various parts, some of which control routine functions. But the important parts that make us into those marvellous thinking machines, we like to think we are, are the two hemispheres or the two sides of the brain: the left and the right. Now, the left hemisphere controls the right half of the body, that's right, the left controls the right, and the right controls the left half. Normally, the left half of the brain is dominant.

Now, the left side, which is known as the rational side, controls the ... these functions: language, numbers, linearity, analysis, logic, lists and sequencing.

The right side, which is known as the irrational side, sometimes people call it the artistic side of your brain, controls those things ... er ... which are ... well, less specific perhaps: rhythm ... er ... er ... colour, imagination, daydreaming, space: spatial dimension, three-dimensional thought ... erm ... seeing collections of things as one, as a whole. One interesting thing is that left-handed people often have a dominant right hemisphere, and in this case the priorities of the things I've just mentioned are all reversed.

The corpus callosum is very important. That's corpus CORPUS, callosum CALLOSUM – you should make a note of that, it's very important – that's the link between the two hemispheres in the brain and it's the key to successful thinking, linking the two parts of the brain, so you don't use them independently.

By the way, you ... you could try this experiment – you'll see the two halves being used. Ask someone two questions, one to do with numbers ... you could say 'What's 12 multiplied by 137?', and the other one to do with space. For example, you could say, 'What piece of furniture is directly above this chair in the room upstairs?' OK? Now, while they're trying to answer the first question, that was the ... the numbers one, they'll probably look to the right to prevent being distracted by visual information, and while they're trying to answer the second, that's the spatial one about what's upstairs above the chair, they'll probably look to the left. But of course, some people just close their eyes and that ruins the whole test!

According to experts, as we get older our memories do not get worse. Er ... that's just an old wives' tale. In fact, we forget things at *all* ages. Now, if you *expect* your memory to be bad or to get worse, it probably will. Lack of stimulation, brain exercise and lack of interest can mean that you forget things more easily. Lack of concentration simply. Ah, lack of fresh air can also lead to your brain being less efficient because it gets starved of oxygen, and an unhealthy lifestyle – take note – can also damage your brain: er ... alcohol, smoke, um ... pollutants in the air like lead, er ... chemicals in food, they can all add to a generally deteriorating condition of the brain.

You've probably heard a lot of people say, 'I'm not brainy' or 'That's too difficult for my brain' – but this is not true because everyone's brain has an equal potential.

There are a few rules – Golden Rules of brain power. One: use your senses. Don't only think in an abstract, logical way. Try to imagine a problem visually. Second rule: use both halves of your brain. For example, if you're faced with ... er ... an abstract, logical problem, try thinking about it imaginativ ... er ... try thinking about it imaginatively. Or if you're faced with a creative problem, try to analyse it. Think logically about it. And don't ever say you *can't* solve a problem because your brain is just as good as anyone else's.

(Time: 5 minutes 45 seconds)

13.7 Chapter One *Reading*

A The text is from *Mr Norris Changes Trains* by Christopher Isherwood.

Answers

1 A   2 C   3 C   4 B   5 C   6 C   7 A   8 A   9 C   10 D

B

A description of the stranger:

The stranger seems very nervous as though he is scared of the writer. He is wrapped up in his own thoughts and rather unwilling to talk to the writer. He is smartly dressed, has small pale well-manicured hands and a charming smile. His teeth are like broken rocks.

13.8   Exam practice   *Passage with gaps*

▶ In the exam, this kind of exercise is more likely to be a narrative of some sort.

Answers

1 about	11 being
2 an	12 her
3 of	13 rather
4 In	14 very/extremely/terribly, etc.
5 of	15 that
6 from	16 marriage
7 in	17 gets/receives/has
8 out	18 like
9 without	19 life
10 one	20 relations/relatives/acquaintances/colleagues

▶ Perhaps ask the class to guess who the two people are.

▶ Further advice to students:
Note that where more than one answer makes sense and fits grammatically, you do get a mark for whichever one you choose, even if one of them is 'better' in the context. However, you should never write more than one word in each gap, or present the examiner with alternatives.

13.9   Five students   *Listening*

A 📼 In this part there is a great deal of writing to do and it is NOT a 'typical exam exercise'. Listening to the conversation will help students to take part in the communication activity in C more confidently.

▶ To make the task easier, perhaps get different groups of students to make notes on different people or different aspects: group A could make notes on appearance, group B on good points and group C on points to be careful about – then they can form groups of three to exchange information later.

⟫→

Answers

	Appearance	Good points	But be careful!
PAUL	Tall, slim, fair hair, friendly face, lovely smile	Helpful, speaks fluently, interesting ideas	Makes mistakes, speaks first and thinks later
SUSAN	Dark hair, dark eyes	Lively, quick, bright	Doesn't always talk in English, sometimes talks too much
MARIA	(Susan's sister) Looks similar but longer hair and plumper	Sensible	Sulks when she makes mistakes, feels inferior to Susan
HELEN	Pretty, nice smile	Good written work, laughs at jokes	Shy–needs encouragement– own little world
PETER	Older, moustache, glasses, wavy dark brown hair, jacket or suit	Takes notes, serious, determined to learn	Asks difficult questions

Transcript

Chris: Barbara, before you go, could you tell me about these students that are coming into my class?

Barbara: Oh, yes. Now, let me think, well there's ... er ... Paul. He's ... er ... he's the tall slim ... slim lad with fair hair. Very ... very friendly face, lovely smile ... He's ... er ... particularly good with group activities, he's a very helpful person to have in the class and very helpful with the other students. He ... er ... speaks fluently, but does make a lot of mistakes! Doesn't seem to mind making mistakes, mind you. He asks a lot of questions ... er ... tends to speak first and think later, he's a bit impetuous. But he's got lots of interesting ideas.

Chris: Good.

Barbara: Er ... Susan ... Susan. Now, she's very lively, quick, very bright. Now she talks all the time but not always in English.

Chris: What, is she difficult or anything?

Barbara: N ... no ... She's quite young but she does behave in quite a grown-up way really for her age. She ... ah ... it can be a bit difficult to actually shut her up sometimes and make her listen to you but she's ... er ...

Chris: Ah, right.

Barbara: She's ... er ... very nice. And she's ... um ... what does she look like? Just as ... yes, she's dark hair, dark eyes.

Chris: Right, well ... er ... is there ... any other girls in the ...

Barbara: Yes, there's Maria, that's Susan's sister.

Chris: Yes.

Barbara: Actually, it's quite difficult to tell them apart although ... er ... Maria is slightly older. She's a bit ... a bit plumper and has longer hair ... than Susan. Er ... she's not quite as bright as her sister and I think that makes her feel a bit inferior really. Well, you know, she sulks a bit when she gets things wrong or if she misunderstands you. But on the whole, very sensible girl.

Chris: OK.

Barbara: Then there's, oh, Helen. Er ...

Chris: Er ... Helen, Helen, Helen, Helen ...

Barbara: Yes, she's very very pretty with a ... with a nice smile and she's ... but she ... she's quite ... quite shy and quiet, so you have to sort of encourage her a bit. And she's very bright. Er ... does tend to seem ... well, she seems a bit wrapped up in her own little world but the ... er ... written work she does shows that she's learning a lot. Oh, she laughs at my jokes, too.

Chris: Oh, hope she laughs at mine!

Barbara: Yes. And then there's Peter, who's older than the others. He's sort of ... um ... a bit more distinguished, he's got sort of moustache and spectacles and wavy dark brown hair. And he usually wears a jacket and sometimes a suit. Very smart and very ... takes notes all the time and very serious and determined to learn as much as possible. He also ...

Chris: Oh, soon put a stop to that!

Barbara: Ah, but he asks quite difficult questions. He doesn't ... doesn't mean to be nasty but if you're not careful, he can catch you out.

Chris: Well, thanks, Barbara. It's all up to me now, isn't it? Have a good holiday, won't you?

Barbara: Thanks.

Chris: Bye.

(Time: 2 minutes 30 seconds)

B   Perhaps take this further by getting each group to describe their fellow members to the class. They should do this without naming them or revealing whether the person in question is a 'he' or a 'she' – they can be referred to as 'this person'.

The rest of the class should guess who is being described at the END of each description.

C   [▓] In this information-gap activity, each partner has a group of people to describe. Make sure no one peeps at the other's picture and DON'T give the game away ...

Activity 38 contains a photo of a group of people to describe.

Activity 49 contains the *same* photo but in mirror image!

Each person should make notes.

At the end of the activity get everyone to compare notes to see how well they both described the *same* people!

13.10   Describing people   *Composition*

A   Although the first paragraph is probably the most interesting to read, perhaps the second is more the kind of paragraph that your students should be encouraged to write – long complex sentences often lead to pitfalls and errors.

Instead of repeating 'He' so much, giving the person a name would reduce the dullness of the second and even the third paragraphs.

B

Model paragraphs (Many variations are possible.)

```
He is a slightly overweight man in his mid-thirties. He
is terribly selfish and even dishonest but his worst
feature is that he loses his temper whenever people
disagree with him.

She is a very thin lady in her late fifties. She does
tend to be rather absent-minded but she has a delightful
sense of humour and is always ready to help other people
with their problems.

He is 18 years old and very athletic. He really loves
sport and his favourite game is football. In his spare
time he enjoys going out with his friends and
particularly going to the cinema.

She is 16 years old and a very studious young woman, who
enjoys reading. She has four brothers and two sisters.
When she leaves school, she hopes to go to university,
where she wants to study engineering.
```

© Cambridge University Press 1990

C   Exam conditions in class – or to save time, as homework. There are model compositions for the first three topics only, as the details of the fourth depend on a particular book.

Model compositions

```
I remember the first time I met Tim. He was sitting on a
bench in the park, looking very depressed and cold. He
hadn't got a coat on and it had started to rain.
Normally, I don't think I'd have stopped to speak to a
complete stranger who looked like that - not that he
looked like a tramp or anything: his shoes were well
```

polished and his clothes were quite smart. But on an
impulse I stopped walking and said to him, 'Are you OK?'
in a sympathetic voice. He said he was but I sat down
beside him and he started telling me how his wife had
just locked him out of the house after a row and so he
was sitting in the rain waiting for her to calm down and
let him in again. I suggested that we went somewhere warm
and dry, so we found a nearby cafe and continued our
conversation. And that was how I met Tim - the man who
was later to become my worst enemy.

> 48 West Green Lane
> Brompton
> Herts   England
>
> 17 May 19##

Dear Maria,

    As this is my first letter to you, let me
begin by introducing myself: my name's Susan Underwood
and I live with my parents in a detached house in
Brompton, which is a little town about 40 km north of
London.

    I have curly fair hair, blue eyes and a round
freckled face. I'm quite tall and a bit overweight at the
moment! I enjoy listening to classical music and going to
the cinema. Of course I also watch TV - especially the
old movies they have on.

    I'm still at college and I'm studying for a
diploma in hotel management at Brompton Technical
College. If I pass my final exams next summer, I hope to
get a job somewhere abroad for a year to get experience
of foreign hotels and learn a useful foreign language.
I'm really looking forward to starting work, even though
the course I'm doing is excellent.

    That's about all I can think of to tell you
about myself. Do write back and tell me all about
yourself. I'll write again soon.

    Yours truly,

Sue

The two people I admire most are my aunt and uncle. They are my mother's sister and her husband and they have a small farm in the country about 200 km from where I live.

My aunt is quite tall, she has wavy black hair and wears glasses. She has a round, friendly face and smiles quietly to herself while she's working - even when she's cooking or washing up! She has two children, who are two and four years old. Amazingly, she is able to look after them and do all her work in the home and on the farm and she never, never loses patience or gets cross. That's what I admire in her.

Her husband is quite a short man with attractive brown eyes who always behaves charmingly even when people are not pleasant to him. He's busy every day of the week from morning till evening. Whenever I go to visit them he encourages me to help with the work, and with him even routine jobs seem fun. That's what I admire about him - he makes work seem a pleasure.

© Cambridge University Press 1990

13.11   That's a problem!   *Interview exercises*

A   This could be done in pairs, with one person asking questions (in the role of 'examiner') and the other playing the role of 'candidate'.

B   [⚒] Working in groups of three, students have to suggest how to solve various problems.
The problem in Activity 31 is:
> You're locked out of your car at 2 a.m. and your house keys and money are inside.

The problem in Activity 36 is:
> You've run out of cash during a holiday in a foreign country, you have no traveller's cheques or credit cards and no friends in the country.

The problem in Activity 50 is:
> Your excursion coach has left without you, leaving you stranded in the middle of nowhere in the rain. All your money and your raincoat are on the coach.

▶ Here are some more dilemmas to suggest if a group runs out of ideas:

- You have got someone else's suitcase by mistake.
- You're stuck in a lift and there's no one else in the building.
- Your guests arrive for dinner/a party on the wrong evening.
- Your weekend guests arrive the wrong weekend, just as you're setting off somewhere else.

▶ If you want to simulate exam conditions, get the class to work in pairs for **B** (looking together first at Activity 31, then 36, then 50). Rather than role-playing, get them to discuss what they would do in each situation described.

13.12   Grammar revision   *Exam practice*

A   Question 4 is particularly tricky – in the exam there are often one or two questions in this kind of exercise which are difficult or in which there are hidden difficulties.

Answers

1 It's important/essential/necessary to be more polite to people.
2 The letter (that) she wrote (to) me said (that) she never wanted to see me again.
3 He's such a dull person that people fall asleep while he's talking.
4 In spite of her father's wealth he doesn't want to marry her. / In spite of her being the daughter of a rich man, he doesn't want to marry her.
5 If you don't write to him you'll lose touch with him.
6 She told me (that) she was leaving and (that she was) never coming back.
7 Her brother is much less amusing than her. / Her brother isn't anything like as amusing as she is.
8 They have known each other for ten years.
9 While her husband was away, she was very lonely.
10 Everyone still seems to like him although he's a liar and a cheat.

B

Suggested answers

Chris: Hi, Robin.
Robin: Hello, Chris, what's up? Are ₁ **you feeling all right?**
Chris: Not really, no. I feel a bit depressed.
Robin: Oh dear. Why ₂ **do you feel / are you depressed?**
Chris: It's my family again. My Uncle George is staying with us again.
Robin: I see, but what ₃ **is the problem with him?**
Chris: Oh, *he's* all right. It's just that my father simply doesn't get on with him. If they're in the same room one of them starts an argument.

Robin: Can't ₄ **you persuade them to stop arguing / to make up their differences?**

Chris: They wouldn't take any notice of me. And to make matters worse, Uncle George is sleeping on the spare bed in my room.

Robin: Why ₅ **does that make matters worse / do you find that so annoying?**

Chris: He snores and I can't get to sleep.

Robin: How ₆ **long has he been staying with you?**

Chris: He arrived on Sunday.

Robin: And how ₇ **long is he going to stay?**

Chris: Another three weeks at least. Until he gets another ship.

Robin: What ₈ **does he do / do you mean?**

Chris: He's a merchant seaman. He always stays with us when he's on leave.

Robin: Well, you'd better ₉ **put up with it!**

Chris: Yes, I'll have to, I suppose! I'm going to be spending a lot of time away from home until he goes back to sea.

Robin: You could ₁₀ **come round to my place / share my room / spend the evenings with me while your uncle is staying.**

Chris: Really? That'd be wonderful. Thanks a lot.

▶ For more speaking and listening activities on the topic of people, see *Ideas* Units 1 and 16.

14 The past

▶ Although the exercises in this unit can be used for a mock exam, it would be more realistic to use test papers from *Cambridge First Certificate Practice 3* for this, especially as regards the length and timing of each paper. The exercises in this unit are best used as revision and not as tests.

14.1 to 14.3 contain Vocabulary and Reading Comprehension exercises (Paper 1).

14.4 contains Composition exercises (Paper 2).

14.5 to 14.9 contain Use of English exercises (Paper 3).

14.10 to 14.12 contain Listening Comprehension exercises (Paper 4).

14.13 contains Interview exercises (Paper 5).

▶ If your students are doing Papers 4 and/or 5 some time before they do the written papers, make sure they are prepared for these by starting this unit at 14.10 or 14.13.

14.1 Vocabulary and grammar

Reading comprehension

▶ The first part of Paper 1 in the exam consists of 25 questions on vocabulary, grammar and usage. (As students have to *read* the information in each question and interpret it correctly in order to choose the best alternative, it does involve reading comprehension.)

Answers

1 C 2 A 3 B 4 B 5 B 6 A 7 C 8 B 9 A 10 D
11 A 12 A 13 B 14 D 15 B 16 C 17 A 18 D 19 A
20 B 21 A 22 A 23 D 24 B 25 B

▶ In the exam, students should spend about 25 minutes on this exercise. Each question is worth one mark (total 25 marks), but the questions based on the passages are worth two marks each (total 30 marks).

14.2   1900

Reading comprehension

Discuss whether your students prefer to read the text first or the questions first. Which do you recommend?

Answers

1 B   2 D   3 B   4 C   5 A

▶ Some discussion questions:
- Do you ever read history books? Why/Why not?
- What will life be like in the year 2000?

14.3   The Lost Viking Capital

Reading comprehension

Answers

1 D   2 A   3 C   4 A   5 C   6 A   7 A   8 D   9 D   10 D

▶ Some discussion questions:
- Has anyone visited anywhere like Jorvik Viking Centre? What was it like?
- Would you like to go to York? Why/Why not?
- Do you find conventional museums interesting? Why/Why not?

14.4   Under exam conditions

Composition – 1 ½ hours

Go through the exam tips given in the Student's Book with the class – do you and they agree with the advice given there?

A   If your students have been studying one of the prescribed books, add a question on the particular book as question 6 in the Student's Book.

B   Give a final mark for the two compositions using the marking scheme on page 219.

Point out what particular points each student should be careful about in the exam: what are each student's typical 'careless mistakes' of spelling and grammar that they should notice when checking their work?

▶ Discuss with the class what types of questions they feel more confident about (e.g. writing an informal letter) and which they feel diffident about (e.g. writing an essay).

14.5   Fill the gaps
Use of English

Answers

1 less	11 seen/observed
2 spend	12 another
3 sister	13 upside
4 mention	14 down/along
5 myself	15 through
6 provided/providing	16 barking
7 company/protection	17 trying/managing
8 distance	18 share
9 scared/frightened	19 promise
10 behind	20 case

14.6   Grammar revision
Use of English

A   The advice about checking for mistakes is equally valid for the Directed Writing exercise too – and other exercises in Paper 3.

Mistakes corrected

1 **Careless mistakes and slips of the pen:**
   A The castle contains many treasures and paintings.
   B I wonder **which** of the **mistakes** is most **serious**.
   C My brother and sister **have** brown eyes but my eyes **are** blue.
   D Could you tell me what time **it opens**?
   E Who **paid** for the ticket?

2 **Mistakes that are harder to notice:**
   A After visiting the museum he **didn't/did not have** very much time left.
   B His hair is very long, it's time for him to **have it cut**.
   C I **have been** waiting for you **for** four hours.
   D They **had** never visited Rome before their first visit in 1987.

E She **has never written** a letter by hand since she **bought** a word processor.

F I **have been** learning English **for** five years.

G A **suspicious person / suspect** is **being questioned** by the police.

H Before they **went** out they had been **watching** the news on TV.

B

Answers

1 During your holiday I'll be busy working.
2 It's ages since I saw my old school friend.
3 I hadn't been to / visited North America before.
4 The Pyramids were built by the ancient Egyptians.
5 Soon she'll have to give up her job.
6 We found out that the office was closed due to illness.
7 We managed to reach the top of the hill in spite of the heat / although it was hot.
8 By the time you arrive, I'll be ready.
9 You shouldn't / oughtn't to have put so much salt in the soup.
10 It's so salty (that) I can't eat it now.

14.7 Word-building revision   *Use of English*

A

Answers

1 impatience	5 unemployment
2 unselfishness/selflessness	6 encouraged
3 replacement	7 disagreeing
4 irresponsibly	8 sharpening

B

Answers

1 unpredictable	6 certainty
2 unforgettable	7 likelihood
3 daily	8 memorable
4 photographic	9 unfashionable
5 probability	10 difficulty

14.8   Unusual exercises   *Use of English*

Discuss the exam tips with the class. What other 'new' types of exercise
have come up in recent exam papers? (Ask a colleague, if necessary.)

A

Answers

1 made it up	4 made off with
2 make do	5 done
with	6 making for
3 done up	

B

Answers

1 title	4 columns
2 margin	5 volumes
3 index	6 bookmark

C

Answers

1 fortnight	4 fifth
2 dozens	5 quarter
3 doubled	6 century

14.9   Problem solving /   *Use of English*
       Directed writing

A and **B**   Under exam conditions, this exercise should take 35 minutes
or so, including time for planning and checking.

In this kind of Directed Writing exercise, there is not necessarily a 'best
solution'. In this case, there are certainly equally valid reasons why the
Meiers should go to York or to Cambridge. The model answer below is
130 words long, rather longer than required according to the
instructions in **B**.

Model answer

I think the Meiers would enjoy spending Sunday in
Cambridge, because the two-hour journey to York would
take four hours out of their day. I know this would
disappoint Richard, but never mind.
       Once in Cambridge Helen would enjoy seeing the
paintings in the Fitzwilliam Museum and Kettle's Yard,
but this would not appeal to her father. I think Helen
and her mother, who isn't a keen walker, should
concentrate on the museums before lunch, while Richard
and his father go for a walk beside the river and walk
through the old colleges. They could meet for lunch,
perhaps in a pub by the river, and after lunch hire a
boat on the river before going together to admire King's
College Chapel and then catching the train back to
London.

© Cambridge University Press 1990

14.10   I remember . . .   *Listening comprehension*

📼 Follow an exam-style procedure for all three of the listening
exercises in this unit:

1 20 seconds before each exercise for reading the questions.
2 An uninterrupted first playing.
3 20 seconds before the second playing.
4 An uninterrupted second playing.
5 20 seconds after.

Answers

1 C   2 C   3 C   4 A   5 B   6 D   7 A   8 B   9 D   10 C

▶ Ask the members of the class to tell each other about an experience
from their childhood that they'll never forget.

Transcript

Liz: I remember when I was very little, about three or four, my brother used to
      take me to the local playground. He was a bit older than me. And he used
      to look after me while I went on the swings and, you know, the slide and
      things. Well, one afternoon I went out with him after tea and I was sitting
      on one of the swings with my teddy bear and I was swinging away and
      talking to Teddy, you see, when it gradually dawned on me that I was all
      alone and that my brother had left me by myself and there was no one else
      in the playground at all. And it was starting to get dark. Then – ooh, I can

remember it, it sends shivers down my spine even now – I saw this big fierce dog sniffing around the swings a . . . and as I was going backwards and forwards it started to bark at me. Well, first I sort of, you know, tried to be terribly brave and I wanted to make it go away so I shouted at it and it took no notice and started, you know, jumping up at me and trying to bite, well not me, but I think it was my teddy bear. Well, I started to cry and scream and got in a terrible state sort of trying to climb up the swing and . . . and no one came and it was getting darker and darker. And . . . er . . . oh, I was in such a state. Well, eventually I saw my Dad running towards me waving a big stick and shouting at the dog and he chased the dog away and took me in his arms and I . . . I clung onto him and he held . . . held me and I cried and cried and cried until eventually I suppose I stopped. Well, I never saw the dog again but I always made sure that, you know, after that there were other people in the playground when I went. And well, of course, later I realised that my brother hadn't abandoned me to be eaten by this dog. I suppose he must have run back home to fetch my father and . . . and er . . . I suppose he must have been very frightened too. But he obviously felt very responsible for me and he ran home to get help. But since then . . . whew . . . I've always been so careful with dogs and I've never trusted them.

(Time: 1 minute 50 seconds)

14.11   **The slave trade**   *Listening comprehension*

Answers

TRUE statements: 2   4   5   6   7   9   10   12   13   16   17   18
FALSE statements: 1   3   8   11   14   15

Transcript

Presenter: Good afternoon. We have with us Professor Nicholson, who is the author of a new book on the slave trade and he's going to tell us something about it. Professor Nicholson.

Professor: Thank you. Well, first of all I think I ought to clear up a bit of a misunderstanding. People normally mean when they talk about the slave trade the buying of Africans from other Africans by Europeans for sale to other Europeans. But of course, there are much wider implications. You see, slavery seems to have existed in many societies at all times in history – perhaps it always will. You see, even today there are people in some countries, who can't officially be described as slaves but who are still slaves in all but name.

Presenter: Can you tell us a little bit about the origins of the first African slaves?

Professor: Yes, indeed. The . . . the first African slaves were brought to Portugal by the Portuguese in 1434 and the Portuguese in fact dominated the slave trade right up until the . . . er . . . 18th century. After the establishment of colonies in Brazil, slaves were shipped over there to work in the plantations, particularly in the 17th century. And also, of course, the English needed slaves for their plantations in the West Indies. And by 1700 the trade was dominated by England and, of course, by France. Then, in the 18th century six million slaves were shipped across the Atlantic because the ... the colonies in North America depen ... depended on slave labour to produce the sugar crops and tobacco and cotton and so forth for the ... for the European market. Altogether ... er ... the estimate is that about ten million people were sent from Africa, but of course, not all arrived and certainly not all survived for very long even if they did arrive safely.

Presenter: What were the conditions like?

Professor: Well, aboard ship, of course, the conditions were absolutely unspeakable, absolutely unspeakable. You see, on some ships only a handful of people arrived alive.

Presenter: Mm, and in the plantations?

Professor: Well, the conditions there were equally horrible. In fact they were so bad that many of the slaves only survived for a few years. Gradually, of course there ... there grew up a movement in Europe – Wilberforce and so on – a ... a ... against the slave trade but it ... it wasn't until 1809 that English ships finally stopped taking slaves from Africa to North America and the West Indies.

Presenter: And when were they actually set free?

Professor: Well in the ... in the Americas they weren't set free until ... er ... quite a bit later on. 1833 in the British colonies and then 1865 in the USA. But of course, before that many slave owners did set their own slaves free of their own accord. In fact ... in fact it's interesting, in 1822 in West Africa a state was ... um ... was set up for slaves who were in fact freed and sent back there and of course the ... er ... the state has the name Liberia, which is quite apt, isn't it?

Presenter: Yes, indeed. Professor, I'm sorry, I'll have to stop you there because we're out of time. But thank you very much for talking to us.

Professor: Thank you.

(Time: 3 minutes 5 seconds)

14.12   Gipsy signs   *Listening comprehension*

Answers

1 Beware of the dog

2 Fierce dog

3 Friendly people

4 Friendly, generous people

5 Very friendly, generous people

6 Work to be had here

7 Gipsies not liked

8 Nothing to be had

9 Work available with good pay

10 These people will buy from you

11 This place has been robbed ///

Transcript

Guide: … and the gipsies also had a whole system of communications of … of … way of communicating with each other as well. When they went from house to house around the country they left behind chalk marks on the wall … um … and these were messages for any other gipsies who came along later. Now, these signs were useful because, for one thing, many gipsies were illiterate in those days but also the signs couldn't be understood by the country people, they were only intelligible to the gipsies themselves.

Now, I'll show you some of the signs, I'll draw them on this board. Now, if there was a dog at the house then they used this sign, see: a triangle. If it was a fierce dog then they put a horizontal line through the triangle like this. If the people in the house were friendly, then they'd draw a circle, like so.

Now, what do you think this one meant? This is a circle with a dot in the middle. Now, I wonder what that meant?

Man: Angry? Angry neighbours?

Guide: No, no, no. It meant 'friendly and generous people'. Now, what about this? This is a circle with a dot in the middle and a line underneath and this meant 'very friendly and very generous people'. Now, this one, this is a circle with a horizontal line through it and this meant 'work to be had here'.

Now, if a house was known to be unfriendly, then they would leave a sign like this, this is a vertical line with two horizontal lines and that meant 'gipsies not liked', so they could steer clear of that one. Now, I wonder what you think about this one? This is a very common one: it's a cross made with one vertical line and one horizontal line. What … what do you think that might have meant?

Woman: No idea.

Guide: Any ideas? It meant 'nothing to be had' at this house, so again they could … er … they could go on by and not waste their time knocking on the door. Um … here's another one. This is a circle with two horizontal lines and … er … probably fairly uncommon in those days, this one meant 'work available and good pay'. So they'd obviously stop there. Er ... now, three horizontal lines – any ideas what that might be? No? Now, this was a very hopeful sign for a gipsy because this meant 'these people will buy from you' so it would be well worth your time stopping by here. Now, here's the last one: three slanting lines, like this. Anyone care to guess? This was a very important one for the gipsies. Three slanting lines means 'don't stop here because this place has been robbed' ...

(Time: 3 minutes 15 seconds)

14.13   A long time ago ...   *Interview exercises*

▶ To simulate a real interview, perhaps enlist the aid of another teacher who will play the role of 'examiner'.

A   [📷] The photos in Activities 14 and 21 show different scenes. You may prefer to have both partners looking at both of the photos and talking about the differences between them.

The photo in 14 shows an unemployed man on a bike looking for work in the 1930s.

The photo in 21 shows some children sheltering in a trench during an air raid in the Second World War.

B   In the exam, students should read this kind of advertisement through before discussing it. They won't be asked 'comprehension questions' but may be asked to react to the content of the text.

C   In the exam the examiner might ask questions like these to 'get people talking' – they aren't intended to test students' knowledge about the particular subject.

(In case your English history is rusty: 1066 – Norman Conquest and Battle of Hastings; 1588 – Spanish Armada.)

▶ For more speaking and listening activities on the topic of the past and history, see *Ideas* Unit 9.

14.14   Last minute advice

Now's the time to make sure everyone in the class knows what their weaknesses are. Recommend or do in class relevant exercises from *Cambridge First Certificate Examination Practice 3*. Students should concentrate on improving the areas they are weakest in, and not spend time on exercises that practise things they know well.

Give everyone a last-minute pep talk and remind them …
    Not to spend too long on any one question
    Not to panic when there are any words or questions they don't
        understand
    Not to get flustered if time seems to be short
And remind them to …
    Read all the instructions carefully
    Make notes
    Check written work for mistakes
    And show the examiner how much they know!

Further reading

Cambridge First Certificate Examination Practice 2 Student's Book, Cambridge University Press, 1986.

Cambridge First Certificate Examination Practice 2 Teacher's Book, Cambridge University Press, 1987.

Cambridge First Certificate Examination Practice 3 Student's Book, Cambridge University Press, 1989.

Cambridge First Certificate Examination Practice 3 Teacher's Book, Cambridge University Press, 1990.

Hindmarsh, Roland, *Cambridge English Lexicon*, Cambridge University Press, 1980.

Jones, Leo, *Ideas*, Cambridge University Press, 1984.

Jones, Leo, *Use of English*, Cambridge University Press, 1985.

Murphy, Raymond, *English Grammar in Use*, Cambridge University Press, 1985.

Swan, Michael, *Basic English Usage*, Oxford University Press, 1984.

Swan, Michael, *Practical English Usage*, Oxford University Press, 1980.